Opposing Fascism

Community, Authority and Resistance in Europe

This innovative volume draws together in a wide-ranging collection a series of new perspectives on the everyday experience of Europeans in the 'age of fascism'. The contributions go beyond the conventional stereotypes of organised resistance to examine the tensions and ambiguities within the communities, both national and local, that opposed fascism. The authors show that under the pressures of civil conflict, occupation and even everyday life, motives were rarely as pure and political alignments seldom as straightforward as our reassuring collective memories of fascism and war have led us to believe.

The combination of original research and engagement with current debates makes this collection invaluable both for researchers in the social and political history of World War II and for students of modern European history.

TIM KIRK is Senior Lecturer in History, University of Northumbria at Newcastle. His previous publications include *Nazism and the Working Class in Austria* (Cambridge, 1996).

ANTHONY MCELLIGOTT is Lecturer in Modern History, University of St Andrews. He is the author of *Contested City: Municipal Politics and the Rise of Nazism in Altona, 1917–1937* (Ann Arbor, 1998).

Opposing Fascism

Community, Authority and Resistance in Europe

Edited by

Tim Kirk and Anthony McElligott

 **CAMBRIDGE**
UNIVERSITY PRESS

PUBLISHED BY THE PRESS SYNDICATE OF THE UNIVERSITY OF CAMBRIDGE
The Pitt Building, Trumpington Street, Cambridge CB2 1RP, United Kingdom

CAMBRIDGE UNIVERSITY PRESS
The Edinburgh Building, Cambridge CB2 2RU, UK
http://www.cup.cam.ac.uk
40 West 20th Street, New York, NY 10011-4211, USA   http://www.cup.org
10 Stamford Road, Oakleigh, Melbourne 3166, Australia

First published 1999

Printed in the United Kingdom at the University Press, Cambridge

Typeset in Plantin 10/12 pt [VN]

A catalogue record for this book is available from the British Library

ISBN 0 521 48309 3 hardback

Contents

v

Contributors

NEIL BARRETT   formerly Lecturer in Government at the University of
Manchester, now works in industry. He recently submitted a doctoral
thesis on the nature and causes of political stability and instability in
interwar Britain and has published work on the Communist Party of
Great Britain and the British Union of Fascists and the dynamics of
Jewish intra-communal responses to the BUF in and around Manchester.

MIKE CRONIN   is Senior Research Fellow at De Montfort University,
Leicester. He is author of *The Blueshirts and Irish Politics* (1997) and editor
of *The Failure of British Fascism: The Far Right and the Fight for Political
Recognition* (1996). He is currently completing a monograph entitled
Sport and Nationalism in Ireland for publication in 1998.

HELEN GRAHAM   is Reader in Spanish History at Royal Holloway College, University of London and author of *Socialism and War. The Spanish
Socialist Party in Power and Crisis 1936–39* (1991). She has published
widely on the Spanish civil war and, with Jo Labanyi, is co-editor of, and
contributor to, *Spanish Cultural Studies* (1991). Her research interest is in
the social and cultural history of Spain in the 1930s and 1940s.

NICK HOWARD   is Lecturer in Social and Industrial Studies, Department of Continuing Education, University of Sheffield. He has published
articles on the German labour movement in a number of scholarly jour-
nals, and recently contributed to Colin Barker and Paul Kennedy (eds.),
To Make Another World – Studies in Protest and Collective Action.

TIM KIRK   is Senior Lecturer in History at the University of Northumbria, Newcastle upon Tyne. He is author of *The Longman Companion to
Nazi Germany* (1995) and *Nazism and the Working Class in Austria* (1996)
and co-editor with Malcolm Gee and Jill Steward of *The City in Central
Europe. Culture and Society from 1800 to the Present* (1998). He is currently
working on the Nazi new order in Europe.

YVES LE MANER   *agrégé d'histoire*, is a *correspondant départemental* of the Institut d'Histoire du Temps Présent (CNRS) for the Pas-de-Calais where he researches the history of northern France and the Second World War. He is the author of *Histoire de Pas-de-Calais, 1815–1945. Mémoires de la Commission départementale d'Histoire de d'Archéologie du Pas-de-Calais,* vol. III (1993).

ANTHONY MCELLIGOTT   is Lecturer in Modern History and Fellow of St Leonard's College at the University of St Andrews. He is co-author of *'Hier war alles nicht so schlimm!' Wie die Nazis in Hamburg den Alltag eroberten* (1984) and author of *Contested City. Municipal Politics and the Rise of Nazism in Altona 1917–1937* (1998) and *Modernity and Crisis 1900–1945: The German Experience* (forthcoming). He is currently writing a major history of Germany in the early twentieth century, and is researching rape and murder in interwar Munich.

MARK MAZOWER   is Reader in History at the University of Sussex. He is the author of *Greece and the Interwar Economic Crisis* (1991), *Inside Hitler's Greece: The Experience of Occupation, 1941–1944* (1993) and *Dark Continent: Europe's Twentieth Century* (1998). He is editing a collection of essays on the Greek Civil War and he is currently working on Greek–Jewish relations in the 1940s.

PHILIP MORGAN   is Senior Lecturer in European History at the University of Hull. He has contributed articles on Italian fascism to scholarly works, he is the author of *Italian Fascism 1919–1945* (1995), and he is currently writing a history of Italy from the fall of Rome to the present day.

HANNES SULZENBACHER   is a curator and exhibitions organiser at the Jewish Museum in Vienna. He is co-editor of *Juden Fragen Jüdische Positionen von Assimilation bis Zionismus/Jewish Attitudes from Assimilation to Zionism* (1996) and *The Jewish Museum, Vienna* (1996). He has published widely in the fields of Jewish history and cultural history in the twentieth century.

PERRY R. WILLSON   is Lecturer in Italian History and Language at the University of Edinburgh. A founder member of the editorial committee of *Modern Italy,* her publications include a number of articles on women under fascism and *The Clockwork Factory: Women and Work in Fascist Italy* (1993). In 1992–3 she held a Jean Monnet Fellowship at the European University in Florence. She is currently researching the *massaie rurali,* the fascist mass-mobilising organisation for women.

Preface

This book had its origins in History Workshop 26, held at the University of Northumbria at Newcastle in 1992. Most of the chapters were presented as papers in a conference strand on 'Popular Resistance to Fascism'. The aim of this strand was not to assemble a series of papers which would provide a systematic or representative 'coverage' of the theme for all parts of Europe; that would have been impossible in any case. It was, rather, to invite papers which re-examined the perspectives of the postwar historiography of fascism, a theme which has only slowly begun to free itself from the taboos and political imperatives of the Cold War. There were important gaps in the geographical range of the collection, and new contributions had to be solicited. The intention in doing so, however, was never merely to fill a national or regional gap but to extend the range of critical perspectives and new approaches. The editors would like to thank the original conference participants for their patience with this process, and the authors of the additional chapters for the efficiency with which they delivered their contributions. We should also like to thank Sarah Kane, who translated Yves Le Maner's article. Thanks are also due to the University of Northumbria Small Research Grants Committee for its support during the preparation of the manuscript for publication; and to the Department of Historical and Critical Studies at the University of Northumbria, and the Research Committee of the School of History and International Relations at the University of St Andrews for their financial support for the translation of Le Maner's article. Both universities also provided important technical and administrative support. Last but by no means least we should like to thank Liz Harvey for her encouraging critical advice on the manuscript.

Introduction
Community, authority and resistance
to fascism

Tim Kirk and Anthony McElligott

I

Increasingly, history impinges on the attention of the public through the celebration of anniversaries as conveyed by the media. In Europe at the end of the twentieth century this form of commemoration has been dominated by the fiftieth anniversaries of the origins and course of the Second World War: the appointment of Hitler as chancellor of Germany in 1933, the outbreak of war in 1939, the liberation of Europe from fascism in 1945. Commemorating recent history in this way has not been unproblematic for the leaders of post-war western Europe. Indeed, two such public anniversaries celebrated in Europe in 1994 threw the problem into sharp relief. Britain and France celebrated the D-Day landings in June with their former war-time Allies, but Germany was excluded, and commemorated alone the bomb plot against Hitler in July. In its own way, each of these events reiterated powerful points in our collective and public memory of fascism and the war. For the Allies, the conflict had been one of nation against nation and was decided on the battlefield by Allied forces and armed resistance organisations operating as adjuncts of those armies. That version of the war excluded the idea of a broader resistance to fascism on the continent (including Germany itself). For many Germans the conspiracy to kill Hitler in July 1944 symbolised the existence of the 'good German', and to celebrate it fifty years later was an important reassertion before the rest of Europe that there had been decent Germans among the country's leaders, and that Germany had a 'usable past'.[1]

The D-Day anniversary celebrations represent a nationalising of the conflict between fascism and anti-fascism which conveniently buries the social and political antagonisms which were unleashed at the end of the First World War. These antagonisms were acted out at some level in every community across the continent during the course of the next thirty years, from the revolution in Petrograd to the street battles between

1

Mosley's Blackshirts and anti-fascist demonstrators in London or Manchester. Similarly, the historiographical appropriation of the struggle against nazism in Germany itself by the country's compromised elites on the one hand, and political organisations on the other, eclipses the *popular* resistance against nazism before 1933 and against the Hitler regime.

Both of the commemorative occasions mentioned above furnished the opportunity for the restatement of the elite historiography of fascism and the war which had been established immediately after its end, but which has been increasingly challenged by a vigorous historiography of popular resistance since the mid 1970s, most notably in Germany itself.[2] In the light of this restatement, it seems appropriate here to restate too that alternative tradition and, through the contributions in this book, to apply it not only to Germany but to those communities in other parts of Europe where fascism was resisted.

II

Interwar fascism was a pan-European phenomenon. No country in Europe was without its fascists or fascist sympathisers, and none without its anti-fascists. The history of fascism, however, was more than the success or failure of explicitly fascist parties in national contexts. It was part of a broader European consensus on the radical right among those who had been dismayed by the political character of the Europe which emerged from the First World War: a consensus founded on uncompromising hostility to 'bolshevism' in all its perceived forms, both at home and abroad. In many parts of the continent (though less so in the British Isles) traditional state authority was in crisis, and seeking to regain the initiative from a broadly democratic left.[3] The role of fascism in this project varied according to national circumstances. In Italy and Germany fascism came to power with the support of conservative elites. But in most of eastern and southern Europe, for example, it was marginalised because traditional elites succeeded in restoring their authority by establishing recognisably modern dictatorships without the need for a populist party which could mobilise popular consent. This was effected very quickly in Hungary, for example; and in Romania the Nazis themselves dispensed with the collaboration of the indigenous fascists. But even in these societies, fascism, together with its outward trappings and its ideology, exerted considerable influence. Thus, in Greece, Metaxas' regime encouraged the Greek youth movement to adopt the full panoply of fascist uniforms and ceremonial.[4]

Sympathy for fascism, and for the broader corpus of ideas which it shared with other groups on the radical right, was thus widespread in

Europe. Mussolini and Hitler were treated with relative sympathy by conservative public opinion during the 1920s and most of the 1930s.[5] Much of this earlier sympathy was forgotten after the Second World War or, as we have noted above, suppressed by a post-fascist historiography that redefined the acute social conflicts which fascism and anti-fascism most starkly expressed as, quite simply, no more than another war with Germany. At its crudest, this is an interpretation in which only the Germans are demonised. According to A. J. P. Taylor, nazism in Germany was not an 'accident' in history (*Betriebsunfall*), or a case of 'bad luck'; rather 'It was no more a mistake for the German people to end up with Hitler than it is an accident when a river flows into the sea'. And, Taylor added: 'No civilised nation has such a record of atrocity.'[6] This is a perspective in which the nations of occupied Europe experienced a passage from repression and victimhood to a liberation in which national resistance movements performed the duty of rescuing national honour. This experience of occupation, resistance and liberation was claimed even by Austria and Italy, and the role of the resistance as a keeper of the national conscience even extends to the historiography of Germany itself.[7]

There was something to be said for this kind of historical representation after 1945. Above all, fascism was defeated in the end by the Allied armed forces. The European order which replaced it was explicitly anti-fascist, not only in its rhetoric and symbolism, but in its constitutional origins and the character of its political arrangements. Most early post-war governments across Europe were legitimated by the presence of 'resisters' in office. In Yugoslavia and Albania the resistance actually formed governments. In Czechoslovakia it was part of a leftist coalition based on the model of the pre-war Popular Front. In Italy, the resistance leader Ferriccia Parri emerged as prime minister in the country's first post-fascist coalition government in June 1945; in France communist resisters also served in the government until their expulsion in 1947 with the onset of the Cold War.[8] Thus the black and white mythology of resistance and collaboration was not only an important commemoration of the heroism of the resistance, but an essential one in constituting stable post-war national communities.

But official resistance history necessarily obscures as much as it reveals, as indeed does the general political history of the period. The years between 1917 and 1945 have been frequently summed up in simple generalisations expressive of the *histoire événementelle* of high politics, such as 'the age of the dictators' or 'the age of ideology'; and where the majority of the population appears at all, it is as a malleable 'mass' transfixed by a demagogic genius.[9] By defining fascism so narrowly we also define resistance narrowly, and exclude, or conceal behind the periodisation of high politics or declared war and peace, the common experience of the majority of Europeans in the 'age of fascism'.

III

It is an axiom that these experiences were situated in the immediate community in which people lived – what Helen Graham in chapter 4 calls the *patria chica*. However, 'community' is an elusive construct, even though it is often taken for granted by historians. At its very basic level, it is recognisable as a geographical entity, such as the village or urban neighbourhood. At another level, a community can be defined by shared aspirations articulated in the prescribed goals of a political party; at a more abstract level, it can be notional or 'imagined': not only the 'imagined community' of compatriots who have never met each other, but also the putative or implied community based, for example, on gender or sexual orientation.[10] None of these communities are homogeneous constructs: all of them are socially stratified, bear fault-lines of gender or class and, whether in the case of the village or the nation, retain clear hierarchical structures of authority. What binds them together is the existence of what sociologists term a 'commonality of goals', that is, a subjective consciousness that certain overriding interests transcend their internal differences.[11] Not that a 'commonality of goals' presupposes constant unanimity. Common goals are defined instead in a continuous process of negotiation between competing groups – or communities within the community – with very divergent interpretations of what its common purpose is.

In inter-war Europe this was particularly evident in the conflicts between those espousing a republican ideal of the state (and, indeed, defending the republican state itself), and those wishing to impose or re-impose an authoritarian conservative concept of the national community. Finally, common goals might be imputed to a community by an external agent: the Communist Party activist, for example, who sought to discipline the inhabitants of the rural hill village or working-class neighbourhood and bind them to the party's own agenda.[12] Negotiation would then take place between representatives of competing sources of authority, both internal and external to the community itself (for example, village elders, political activists or agents of the state). Where accommodation was impossible, conflicts arose in the form of resistance to imposed authority of whatever kind, and this helped crystallise the common purpose of the community in the consciousness of its members.[13]

One such competing group, which was both part of the community and simultaneously representative of, and sustained by, external forces, was fascism itself. For, although fascist parties represented national – and nationalising – movements, their emergence and rise to power were predicated upon local conditions. That is to say they were rooted in local communities. In Italy, the *Fasci* were very much regional organisations with leaderships responding to specific local conditions. Even after Mussolini came to power, localism continued to be a dominant feature. The same can be said of National Socialism in Germany where, in spite of attempts by the party leadership in Munich to impose central discipline, some degree of regional autonomy prevailed.[14] This meant that the struggle over fascism was rooted in the very communities within which it was incubated. During its rise to power fascism was able to wear down resistance at the local level and this process of attrition prepared the ground for a national take-over of power. But even when this had been achieved, fascist authority continued to be mediated – and resisted – at the local level.

For there was no 'national resistance' to speak of, even in occupied countries where a united struggle in defence of national independence has been subsequently identified by historians.[15] Michael Geyer is therefore right to locate the problem of resistance historiography in the 'posthumous act – of creating fictitious solidarities where the breakdown of solidarity had become and continued to be the insurmountable issue'.[16] Yet resistance did occur, and it was based on real communal solidarities beneath the level of the nation.

Communally based resistance to fascism was mostly spontaneous, and usually displayed what Jacques Semelin has termed 'civil goals' aimed at preserving the integrity of the community.[17] These communities were never defined in purely spatial terms. To be sure, the communal cohesion of the working-class district or the mountain village depended to some extent on its geographical dimension, and particularly its remoteness or its impenetrability to outsiders, but it also depended on the agreed acceptance of shared values or political orientation. Other types of community had no necessary geographical definition at all, but existed purely on the basis of shared interests or common assumptions. In Semelin's view, resistance is very much dependent upon this kind of communal cohesion.[18]

Semelin also believes that such resistance had to 'start from scratch'; but the contributions in this book show that communities could also call on traditions of resisting authority. And it was these local traditions that formal resistance organisations, primarily those of the European communist parties, sought to organise and channel into a nation-wide resistance. The community was thus a site where political–ideological and personal resistance to oppressive forms of authority intersected.[19]

IV

Resistance to fascism was inseparable from the revolutionary politics which had forced concessions from Europe's established rulers after the First World War. It was rooted in the defence of political gains in the face of the right's determination to reverse them. Resistance began, then, long before fascism could come to power. As Nick Howard's contribution to this collection makes clear, in Germany this conflict began during the revolution of 1918 itself. In his discussion of the servicemen's revolt at the end of the war, Howard argues that the popular challenge to authority from below was so widespread and persistent that Germany's threatened ruling class and the new socialist government were compelled to form a pragmatic alliance. He argues that by suppressing the soldiers' councils and, by extension, the radical element of the revolution, the army and republican government together disabled the potential for the resistance to the destruction of the Republic itself a decade later, leaving the way clear for nazism to triumph.

The authority of the Republic was dealt a severe body blow in 1919 from which it would not recover. For the authority of the elites was reasserted and was used to undermine the democratic polity. In spite of the limitations imposed on the Republic by the defeat of 1918–19, democracy itself had been the principal gain. It guaranteed a degree of popular control over political authority, especially in local communities, by the exercise of the vote. Where these were working-class communities, this usually meant the election of republican administrations.[20] Yet such communities, which had gained considerably from the post-war settlement, now found themselves subject to a two-fold and increasingly co-ordinated attack. In his contribution, Anthony McElligott shows how the judiciary, as one of the principal organs of the conservative state, took advantage of the multiple crises after 1930 to extend its authority over 'rough' working-class communities which were also subjected to pro-longed and increasingly violent terrorism from Nazi stormtroopers. McElligott puts the case for the convergence of the authorities' agenda of intensified social control during the depression with an authoritarian political agenda for the state. Moreover there was a further convergence, he argues, between these conservative agendas and the political goals of the Nazis. He shows how, before 1933, a determined judiciary played a key role in thwarting communal self-defence against fascism by effectively criminalising the politics of working-class communities.

In Britain, too, fascism encountered resistance at the communal level. Drawing on oral testimonies, Neil Barrett's comparative study of the working-class community in Nelson and the Jewish community in north

Manchester reveals the strengths and the weaknesses of community-based strategies of resistance. Nelson was typical of the south-east Lancashire cotton towns targeted by the British Union of Fascists for recruitment during the depression years, in that Mosley's Blackshirts had very little success. Communal solidarities in Nelson proved stronger than nominal political differences that might have undermined the resistance to fascism. In Manchester, however, there were genuine political and generational cleavages within the Jewish community which made resistance more difficult. Young Jews, organised in the Communist Party and in other political groups, adopted a more confrontational activism from the outset; community elders, however, initially had reservations about the political associations of anti-fascism, not least because they threatened to undermine their own authority within the community. The belatedness of their response to the BUF, Barrett argues, was a consequence of the attempt to reassert that authority. In both cases Barrett shows the usefulness of studying local peculiarities for understanding the contours of resistance and the failure of fascism in interwar Britain.

Communal cleavages were not restricted to local communities, but proved to be a disabling characteristic of anti-fascist resistance at the national level. As we have noted above, national resistance movements rarely existed in pure form. Resistance came from a variety of disparate, often mutually hostile groups, whose cohesion in the cause of a common patriotic aim was often nominal at best. Indeed, even where a notional ideological unity appeared to exist, the reality was often more complex. Helen Graham's study of resistance and revolution in Spain illustrates the difficulties in maintaining unity within the ostensibly united front defending the Republic against Franco's military coup. Resistance came, as so often throughout Europe, from the communities which stood to lose, but which articulated and carried out their opposition through a range of divergent social ideologies and separate and distinct political parties. For most rank-and-file participants in the resistance to Franco, initial mobilisation in defence of the Republic was spurred by the possibility of changing and controlling the immediate, lived environment. But the local roots of the resistance movement, privileging community over state, rapidly came to disadvantage the Republic in the evolving conditions of the conflict. Thus while the potential for unity in defence of the Republic was strong, the historically fissiparous nature of the Spanish left and the persistence of localism prevented the formation of a genuinely united resistance. Above all this represented a failure to move beyond the *patria chica* and to '"think" the nation'.[21]

In Ireland, on the other hand, as Mike Cronin argues, the nation was a powerful and decisive rallying point for the resistance to fascism.

Cronin's study focuses on the resistance to the Blueshirts, Ireland's putative fascist movement. He highlights two different responses: the 'official' opposition from the Fianna Fail government, employing the full range of government authority at its disposal; and the 'popular' resistance from various splinter groups under the broad heading of republican socialism, rooted in communal mobilisation. After Fianna Fail's political success in 1932 and the recasting of the Irish state three years later, a 'national community' based on a near comprehensive political consensus came into existence. This not only obviated the need for a *fascist* regeneration of the nation, but also marginalised the Blueshirts, under their extremist leader General Eoin O'Duffy, to such an extent that they were eventually disowned by their own political allies.[22]

The realities of fascist power created a whole new set of power relationships and resistance strategies. The focus of Yves Le Maner's study of the Nord and Pas-de-Calais is not resistance as national liberation, but the impact of occupation on existing local structures of authority and on communal responses to such authority. Le Maner shows how the occupation was exploited by competing levels of the local state (prefectural and municipal) and political groups to reassert their own dented authority within the community at each other's expense. Moreover, the local state became a testing ground for the conflicting authority of the Germans and Vichy. Le Maner explores the ways in which the occupation modified relations between local elites and the population, and assesses the extent to which political attitudes were changed. Some local notables, especially in the countryside, were able to exploit the conditions of the occupation to reassert their 'natural' authority over local communities as the basis for a conservative post-war order.

The political vacuum that accompanied occupation was exploited by existing authorities seeking to reassert their position (often with the help of the Germans), and it also offered an opportunity to aspiring leaders. The politics of resistance was not only a matter of opposing the German occupation, but afforded the opportunity of establishing new structures of authority as the basis for a new post-war social order. Mark Mazower's contribution to this collection focuses upon the power relations within the Greek resistance movement led by EAM/ELAS to the German occupation and the quisling regimes in Athens. He argues that existing histories have represented EAM/ELAS as a sharply politicised, monolithic entity in a way which ignores the social, geographical and cultural realities of wartime Greece. Although the Communist Party clearly dominated the Greek resistance movement and sought to establish a vertical structure of authority, Mazower argues that no central control was ever established. Poor communications and village particularisms meant that local commanders had to improvise. The authority of the resistance movement was frequently questioned by local people even within the areas it nominally controlled. Ultimately it was the compromises of EAM/ELAS as it imposed its leadership in the mountain regions that defined the nature of resistance. Nonetheless, in Greece, as in many other parts of Europe, the experiences of individuals and resistance groups have frequently been appropriated and subsumed into an institutional historiography of resistance, not least by the Communist Party.

Such historiographical appropriation of resistance distorts the nature of historical experience and social identity. Austrian industrial workers, for example, might identify with some of the aims of the Communist Party. However, as Tim Kirk argues in his essay, the KPÖ secured conditional support only among certain groups of workers disillusioned with the Social Democratic Party. Kirk examines the different oppositional strategies, from active resistance to truculent dissent, which remained open to an industrial working class weakened by prolonged economic depression and in the absence of clear leadership after a decade of political repression. His study of the work-place community offers a reassessment of the insistence of recent research that working-class acceptance of nazism was widespread and sustained the regime in power.[23] Yet if the opposition of the working class appeared limited both in intention and impact, their communities nevertheless remained pervaded by an instinctive anti-nazism which was expressed in impromptu responses to particular policies or events.

Community consciousness was related to different kinds of authority: that of its own leaders and that suggested by external agents. It was not only that social democrats and communists asserted political authority and shaped communal identity, but also, by criminalising certain kinds of political behaviour, lawyers and policemen also imposed a cohesion. In the case of an inchoate community, externally imposed definitions might provide the first or only articulation of common identity. Hannes Sulzenbacher's reconstruction and examination of the experience of 'homosexual' men in Vienna between the wars shows how the origins of their shared sexual identity was founded on medical and criminal categories. He shows that by defining sexual norms doctors and lawyers created, from the variety of public, sub-cultural and 'hidden' sexual behaviour, distinct if unstable categories which served not only to determine the boundaries of 'normal' sexual behaviour for the police, but contributed to the development of a community consciousness. Although Sulzenbacher is critical of the notion of a 'single experience', he concludes that resistance among 'homosexual' men to Nazi repression was based on a long experience of negotiating with authority and that repression itself created the very community it sought to shatter. It was a community whose history was suppressed after 1945, both by the authorities and by historians. Nazi anti-homosexual legislation was not repealed until 1971; until then the individual and collective experience of this community under fascism could not be recorded.

The problems of the post-war historiography of fascism are the central concerns of Philip Morgan's and Perry Willson's essays on Italy. In a critique of the *oeuvre* of Italy's pre-eminent historian of Italian fascism, Renzo de Felice, Morgan argues that while there may have appeared to be a measure of political consent for the Fascist dictatorship in Italy, it is impossible to establish that it was genuine. The difficulty, as Morgan demonstrates, is the methodological problems of defining and analysing popular attitudes under the 'totalitarian' conditions of the Fascist system which aimed at mobilising 'consent' in a repressive context. If a qualified consensus was achieved, it was on the basis of the threat of coercion and in the absence of alternatives to the organisations through which the regime sought to mobilise support. Like their counterparts in Austria, working-class communities with grievances against the regime, often economic in origin, recognised the limits of the possible and expressed their opposition, not in ways that resistance activists from the PCI might have wished, but through symbolic gestures of defiance in a tradition of dissent which predated fascism itself. Such symbolic opposition to the regime is excluded from standard histories because it does not accord with the accepted categories of resistance activity.

Historians have found it difficult to abandon their stereotypical expectations of communities with which they are unfamiliar or unsympathetic. Workers who are not violently confrontational or politically docile are difficult for historians to imagine. Similarly, the notion that the contribution to resistance of women performing 'traditional' roles can have the same value and significance as that of armed men has been difficult for them to grasp.[24] Perry Willson argues that post-war histories have recast women's experience, resituating it within traditional gendered relationships. This had much to do with the post-war reconstruction of the *pater familias* as one of the key pillars of authority and stability. Her contribution reveals how, immediately after the war, an iconography of women resisters as 'saints' emerged. While male resistance was 'real', women's resistance to fascism was relegated to the traditional role of support and self-sacrifice. Armed women are either written out or deprived of their female identity, while women in nurturing or caring roles lose any claim to be equal resisters. Willson's approach broadens the discussion of women's resistance in Italy beyond their 'contribution to the anti-fascist movement', to propose a history where *maternage* (mothering) has the same validity and significance as the bearing of arms.

We have argued here that resistance historiography has prioritised the visible and the organised, and that post-war institutions (including the nation state) have appropriated the experience of resisters to their own political agendas. What binds together the studies in this collection is their exploration of the 'hidden history' of communities which do not fit easily into the above paradigm. To recover this 'hidden history' is not only to reveal the experience of a group the validity and significance of whose experience has been denied. The essays presented here have sought to reveal the contradictions and fractures within such communities and the shifting nature of their internal relationships as they came into contact with the new forces of external authority which threatened their worlds.

1 The German revolution defeated and fascism deferred: the servicemen's revolt and social democracy at the end of the First World War, 1918–1920

Nick Howard

Introduction

The November revolution of 1918 was the culmination of a series of struggles protesting against the political and social conditions brought about by the world's first war of industrialised mass slaughter. Strikes, mass desertions and mutinies led to the collapse of the discredited Wilhelmine political system and thwarted the plans of generals, admirals and politicians to prolong the war. Thus the Weimar Republic was born during a revolution to end the First World War.

The main feature of the foundation of the Republic was the disintegration of the entire armed services, together with the powers of the officer corps, the army High Command and its civil service offshoots, that formed the central pillars of the authority of the state.[1] In this chapter, the servicemen's revolts and the interventions by the social democrats are examined from contemporary reports, proclamations and press accounts and from subsequent memoirs and debates. They reveal the widespread advance of the revolution in the army when the Majority Social Democrats (MSPD) and the left-wing Independent Socialist Party (USPD) took office, initially with the general approval of the revolutionaries. After the removal of the Kaiser, however, the social democrats maintained the structures of the central state that the revolutionaries sought to abolish.

In the five months before the events of November 1918, the resistance to the war of growing numbers of soldiers on the western front took the form of widespread desertion and gave impetus to revolutionary changes prior to the outbreak of the naval mutiny at Kiel. By 4 November, the sailors' revolt had become public knowledge as General Scheüch of the High Command bowed to political pressure and had reduced press censorship on 2 November. News of the far more numerous actions against the war by the soldiers had earlier been suppressed. The impact of desertion was examined by the Reichstag Commission of Enquiry in the 1920s and evidence as to its scale points to a massive soldiers' movement of wholesale opposition to the war from August 1918 onwards, against which the generals were powerless. The numbers of deserters were estimated at more than three-quarters of a million[2] and combined with voluntary surrenders, deaths and injuries, they reduced army divisional strengths on key sectors of the western front to a reported one-twelfth of the 1914 levels.[3]

Widespread hunger and exhaustion at home fomented a wave of industrial strikes against the military and political establishment in at least fifty-five towns and cities in January 1918. Opinion among war resisters moved rapidly to the left, though the soldiers' movement generally grew without political party leadership. Later, deserters and mutineers looked to moderates within the left and right of the social democratic movement for guidance. With support from USPD activists and shop stewards from the factories and occasionally from the tiny Spartacist group of supporters of Karl Liebknecht, who was imprisoned as a war resister in 1916, strikers and mutineers set up soldiers' and workers' councils as their instruments for revolution.

Evidence of fascism in the period is minimal, despite the rise of anti-semitic groups during the war.[4] However, right-wing social democrats who organised against the revolution supported their arguments with calls to patriotism, military glory and warnings against 'asiatic bolshevism'. Such slogans encouraged the defeated generals and politicians to hold on to their declining power and similar propaganda was used later by the Nazis in their ideological onslaught against the Republic.

The disintegrating army and the rising tide of revolution

The organisational cells of the revolution, the German Soldiers' and Workers' Councils (Arbeiter und Soldatenräte, ASR), were initiated in two phases. The workers' councils originated in the great munitions strike of January 1918, in which over half a million workers participated under the leadership of workers' committees. The strike was strongly anti-war but was called off after a few days by three right-wing social democrat leaders on the central strike committee: Friedrich Ebert, Philip Scheidemann and Otto Braun, who respectively became Reich president, prime minister of the Republic, and prime minister of Prussia. To discourage further industrial action, the military High Command victimised trade union activists by sending them to the trenches on the western front. Their banishment had the effect of spreading the strikes to the troops.

The soldiers' councils originated in the practice of what Erich Volkmann, a retired army major writing in 1925, called the *verdeckter Militär-streik* or hidden army strike.[5] Mass desertion began in early 1918, and as the sufferings of the war increased, from May to October developed into mutinies on a massive scale. The existence of this movement was hidden from most citizens by censorship, but key industrialists met in private on 23 August 1918 to discuss the significance of pending collapse. The steel magnate Hugo Stinnes informed the Hamburg shipowner Albert Ballin that 32,000 soldiers had deserted in recent weeks, that thousands of conscripts were refusing the call-up, and many more were hiding in the Silesian forests where local women provided them with food.[6] Deserting soldiers could not draw official attention to themselves by the open formation of councils, but in occupied Belgium they gained protection from the size of their movement and were supported by the local population. The mood of the soldiers is reflected in a soldier's poem found in a train:

> It is all a swindle:
> The War is for the Wealthy,
> The Middle Class must give way,
> The People provide the corpses.[7]

Initially the soldiers' and sailors' councils formed a collective voice and an organised means to cope with material and food shortages. Politically, the councils demanded the removal of the Kaiser, full democratic rights and a solution to the problem of the future status of the deserters and mutineers.

On 24 October Generals Hindenburg and Ludendorff issued an order to all troops in the field to continue the war in the west, in defiance of Max von Baden's interim government, which the generals had previously authorised to seek an Armistice. On 28 October the Admiralty moved to prolong the naval war. The interception by revolutionary servicemen of these plans finally brought the resistance movement into the open. Overnight, deserters became mutineers and revolutionaries demanding the removal of the Kaiser and the High Command, an end to martial law, and an immediate democratic government to end the war. The soldiers acted against their officers, stripping them of the insignia of rank, occupying army bases, taking over troop and hospital trains, seizing military stores, organising the retreat and freeing prisoners in the weeks before the Armistice on 11 November 1918. The generals of the High Command prepared rapidly for civil war. Some senior officers, with equal urgency, organised to escape an armed confrontation in the homeland that would lead to the loss of their authority as the national leaders of German society.

Their fears were justified. From spring to autumn 1918, an estimated 750,000 to one million soldiers gave up the war, the vast majority from, or en route to, the western front. After the breakdown of the German spring offensive in June 1918 with the loss of over 400,000 men, the generals tried to replace them by combing out industry and agriculture. Warned that, if he succeeded, much of the forthcoming harvest would have to be sacrificed,[8] General Ludendorff invoked military law to divert workers from farms and factories to the front, thus worsening the food shortages that accelerated the army's eventual collapse. Many strikers in uniform plundered army food stocks on a large scale.

An early sign that desertion had turned to mutiny came on 6 June 1918, when the commanding general of the 41st Infantry Division near Beaumont-Hamel ordered those officers and men refusing to enter the trenches to be shot.[9] The threat, if carried out, had little effect. The same division again refused to fight on 8 August and was one of seven that gave up, leaving a twenty-kilometre section of the Amiens front completely undefended. As desertions increased, so reserves dwindled in the base camps in the homeland and in the armies of occupation. Whole bodies of men surrendered to individual Entente soldiers. Retiring troops met fresh divisions going into action, with shouts of 'blackleg' and 'you're prolonging the war'. Many of the officers lost their influence and were swept along with the rest[10] as the soldiers' movement took on the language of striking workers. However, surrendering did not resolve the problems of hunger at home.

In mid October the army High Command, desperate to keep the Allied advance from entering Germany, called upon civilian politicians in the war cabinet for a sudden round-up of 637,000 men, but to no avail.[11] On 17 October Ludendorff reported many deserters in Mauberge, at that time only twelve miles from the front. Significantly he labelled them as 'shirkers', not as capital offenders under martial law, under which deserters could face the firing squad. Many among the dwindling band of officers were reluctant to take extreme action against these so-called 'shirkers' and face the risk of spreading the revolts. Middle-class recruits to replenish the active officers corps were depleted at the end of September.[12] Dissatisfied with Ludendorff's cover-up, the commander of the Sixth and Seventeeth Army Groups in northern France and Belgium wrote, on 18 October, to the interim Chancellor Prince Max von Baden, insisting that Ludendorff was hiding the truth from the politicians:

Our troops are over-fatigued and altogether melting away in a terrible manner. Very many machine guns have gone missing and there are shortages of trained riflemen and rifles, artillery pieces and gunners, munitions are lacking, lorries lack fuel and our reserves of manpower are already declined to exhaustion. Thousands of pillagers drift around the rear bases. We can no longer withstand heavy enemy attacks because of a lack of reserves, and in each retreat we always have to abandon a large part of our *matériel*. The divisions can, on average, put only one thousand active men into the fight compared with 12,000 at the beginning of the war.[13]

One officer thought he had Russian *bolsheviki* under him, not German soldiers.[14] Generals who feared the spread of revolution on the Russian pattern could do little but report the phenomenon of mass desertions to their superiors. The signal station at Kovno in the east, which intercepted and publicised Hindenburg's call for a last-ditch battle, was in the hands of revolutionaries by 24 October and used its powers to link up the increasingly organised deserters.[15] The movement was in the open politically six days before the start of the Kiel mutiny.

The hidden army revolt in Belgium

Historians have argued that generally the attitudes of front soldiers in the trenches prevented acts of revolt, which began only after the soldiers had marched back in a disciplined fashion to the homeland, there to be subverted by revolutionaries.[16] By this reasoning, the German revolution did not begin until the Kiel mutiny, which the sailors spread to the soldiers via the workers' councils in the towns and cities, and thence to the reserve troops in the base camps. Though this was the situation in the coastal region, some 10,000 soldiers' councils were set up[17] and, by 11 November 1918, 110 towns and cities were in the control of the soldiers' and workers' councils. The sailors had triggered the rapid spread of the revolt, but the actions of the soldiers were more audacious before they reached home from France and Belgium than they were after they came into contact with the organised councils of social democrat workers.

Events in Belgium showed the distinct strengths of the soldiers' revolt. According to Heinrich Brüning, a lieutenant at the time, desertions there were truly a mass phenomenon in the late summer of 1918. He was astonished to find that the numbers of deserters living in groups in cellars in Belgian cities, in attics and lofts, had reached such proportions that the German military police had given up their raids.[18] Everywhere desertion was linked to the food shortage, as the deserters plundered and took control of army food stocks on an increasing scale.

The switch from covert German army desertions in Belgium to open socialist intervention was reported in the contemporary press but has subsequently received little attention from historians.[19] The initiatives of the mutinous soldiers triggered a short-lived insurrection in Brussels and in the larger Belgian towns. Evidence of previous mutinous activity in Belgium came from the working-class conscript, Oskar Hippe.[20] During Hippe's journey to the front as a raw recruit in late September 1918, hundreds of troops demonstrated against the war as they moved towards it. 'Equal rations, equal pay, then the war can stay away!' they chanted. If the officers called for discipline, they replied in unison, 'Out with the light, out with the knife, let him have it within an inch of his life!' Hippe's fellow soldiers removed the ammunition from their troop train, climbed an adjacent hill and shot up the locomotive. Threatened by a shock brigade, they continued to the front, staged their own retreat and commandeered another train to take them to Brussels. There an organised soldiers' resistance to the High Command was being set up.

General Maercker, the commander of the first *Freikorps* authorised by the MSPD, described such behaviour as the spark of revolution flying around the contaminated bases, but denied that any front soldiers took part, insisting that these events took place behind the lines.[21] The *Kölnische Zeitung* put these events in a different perspective, describing how on the barracks square at Beverloo in north-east Belgium, 70,000 returning front soldiers fought with weapons against their officers. They set up a soldiers' council, commandeered automobiles, festooned them in red and drove into Liège, Namur, Brussels and Antwerp, forming soldiers' councils en route. Contacts had been made between deserters and Belgian resisters who helped them to survive, among whom were social democrats whose links with German socialists had saved the lives of two of their leaders, Legros and Colleaux, who had been sentenced to death by the military commandant for spying.[22] Soldiers joined up with Belgian workers from the outer suburbs of the towns and cities. In the city centres, they evicted German civilian officials of the military government, occupied public buildings and court houses, freed Senator Colleaux, broke up Belgian nationalist preparations for victory rallies, removed Belgian, French, English and American flags and raised the red flag.

In Brussels, the soldiers' movement against the military government began on the evening of Saturday 9 November and victory was proclaimed at three o'clock in the afternoon of the following day. The press reported continuous fighting, and forty Germans were killed in central Belgium, in battles in which some Belgians took part on both sides. Armistice day celebrations in the larger towns were overwhelmed by demonstrators who tore down national flags and monarchist symbols. The soldiers drove off a counter-attack led by German and Belgian nationalists and freed military and political prisoners. The Press Bureau of the Workers' and Soldiers' Council in Cologne received telegraph reports signed 'Friend', 'Henry' and 'Nottebohm', to cover the identities of the senders. The short-lived socialist revolution in Belgium proclaimed a republic, demanding a universal and equal electoral franchise. Revolutionary German soldiers marched under the red flag through the working-class suburbs, released French prisoners and joined up with a general strike, arresting the Belgian mayors and senior judges. A leading Belgian citizen declared to the press, 'What has just happened here is far worse than the Great Strike of 1913. You will see that no-one has won the World War but the Socialists and nobody has lost it but the property owners.' In speeches at the strike rallies, speakers declared that reparations for war damages, a central demand of the Allied armistice terms, should not be paid for by squeezing them out of workers' living standards.[23]

The Beverloo and Brussels soldiers' councils set up an internationalist and working-class model for the November revolution but without a revolutionary socialist base to consolidate their gains. For most German soldiers, returning home was the priority and they were preoccupied with organising transport formations and saving German army food supplies needed in the homeland. To accelerate their return to Germany, the Brussels soldiers' council handed their authority to the social democrats in Cologne who ordered them to relinquish the positions of power they had so easily won for the Belgian social democrats. Discipline was difficult to maintain and some soldiers went on a looting spree, damaging city-centre properties, which the soldiers' councils later repaired before they withdrew to Germany.

The Beverloo council also came under the control of the Cologne Soldiers' and Workers' Council, where the middle classes, alarmed at the 'terrible, unplanned nature of the demobilisation' on 8 November had tried to prevent the convening of a revolutionary council in the first place,[24] calling instead for a welfare committee. The Cologne council resisted this move but the social democrats persuaded the middle-class parties to withdraw, promising that they would bring the soldiers under control. They ordered the councils in Belgium to share authority with officials of the International Belgian Relief Agency, administered by Herbert Hoover. Food supplies in Belgium were later organised by the controllers of the post-Armistice Entente food blockade, who were determined to keep food supplies out of the hands of the workers' councils in a starving but revolutionary Europe until bourgeois governments were firmly in place.[25]

The mass withdrawal of the revolutionary soldiers from Belgium, through the Maastricht strip east of Beverloo, began immediately after the Armistice. At the Maas bridges it was resisted by officers with whom fire was exchanged, but after negotiations and the surrender of weapons, the rebels moved into neutral Holland. A British diplomat reported that 70,000 troops under the control of their councils carried huge quantities of food, cattle and clothing on to Dutch trains and organised a return en masse to Germany.

British officers in charge of the Entente armies moving under armistice into Belgium and the Rhineland reported that the German soldiers' councils were 'in charge of everything, including railways, telegraphs, telephones and wireless' and that officers, stripped of their badges of rank, were ordered by the soldiers to use their skills to help the troops to return home.[26] After the withdrawal of the Beverloo and Brussels soldiers' councils, authority was handed over by the victorious Entente armies to the Belgian nationalists and the middle classes. A week after their eviction, mayors and judges were re-instated and the workers' councils of Antwerp, Beverloo and Namur and the executive of the Brussels Central Soldiers' Council were dissolved.[27] On 19 November the Belgian authorities called in the British army to restore order in Namur.[28]

The events in Belgium were replicated in most German cities in these early November days, though it was the MSPD that restored order, not the British army. From press coverage of the formation of soldiers' and workers' councils in seventeen cities and towns over the two days before 9 November, revolutionary sailors linked up with the soldiers in only six cases.[29]

The army in revolt and the prospect of civil war in the homeland

As the revolutionary movement spread in Belgium, and to Germany's main cities, the German Naval and High Commands, faced with acts of armed desertion, of food retrievals and raids on army stores, prepared for civil war. On 2 November, Admiral Ritter von Mann selected loyal submariners in preparation to sink rebellious battleships and three days later unsuccessfully sought cabinet permission for an attack on Kiel by land and sea.[30] The *Berliner Lokal-Anzeiger* reported that, in the aftermath of the mutiny, the ageing cruiser *Schleswig-Holstein* was torpedoed with the loss of 330 lives.[31] On 4 November the Kaiser prepared to lead the civil war and ordered the conversion of his sixty castles into hospitals. On the following day many large industrial enterprises were occupied by the military command. Joffe, the Russian ambassador, was expelled on the same day and on 7 November all officers on leave were recalled by the High Command.[32] The freedom of political assembly conceded by the civilian government of Prince Max on 3 November was cancelled by General Scheüch on 6 November.

On 5 November General Groener, Ludendorff's successor, gave the coalition cabinet his assessment of the situation. Diverting attention from the High Command's troubles in the west, he stressed Germany's vulnerability to bolshevism from the east. Half a million troops had moved from east to west after the armistice with bolshevik Russia on 4 December 1917 of whom around 50,000 had deserted, some after 'bloody confrontations between officers and men'.[33] Erzberger, leader of the Centre Party, contradicted Groener, stating that a bolshevik state of mind was entering the country from the western battlefront. Scheidemann, who had warned in late September that the state of the collapse was so advanced that workers' and soldiers' councils might be meeting in the halls of parliament within a week,[34] now saw 'asiatic bolshevism', coming from 'a land of millions of illiterates with a trifling amount of trade and commerce', as a greater danger than the advancing enemy. 'My party will therefore take care that Germany will be spared from it.'[35]

On 7 November Scheidemann gave his party's view that attempts by the High Command to ban the formation of workers' and soldiers' councils was 'like trying to stop the rain' and urged the government to give the MSPD a greater role in office with powers to restrain their growth. Groener considered the alternatives and discussed with the High Command the measures that might be needed to prevent the revolution from spreading to the army:

I had thought originally of a border defence between the homeland and the army, but it was too late for that. It would have had to be put in hand long ago and now there were no reliable troops in the homeland. Next we discussed the question of *Freikorps*. It was also too late for these to prevent the Revolution, but thanks to the OHL [High Command], over the November days and after they were kept in mind and then proved their effectiveness. Had the *Freikorps* been authorised and built up in August, we would not have had a Revolution. In any case it was now becoming an actual fact that was impossible to stop. The OHL sent one troop section that was holding the rear of the fighting front, back to Berlin. From this troop, the Brigade of Guards, one could expect that the unconditional discipline of the old traditional military concepts could be set against the Revolution. But this measure was of no use, because the battalions sent to Berlin had been disarmed in the homeland before they reached their destinations, by a Division allocated to Verviers [in Belgium] that had marched off without orders.[36]

Revolution was already widespread in the army. On 8 November, Generals Hindenburg, Groener and von Plessen studied the reports:

The councils had seized power in the big cities, on the Coast, in the west and south. The huge magazines and supply depots of all kinds were in the hands of the revolutionaries and the food supplies and munitions that would last only a few days and were needed by the field armies for their journey back, had already been repeatedly intercepted, particularly in Cologne and Munich. The border troops had almost all gone over to the revolution and those despatched there by the Command authorities, who had been pointed out as completely reliable troops, were immediately shot through with the evil influences of the homeland. The troops at base were fully contaminated, and the field army showed traces of subversion. Disbanded troops and uncountable numbers of deserters stormed in many thousands onto the railway lines into Liège and Namur. In view of this situation, the planned advance against the homeland was hopeless.[37]

On the afternoon of 8 November General von Linsingen resigned, after his orders to send aircraft to attack the trains bringing mutinous sailors to Berlin were countermanded by war minister General Scheüch. On 31 October Scheüch had consulted the commander of the airforce over the use of aircraft against the revolution, but was advised that it would be impossible for aircraft to distinguish between friend and foe.[38] However, Scheidemann arranged for the cabinet to send Gustav Noske, a fellow executive member of the MSPD, on a mission of parley to Kiel. He proved that his party could take control of the sailors' mutiny but failed to stop the spread of revolution.

The breakdown of authority to this degree was a real prospect. On 8 November, at Spa the Kaiser proposed to put himself at the head of his army, to seize Cologne and the Rhine and reconquer Berlin. At once the High Command summoned fifty officers with front-line experience to general headquarters in Belgium to assess the strength of the Kaiser's following. Of the thirty-nine who arrived, only one officer said his troops would obey the monarch's orders. Fifteen were doubtful and twenty-three said no. Would the army march against bolshevism in their own country? Nineteen said no, eight did not know and twelve said maybe, if their villages, herds or families were attacked.[39] The High Command, on Groener's advice, rejected the Kaiser's proposal. General von Older-shausen gave a situation report on the military transport. After the order had been made to withdraw from Belgium on 4 November:

The most complete networks and largest railway stations and enormous quanti-ties of supplies got lost. Only three or four days' supplies were left on 8 November. If the advance against the revolutionaries on the Rhine went ahead now with strength, there would doubtless be a long pause in the flow. Since the morning of 7 November, stocks were already on the move in enormous quantities. I produced a map at once after my return from Berlin on the 7th on which the progress of the revolution according to the reports of the line commanders could be made known. On the map were indicated spares depots and the sources of army provisions, so that one could clearly recognise the threat. From a glance at the map on 8 November one learnt that the maintenance of continued provisions was only possible if one operated with the revolutionaries through parleys. The use of force would obstruct the Rhine lines for days and must lead to catastrophe for the army.[40]

Mass desertion, mutiny and the dismantling of the army threatened the social structure of the German war economy. The High Command recognised its total vulnerability to this movement. On 7 November it sent Major von Jahreis from Spa to Cologne to assess the strength of the revolution. Two hundred sailors from Kiel had reached Cologne on the previous night and set up an insurrectionary council.[41] Groener used the major's report as the key to the High Command's strategy for the maintenance of its authority without recourse to armed action. The role of the social democrats was seen as central to the avoidance of civil war. Jahreis summarised the situation in his notes:

Movement set on foot by the Rabble. Terror. Opinion of the mass of the population probably for the announcement of government reform but against this kind of movement. In spite of this, the unconditional surrender of almost all the troops and the population, because the people have lost their nerve. Therefore the next outcome is the Rabble. Moderate and independent social democrats unite, after that cleverly and energetically take the Rabble in hand. The weapons of resigning troops collected, individual people from these troops armed again. Security service herewith organised. Complete success. Order restored. New authorities perplexed by administrative affairs. Therefore Danger, Rabble in short time the new power. Remedy: Re-instatement of the old regime impossible. Mass of the troops depraved, won't shoot. Mass of the population against the old regime. Therefore, support all those guaranteeing order in the new authority.
a) through the former administration's officials.
b) through military authority maintained by hand picked troops to be used as police in the cities.
c) supported by citizens' defence groups from the better elements.

Greatest danger: the homewards turning army with officers who've lost the greater part of their authority.
Proclamation: Fight against terror to guarantee the new authority. Attainment of influence through the officers' corps doubtful, therefore soldiers' councils with extensive rights. Immediately. Don't wait until force is engaged![42]

From this report Groener drew up plans to save the officer corps. On 9 November, the High Command ordered all officers in the west armies to stay at their posts, renounced any intention to unleash a civil war and sought harmony with the new government for calm and security, to spare the homeland from the worst. Weapons could still be used against criminals and plunderers. This order was not to be sent by wireless, to prevent its interception by the revolutionaries. Where soldiers' councils existed, friendly relations should be the objective. The order seemed like a surrender but its purpose was to save the officer corps.

On 10 November, 3,000 soldiers' council delegates assembled at the Busch Circus in Berlin to set up a Berlin executive council for all soldiers' and workers' councils and to endorse a revolutionary council of Six People's Representatives of the MSPD and USPD under Ebert and Hugo Haase for each party. After the withdrawal of Max von Baden, they headed a depleted cabinet of bourgeois ministers of state, including General Scheüch who stayed on as war minister. On the same day, General Groener ordered all armies to set up 'Soldiers' Councils of Trust', elected jointly by the officers and the rank and file, that could guarantee military discipline. The role of these trustworthy councils was clear. They formed the basis for Groener's secret alliance with Ebert made later that day by phone and renewed daily for the ensuing period. The officer corps should disengage, except in the narrowest sense as appropriate, from all economic and social problems and should uphold the commanding authority of the army over the troops. A Soldiers' Council of Trust was set up at the High Command Headquarters and as its mouthpiece a representative of Admiral Scheer's 'lads' was appointed to organise the distribution of thousands of leaflets calling for the maintenance of order and discipline and the protection of food and supply depots under the officers. Where independent soldiers' councils already existed, trustworthy delegates were to be sent from the officer corps to take control.

On 12 November, the Council of Six restored the power of the officers and replaced their insignia of rank in order to organise the demobilisation at a pace that met the requirements of the employers and to place food supplies under official control.[43] Most seriously for the revolutionaries, the decree gave authority to the officers to use weapons to prevent food plundering. However, no official demobilisation order was issued until 19 November, when the Prussian government decreed that soldiers over twenty-four should be released. A general order did not come through until 31 December, which still retained twenty-year-old conscripts.[44] On 12 November, the Council of Six announced that martial law was lifted. However, in practice it continued to be exercised at the discretion of the officers as the fear of famine spread.

The political line of the High Command, voiced by the Council of Trust at Kassel, was published in a leaflet on 19 November. It sought to consolidate the social democrat government of Ebert and Haase, enthused over its intentions to call a parliamentary assembly and offered the collaboration of the officers in the field army, to allow the construction of the new Reich. The leaflet declared: 'We refuse to allow our victory over the old dictatorship to be misused for the building of a new dictatorship, which must lead to a Russian situation.'[45]

Dismantling the army: the soldiers' councils and the crisis in the homeland

After the first phase of revolution, millions of soldiers proceeded to dismantle the armed services, under the duress of hunger and economic crisis. As the soldiers moved from mutiny to massive self-demobilisation, they faced loss of earnings, rising unemployment and shortages of fuel and food. Malnutrition, disease and the threat of famine were spreading, particularly in the mining regions and in many manufacturing towns. Overall food supplies were down to less than half and in some areas to one-third of pre-war levels as a result of the combined effects of Ludendorff's programme and the food blockade. Rationed supplies contained on average one-eighth of the pre-war levels of protein in the second half of 1918.[46] There was a dramatic increase in deaths among those vulnerable to famine. On average, in the month of October 1918, 6,172 people per day died in Germany, excluding deaths on the battlefields, as compared with an annual daily average of 2,542 deaths in 1913.[47]

Before the MSPD came to power, its executive council warned against using 'Russian methods' of enforced food requisitions to deal with the food shortage.[48] Ebert's government threatened those who plundered food supplies or hindered their transportation. It decreed that officials of the old regime must stay in place, property must be protected and food supplies thus maintained.

Meanwhile the leadership of the council movement was unclear as to its own role. Decrees came each day from the Berlin executive of the councils, to be countermanded after the intervention of the Council of Six. On 10 November a new state was declared by the executive council of the MSPD. However, this announcement was over-ruled on 11 November after Ebert's call to existing state and local officials to stay in office. The Berlin executive then supported this move, believing that it could supervise the actions of the officials of the military state. Complaints followed from soldiers' councils that the new bodies set up by the revolutionaries were being stripped of their powers. On 12 November the Berlin executive limited these powers to single factories or troop formations covering domestic matters.

Simultaneously, to maintain the security of the new state, the Berlin executive called for the formation of a 2,000-strong Red Guard to defend the gains of the councils. General von Scheüch, still in office as war minister, opposed this with an order that action committees to maintain sole military authority be set up independently of both the soldiers' and workers' councils and of the political parties. On 13 November, at a meeting of soldiers' council delegates at the Alexander Guards Regiment, the Berlin executive annulled the Action Committees but the call for a Red Guard was defeated by delegates from the Council of Trust on the High Command General Staff, on the grounds that soldiers should stay outside of party politics. The Berlin executive suspended its call for a Red Guard.

However, the Council of Six sent out telegrams on 11 and 13 November restoring the military powers and the prestige of the admirals and generals who had lost the war at enormous cost and defied the authority of the political powers to prolong it on 24 and 28 October. Hindenburg moved his headquarters from Spa to Kassel on 14 November and was greeted by Albert Grzesinski of the MSPD, a full-time executive officer of the Metal Workers' Union and the leader of the local soldiers' and workers' council. He declared his loyal patriotism, affirming that Hindenburg belonged to the German people, whose armies he had led to 'shining victories'.

The restored officer corps moved rapidly to fill the vacuum of authority on the streets. Despite the lifting of martial law on 12 November, an estimated eighty-six people were summarily executed in Berlin, Bremen and Hanover for plundering food and other items over the first three days of the Weimar Republic. Sixteen police were killed defending the royal palace where the kitchens were cleared of luxury foods.[49] Conflicts over self-demobilisation and food requisitions between the councils and the new social democrat–military alliance could not be resolved by military means, without the danger of provoking the civil war the High Command was still anxious to avoid. As later inquiries revealed, the striking soldiers had removed not only thousands of tons of food on their march away from the war, but also nearly two million rifles, over 8,000 machine guns and 400 mine throwers.[50] Under such circumstances, resistance by the state to the activities of revolutionary soldiers and sailors before the declaration of the Republic was minimal. The High Command and its civilian subordinates were helpless against seizures of food from army camps and stores, powerless to prevent rebellions against the officers, the occupation of railway stations, public buildings, local and national newspapers, the sackings of mayors, city and state officials, judges and court officials, the freeing of political and military prisoners, train seizures, the loss of control over communications and, most hurtful of all to the honour of the officers corps, the removal of insignia of rank.

The soldiers' and workers' councils: power without authority

At the high point of the revolution, power was in the hands of the soldiers and workers. The MSPD executive in Berlin moved rapidly to provide the leadership they lacked, but with the intention of depriving them of all immediate power. On the morning of 10 November delegates from the soldiers' councils at the Berlin barracks were persuaded by MSPD functionaries to follow the party's policy of calling for parliamentary elections to replace the powers of the councils. Pending a general election, authority was to remain in the hands of the old state functionaries and the High Command of the officers corps. On 11–12 November, the government brought into office by the revolutionary activities of the soldiers and sailors ordered them to re-submit themselves to the authority of their commanders. The unlawful possession of weapons was made punishable by five years in prison on 14 December 1918. No further gains were won for the soldiers from this submission, apart from those political freedoms already conceded by the Kaiser's government in early October 1918 and re-stated on 12 November by the Council of Six as part of a package of trade union and civil rights. Other social reforms were promised after the elections, which were still months ahead.

The surrender of popular authority was not clear to the soldiers' councils at local level. A severe test of their autonomy came from Bremen within a day of the disciplinary order of 12 November. A group calling itself the 'Bremen Flying Division' was involved in small arms fighting at Hanover railway station after it had executed three sailors and arrested thirty-four others who had been scouring the district for food supplies. A food retrievals expedition of 150 sailors was sent back to Bremen, where the press reported that twenty were subsequently executed under martial law. The authorisation for these killings was, according to Paul Fröhlich, leader of the Hamburg sailors,[51] the responsibility of Robert Leinert, MSPD chairman of the Hanover soldiers' council and later chairman of the First National Conference of Soldiers' and Workers' Councils. However, the Bremen soldiers' council later reported that the 'Flying Division' was a group attempting a putsch in Hanover on its own account.[52] The *Berliner Tageblatt* protested strongly against the arbitrariness of these executions that were made possible by the reaffirmation of martial law as a means to resolve disputes over food supplies.

The re-imposition of the powers of the army officers in this respect, and the re-instatement of mayors and other civic officials, marked an immediate attack by the social democrats on the revolutionary councils.[53] Both wings of social democracy were agreed at this stage on the need to subordinate the councils, despite the sympathy they received from within the ranks of the USPD. It was argued that without the efficiency of the officers and the state bureaucracy the smooth demobilisation of the army and the feeding of the people would be impossible.[54] However, the councils already had both tasks well in hand. The mass demobilisation of the army and the retrieval of its food supplies and of other hidden stocks were organised by the soldiers in disregard of the decrees of the MSPD and without the joint authority of the officers and the state officials who deferred to them.

The real motivation for the measures taken by the MSPD leadership lay in its fear of the revolutionary threat from below, which they feared would open the door to bolshevism. Paradoxically, the vast majority of council activists were social democrats and the MSPD's traditional leadership over the working class made them the first choice for leadership of the councils. The party built on the loyalty of its followers to restore the lost authority of the officer corps. In so doing, however, the MSPD made inevitable the civil war that was to follow.

Many soldiers' councils objected at once to the restrictions on their revolutionary powers. Councils in Leipzig, Chemnitz, Dresden, Kiel and Bremen protested, on 14–17 November, that the restoration of the authority of the officers would lead to bitterness and unrest, not to improved efficiency and law and order.[55] In Leipzig the move was seen as the beginning of a counter-revolutionary tendency.

After the executions in Hanover and Bremen, many returning soldiers who had organised food retrievals ignored the councils as centres for food re-distribution. Others became angry at the return to officer control and fought to prevent it, or expelled the middle-class party representatives who attempted to dominate the councils from within. Thus the soldiers on the council at Stargard in Pomerania, on receiving the news that the officers were mobilising soldiers returning from the front to attack their council, boarded the troop trains and persuaded them to boycott the mayor's official reception. When a later attempt was made to retake the base, the soldiers' council set up machine guns around the station and successfully kept it at bay.[56] This base was led by Wilhelm Necker, newly recruited by the USPD. A campaign of public lies alleging corruption and bolshevik depravity preceded the failed attack.

In some cities, the middle classes moved into the soldiers' and workers' councils with the intention of immobilising them. In Bonn, middle-class parties were given parity on the soldiers' and workers' councils with the MSPD. In Greifswald, the head of the police and the local battalion commander were put at the head of the councils. In Dessau and in the smaller towns in Saxony, Hesse, Thuringia, Mecklenburg, Pomerania,

Westphalia and East Prussia, local company directors sat on the councils. Where this tactic failed, right-wing newspapers urged the middle classes to set up citizens' councils to oppose the soldiers and workers. In Leverkusen, a centre of the chemical industry, a detachment of bourgeois delegates including Carl Duisberg, the director of Bayer, infiltrated the council of soldiers and workers.[57]

Both the middle classes and the social democrats preferred to tackle hunger through the semi-controlled market arrangements of the Reich Food Office, headed by Emanuel Wurm, the new USPD minister of food, who was denied the dictatorial powers he required. The revolutionary council at Kovno urged the soldiers to by-pass the old state machinery and to take control of the operation to retrieve the food stocks of the armies of the western front. On 16 November, Kovno sent a message to all soldiers' councils urging restraint in the use of trains for self-demobilisation, as the prior task was to retrieve the army's enormous foodstocks in the west to prevent a disastrous famine.[58]

However, growing hostility to the councils in the press and from the social democrat–military alliance caused many returning soldiers to act independently of the councils, rushing homewards without waiting for demobilisation papers and on the way selling and directly distributing commandeered food stocks at the railway stations or in the city centres. News reports from as far apart as Belgium, Bochum and Reichenhall described German and Austrian soldiers selling flour, sugar, coffee, rice, dried fruit, cigarettes, clothing, sheepskin, cows, sheep, horses, goats, footwear and weapons, mostly at bargain prices. The press described events in Reichenhall as 'hamstering' (hoarding) on a grand scale, a wartime practice for city dwellers, who had descended in hundreds upon farms and villages buying, bartering or scrounging food. These informal methods circumvented both rationing and the more exploitative aspects of the black market, which nevertheless also flourished in the wealthier quarters. French intelligence agents reported in early January 1919:

Immense stocks of all sorts in the army magazines have become the loot of the soldiers. The latter are to be seen in all the large towns of Germany as well as Berlin selling cocoa, tea, flour and potatoes which are punctually delivered – life in Germany tolerable because hidden stocks are coming to light without difficulty.[59]

The speed of the demobilisation process, and the resulting fall in the army's demand for meat, enabled German butchers from the beginning of February 1919 to increase the weekly meat ration by 100 grams and to continue the wartime extra allowance for heavy industrial workers.[60] However, these changes in the pattern of activities of the soldiers' movement after 10 November did not represent real progress towards their revolutionary objectives of removing the powers of the old state. In fact they marked a retreat before the MSPD's determination to protect that power. The revolutionary left was in a very weak position in resisting the attack on the councils. At the very peak of the revolution in November the Spartacists had a mere fifty members in Berlin.[61] Lacking an independent organisation and having no clear forward plans, the revolutionaries in the soldiers' councils simply began to demobilise themselves by hastily dismantling the bulk of the armed services. Groener wrote to Ebert on 14 December 1918 complaining of the helplessness of the High Command: 'If the authority of the state is not restored, the whole army must disintegrate. The soldiers' councils must disappear.'[62]

The MSPD struggled to prevent the disintegration of the state. Ebert tried to mobilise the many regiments of front soldiers still returning from the battlefields against their own councils. Civic receptions on the Stargard pattern were arranged in Berlin, but the soldiers, despite their adherence to discipline during their march home, simply dispersed themselves on arrival without awaiting orders or passes of release.[63] Nevertheless, their return in an orderly fashion enabled a powerful militaristic myth to be created that aimed to discredit the revolution. Ebert's speech to home-coming soldiers in Berlin on 10 December disregarded the role of the councils in the revolution and praised the army's undefeated glory.[64] Force was used against the revolutionaries by nationalist officers who arrested the Berlin executive of the councils on 6 December, but unarmed protesters freed them. The same officers then murdered fourteen demonstrators, thus stoking the fires of civil war. Within ten days of this attempted putsch, workers were murdered by security patrols in Dresden, Gladbeck and Essen.

From January 1919 to March 1920, the MSPD, fortified by its success in the election for a National Assembly on 19 January,[65] gave Noske, its new minister of war a free hand to unleash Maercker's *Freikorps* on the councils and their followers. The High Command was now armed for the civil war it had dreaded in November. Two days after the election Groener complained to the cabinet that the army in the west had vanished and only 130,000 men remained in the east. With the disappearance of the army had gone the strength of the soldiers' movement, which was now dispersed and disorganised; its activists were confused by the attacks on them from the social democratic leadership, despite the votes most of them had given to Ebert. Bloody repression followed against those left-dominated councils that resisted take-over and dissolution in Bremen, Munich, Halle, Brunswick, Leipzig and Hamburg. Those that survived in central Germany and the Ruhr as strike committees, or which supported workers resisting low wages, long hours and hunger, were also violently suppressed. Greater Berlin, with its population of 3.9 million and 30,000 deserters was under military law from 3 March to 5 December 1919. A general strike broke out on 5 March, food shops were attacked and five police died quelling food riots. At once, *Freikorps* armoured cars and artillery, supported by aircraft grounded the previous November, attacked the working-class districts of eastern Berlin, at a cost of between 1,500 and 3,000 lives. Some remnants of the soldiers' movement in the republican army defended the area, but were overwhelmed by Germany's 'real soldiers' revived by Noske.[66] Estimated deaths in this one-sided civil war were put at 15,000 throughout Germany.[67] Paul Fröhlich, in his diary of events over the period from December 1918 to the Kapp putsch of 1920, recorded forty-six bloodbaths and massacres perpetrated by armed soldiers against workers. There were seventeen states of siege, and twelve hunger riots in districts where rebels were deliberately starved of food. There were also some 5,000 strikes in 1919, including those of bank officials and office workers.[68]

The final wave of the soldiers' movement confronted generals and right-wing nationalists who staged the Kapp putsch in March 1920. They brought it down within a week by general strikes and armed resistance.[69] However, the putschists avenged the earlier defeat of the officer corps when General von Watter's *Freikorps* of 120,000 non-commissioned officers and right-wing students invaded the Ruhr and for months waged bloody terror against the striking communities. President Ebert gave the army's new commander, General von Seeckt, power of courts martial against trade union activists and other rebels in the Ruhr. The massacres were followed by the re-building of the regular army, which also recruited groups of the *Freikorps*. The defeat in the Ruhr marked the end of the servicemen's revolt, though its immobilisation had begun when political authority was handed to the MSPD and the USPD at the Busch Circus on 10 November 1918.

The communities of the soldiers in revolt and in self-demobilisation were transient. On 18 November 1918, recognising their own lack of control, the state authorities gave authority to the soldiers' councils to issue discharge papers, pay travelling allowances out of local government funds, and to find accommodation and priority travel on the railways, in order to accelerate the demobilisation process. In a move initiated by Haase, wholesale amnesty was granted to deserters.[70]

By rapidly re-integrating soldiers and sailors into civilian life, Germany's rulers were following a policy described by the commander of the naval base at Kiel as 'letting off as much steam as possible from the now overheated, seething boiler'.[71]

The steam did not evaporate; nor did the revolutionary crisis vaporise. The employers were not ready to buy social and industrial peace at any price. Some employers, in particular the coal owners, encouraged by the direct attacks on the councils by the High Command, staged counter-attacks against the revolution and demanded longer hours than under-nourished workers were prepared to give. The mining companies sparked off waves of strikes that were put down with force by the newly restored military authorities.[72] Following the bloody suppression in January 1919 of the Liebknecht uprising in Berlin, itself partly provoked by the decision of the MSPD to refuse demobilisation to soldiers aged twenty and un-der,[73] unemployed workers and other protesting marchers were shot down in Munich, Hamburg, Dresden, Stuttgart, Nuremberg, Bremen, Buer and Wilhelmshaven.

The communities of five million ex-servicemen, brought together in their massive rush to dismantle the authority of their leaders, continued as working-class communities based not on the nationalist myth of the front soldier, but on the solidarity of the strike, in or out of uniform. They grew hostile to the Weimar Republic and to the MSPD, the party that procured their defeat. In the June 1920 election, after their punishment by General von Watter for having struck and fought to save social democracy from the Kapp putsch, five and a half million voters deserted the MSPD, the political partner in the military alliance that had defeated the revolution. Most went over to the left-wing parties.

Conclusion: from failed revolution to nazism

The conditions for revolution are not one-sided. A trial of strength between the mass of people who no longer wish to endure the old system of authority is matched against those in power who can no longer con-tinue to exercise it. Power and authority throughout the German Empire during the First World War required absolute obedience to the orders of the High Command, at work and in the services. Once the soldiers refused to obey instructions and the officers failed to carry them through, the war aims of the ruling class became unattainable. Despite a fighting retreat from August to October 1918 by remnants of the army in France and Belgium, the generals knew the war was lost after 8 August 1918. In turning to the social democrats to secure the peace, the High Command was forced to surrender its power of command to the soldiers' councils, in the hope that the MSPD would bring them into line with the nationalist interest and restore control to the officers. After the servicemen's revolt, however, the social democrats could no longer deliver obedient and loyal workers to the rulers of the defeated Republic. The exodus of the revolutionaries to the USPD and the KPD in the elections of 1920–24, caused Ludendorff and his industrialist allies to search for a new force through which to impose their authority, and to undermine that of the social democrats who had rescued the generals from political oblivion in November 1918. They found it eventually in the Nazi Party. Tragically, millions of Germans who had witnessed the MSPD's betrayal of the servicemen's anti-war movement and who later felt betrayed during the great inflation of 1923, came to believe in the myth of an undefeated army.[74]

Few gave credence to such ideas at the peak of the revolution. The Berlin newspaper, *Die Welt am Montag* reported that a thousand nationalists rallied in Berlin on 4 November 1918, shouting 'Down with the Jews, long live Ludendorff!' Several hundred soldiers and workers singing the Internationale and crying 'Long live Liebknecht!' dispersed them without force. Within nine weeks, however, the same racists and nationalists were applauding the murders of Liebknecht and Rosa Luxemburg, lynched by guard officers after the formation of the *Freikorps* that Groener wished had been available to crush the revolt in August 1918.

2 Dangerous communities and conservative authority: the judiciary, Nazis and rough people, 1932–1933

Anthony McElligott

The transition from a liberal democracy to an authoritarian state in Germany began in 1930 and culminated in 1933 with the establishment of Hitler's dictatorship. A vital component in this process was the court-room practice of German judges and state prosecutors. The judiciary, guided by its own set of political values and social prejudices, waged a campaign against 'rough' working-class communities thought to be the loci of social and political challenge to the authority of the state. In doing so, it found itself in alliance with the Nationalsozialistische Deutsche Arbeiterpartei (NSDAP), itself locked in a struggle for control of such communities.

This chapter explores the complex relationship between judicial authority and communal resistance to nazism. In order to do this, it takes a particular case of political violence from the summer of 1932, the 'Altona Bloody Sunday' and its judicial aftermath as illustration.[1] The so-called 'Altona Bloody Sunday trial' began on 8 May and ended on 2 June 1933 in death sentences for four of the fifteen defendants. These were the first judicial killings of the Third Reich and anticipate the flood of miscarriages of justice that followed the introduction of the *lex van der Lubbe* in 1934.[2] But, as we shall see, the 'Bloody Sunday' trial was not solely a *Nazi* miscarriage of justice.

By way of introduction, a brief overview of the political position of the judiciary in the transitional period from the Weimar Republic to the Third Reich is presented. This is followed by a discussion of the crisis of authority in Germany during the final months of the Weimar Republic. Here, the events of the 'Altona Bloody Sunday' are summarised, as too is the political role of the special courts (*Sondergerichte*) set up to deal with political crimes. The introduction of the *Sondergerichte* in August 1932 and again in March 1933 is assessed in the light of the crisis in a third section of this chapter. And finally, in the fourth and fifth sections, we return to our case study of the *Sondergericht* in Altona, its handling of the trial, and the wider implications of judicial practice for neutralising communal forms of resistance to nazism and for the reassertion of conservative authority in 1933.

I

The degree to which the German judiciary had been 'nazified' by the early 1930s is still the subject of debate among historians. Until recently, many historians would have agreed with Gerhard Kramer, among others, that the German judiciary either 'stood at a distance to National Socialism'; that its members were really 'courageous resisters'; and that they were collectively forced into becoming the reluctant and unwilling tool of the Nazi regime.[3] But in the light of research since the early 1980s, a number of historians now adopt a more critical approach than the above positions suggest.[4] However, the view, first posited by the exiled leadership of the Social Democrats in early 1935, that since 1933 'Justice has lowered itself to become the prostitute of politics', still finds a wide hearing. Although critical of the judiciary for apparently abandoning its principles in the interests of self-preservation, this position ultimately exonerates the German judiciary from full culpability for the crimes of the Third Reich because it assumes that the legal system and its personnel became increasingly subject to Nazi manipulation (*Lenkung*).[5]

And yet some contemporaries, such as the social and political scientists Emil Gumbel and Franz Neumann, were acutely aware of the judiciary's highly manipulative and partisan role in the political life of both the Weimar Republic and the Third Reich. In the 1920s, its members, apart from a small handful, remained sullenly resentful of republican democracy and indeed sought actively to undermine it. Recently, the legal historian Klaus Marxen suggests that the court-room activities of the judiciary under the Third Reich were not subordinated to the political imperatives of the regime, but vice versa: that politics underwent a process of what he calls *judicialisation*. This is to argue that rather than being the tool of the Nazis after 1933, the judiciary actively participated in the shaping of politics wherever their interests dovetailed with those of the Nazis, at least until the later 1930s.[6] This model is also germane to politics before 1933.

Before March 1933 the majority of German judges and state prosecutors kept their distance from the NSDAP, aligning themselves instead with the politics and views common to the ultra-conservative and nationalist camp. Even after joining the party in the opening years of the Third Reich, many judges and lawyers still managed to retain a degree of autonomy, in spite of political pressure from the Nazis. Nor were the various sections of the German legal profession either comprehensively or equally affected by the process of co-ordination (*Gleichschaltung*) and the purges that accompanied this process.[7]

Lothar Gruchmann, whose work on the judiciary is the most authoritative to date, shows that there was a widely differing practice between the *Länder* in implementing the Law for the Restoration of the Professional Civil Service and the Law for the Admission to the Practice of Law, both passed in April 1933. Although Prussia proved to be the most draconian state in implementing these laws, he demonstrates how their overall impact was a lot less dramatic than hitherto thought. Those most affected by the new laws in Prussia – as indeed elsewhere in the country – were the Jewish members of the legal profession working at the thirteen provincial high courts (*Oberlandesgerichte*). They formed the great majority of the 11 per cent and 16 per cent of lawyers and notaries respectively who were purged. Gruchmann shows that judges and state prosecutors, enjoying higher civil servant status (*höhere Beamte*), were less affected by the laws: barely 2 per cent were purged and, again, those who were were mostly Jewish. Gruchmann's study, therefore, together with other research, shows that there was little discontinuity in personnel from one regime to the other.[8]

The judicial administration of the province of Schleswig-Holstein was hardly affected by the changes of 1933. To be sure, the province's long-serving chief state prosecutor in Kiel, Dr Peter Hansen (1921–33), was replaced by Dr Viktor Sauer, a nationalist and jurist of the 'old school', as was the province's chief judge, Dr Gottfried Kuhnt (1928–33), by Dr Karl Marten. But the personnel at the county court in Altona, which came under the chief prosecutor's jurisdiction, appear to have remained unaffected by the political change in 1933. It is also important to note that the replacements for purged personnel were not necessarily fanatical Nazis. Indeed, experience usually took precedence over party membership, which explains why less than half of the fourteen new provincial state prosecutors (*Generalstaatsanwälte*) after 1933 were Nazis.[9] The relevance of this for our argument will become clear below.

Of course, continuity in personnel did not necessarily mean continuity in court-room practice (*Rechtsprechung*), but this too was largely the case. Contrary to the traditional view positing a rupture in the role and practice of the courts between the Weimar Republic and the Third Reich, the evidence suggests less disturbance in the verdicts of the courts, especially in the crisis years of 1932 and 1933 when the *Sondergerichte* came into operation. These courts provided Germany's conservative judiciary with the necessary means to harden the criminal code, which, in their view, had grown flabby and weak in the liberal climate of the Weimar Republic.[10]

II

The Weimar Republic was beset by multiple crises of authority during the depression. On the one hand, the Republic was pressured from below as political battles between the left and right shifted to the streets from mid 1929, challenging the authority of the law (a report by the Reich interior ministry listed at least fifty-three violent clashes between political parties in the period from 25 July to 17 November), and the Republic itself was targeted for attack by Nazis and Communists.[11] According to a Social Democrat source, up to the end of December 1931 the Nazis had committed 1,484 violent acts which had left 62 persons dead and 3,200 injured; fourteen newspaper buildings ransacked, and eleven reporters and editors and five newspaper vendors injured.[12]

On the other hand, the democratic structure of the Republic was challenged from above by conservative forces within the higher levels of the Reich administration. From 1930 they took advantage of the economic and political crises to reassert executive jurisdiction over the state at the expense of the elected legislative assemblies. This conservative challenge had considerable success under the chancellorship of Heinrich Brüning, whose tenure in office saw the erosion of parliamentary politics; it was then intensified after the forced demission of the Prussian government in July 1932 at the hands of von Papen. From the summer of 1932, the reassertion of conservative authority and Nazi political ambitions began to fall into closer alignment.[13] The alliance was helped by the mostly futile actions of the German Communist Party (Kommunistische Partei Deutschlands, KPD), in particular to proselytise the police and the armed forces in preparation for a communist uprising.[14] As a result, working-class resistance to the Nazis at communal level was increasingly identified as anti-state activity.

The Weimar state was unable to curb the intensely violent popular politics that characterised these years. The election month of July 1932 in particular saw maimings and deaths perpetrated on all sides that shocked a German public that had become all too familiar with violence. In Prussia alone during June and July, there were an estimated 461 violent incidents resulting in eighty-two deaths.[15] Much of this toll was the result of the murderous street battles as local communities resisted columns of Nazis as they staged so-called propaganda marches (*Werbemärsche*) through mainly working-class districts of towns and cities. By early 1932 German politics had assumed the 'character of warfare between skilfully manned and thoroughly disciplined forces', according to one American observer. The cosmopolitan Count Harry von Kessler noted in his diary: 'Day for day and Sunday for Sunday – continuous Bartholomew night' as political opponents fought out their differences on the streets in mid July.[16]

The list of casualties grew longer as the Reichstag election set for 31 July 1932 drew closer. During the ten days before, there were 300 separate incidents of political violence leading to around thirty deaths and hundreds of injuries. On 10 July, a Sunday, street battles broke out in a number of cities throughout the Reich; one of the worst clashes was in Breslau, where at least eleven lives were claimed. The political situation in Schleswig-Holstein was particularly brittle, with the eye of the political storm in Altona, the province's largest city, with its reputation as a 'red citadel'.[17]

Altona was part of the manufacturing conurbation and port complex centring on Hamburg and was a stronghold of the left. While its administration was dominated by the Social Democrats (Sozialistische Partei Deutschlands, SPD) until 1932, key districts of the city, notably the old run-down quarters of the Altstadt, were identified by contemporaries as communist-controlled territory. The state secretary in the Prussian Interior Ministry, Rudolf Diels, noted shortly after 'Bloody Sunday': 'There is hardly another city in Prussia in which the political parties define so completely the character of the individual districts as in Altona.' Thus in every election during the Weimar period, the KPD consistently achieved results in the Altstadt that were well above levels for elsewhere in the Reich. Conversely, there were other districts in Altona which represented havens of conservative nationalism that eventually provided the bedrock of support for the Nazis.[18]

The Altstadt was destined to become the site for some of the worst scenes of violence to mark the demise of the Republic. The climax came on 17 July 1932, when some 7,000 Nazi Brownshirts attempted to march through some of the so-called 'purely communist and meanest streets' of its poorer neighbourhoods, notably the fish market district to the south and the central area just to the north of the quayside. Most of the Communist Party's offices and meeting places were located precisely here. Indeed, the streets of this area comprised a dense network of communist hangouts, that was underpinned by a consistently solid electoral support. The outcome of this attempted march was eighteen dead and over one hundred wounded.[19]

Blame for the deaths was credited to communist gunmen of the Red Front Fighting League. The police authorities claimed that in a premeditated attack their officers had come under a barrage of sniper fire from the rooftops and windows of the houses lining the narrow streets through which the Nazis marched. Thus the authority of the state had been made as much the target for communist insurrection as the Nazis had been the object of communal repulsion. A picture of the law besieged by an alliance of communist gunmen and an insurgent community quickly emerged in official reports.[20]

The idea of an insurgent working class, which was both insubordinate and contemptuous of authority, seeking to openly wage war on state and society, was firmly planted in the minds of conservatives. Chancellor Franz von Papen's cabinet referred to a 'civil war situation', and portrayed the state as endangered from the combined forces of communism and social anarchy.[21] In his assessment of 'Altona Bloody Sunday', Dr Diefenbach, Altona's commissarial chief of police for the eight critical months from 24 July 1932 to 28 March 1933, stated that the communists and local population had not acted from self-defence, but instead had set out to deliberately 'strike a blow at authority in order to weaken the state'. In his view 'only stern and consequential measures can restore respect and obedience' and thus bring the rebellious working class to heel.[22]

Meanwhile the Nazis, who had been the original cause of the trouble, metamorphosed into victims of working-class rowdyism and communist violence. For instance, four days before the massacre, Joseph Goebbels, ignoring entirely the fact that much of the violence of that summer was being generated by his own movement, wrote in his diary of the 'red murder raging through the country'. And on hearing the news from Altona of the deaths of two stormtroopers, Heinrich Koch and Peter Büttig, he expressed his horror, exclaiming, 'The KPD attack in an organised assault upon our marching SA – Civil war is declared. When will the state act?'[23]

Goebbels did not have too long to wait for the answer to his question. Three days later, taking events in Altona as the pretext for reasserting state authority, Chancellor von Papen, his interior minister, Wilhelm von Gayl of the German Nationalist People's Party, and the army minister, General Kurt von Schleicher, took events in Altona as the excuse to dismiss the Prussian coalition government led by the Social Democrat Otto Braun, on 20 July. Von Papen's constitutional *coup d'état* stepped up the counter-offensive against the left and its allies and, indeed, against the remnants of republican parliamentary democracy. Thus the ramifications of 'Altona Bloody Sunday' went far beyond its local boundaries, shaking the foundations of Weimar democracy.[24]

However, the purging of the alleged 'red system' in Prussia and its replacement by a commissarial administration with special powers to 'restore law and order', while accepted by Goebbels as a step in the right direction, was still not enough to satisfy everyone. An editorial in the Nazi provincial newspaper, the *Schleswig-Holsteinische Tageszeitung*, lamented the weakness of Weimar justice, and promised retribution for the deaths of the two SA men. The writer stated: 'It cannot be vengeance if this or that person gets three months' prison for the illegal carrying of weapons. Vengeance must be radical. The whole murderous communist plague must be cleared out!' He avowed that 'there would be no pardon and no half-measures'.[25]

III

During this phase of reasserting authority and control – from the summer of 1932 to the early months of 1933 – a string of legal measures were taken to neutralise opponents of the conservative right. These began with the emasculation of parliamentary government, starting with the Emergency Decree that dissolved the Prussian government on 20 July 1932 and concluded with the Enabling Act of 23 March 1933. Together these reactionary measures formed a cycle of legal changes to the constitutional life of Germany which, to paraphrase Ernst Rudolf Huber, were designed to defeat the 'old enemy', the republican left.[26] A critical part of these measures included the introduction of special courts by decree on 9 August 1932.[27] The introduction of these *Sondergerichte* would enable Germany's conservatives to reassert their authority after having been forced to retreat in 1918 with the collapse of the 'inner front' without having to resort to extra-legal violence.[28] Using the judicial process stripped of democratic controls, conservatives would be able to regain the initiative over the political situation. At Nuremberg in 1946, von Papen would seek to exonerate these courts by stating that they were simply an 'expeditious' response to the breakdown of law and order in 1932.[29] The attempt by von Papen to omit reference to a political strategy in the practice of these courts, abetted the idea of an unpolitical judiciary, and was welcomed by it in its attempt after 1945 to distance itself from Hitler and the Third Reich. But, as Franz Neumann has argued, 'Law is the most pernicious of all weapons in political struggles, precisely because of the halo that surrounds the concepts of right and justice.'[30]

Similarly, when the *Sondergerichte* were re-introduced on 21 March 1933, this was as part of this continuing concerted political strategy. During the cabinet meeting immediately prior to their re-introduction on 21 March, Franz Schlegelberger, the secretary of state at the Reich Justice Ministry, pledged judicial support for the 'present government of national renewal' in its fight against 'treasonable' acts.[31] A leading jurist in the

Justice Ministry who had joined the NSDAP in the autumn of 1932, Dr Crohne, wrote in *Deutsche Justiz*:

> The *Sondergerichte* are called upon in peacetime during periods of political tension to ensure that restless spirits will be warned or removed through a speedy and emphatic delivery of penal authority and to ensure that the smooth running of the state machinery will not be disturbed. . . . The sentences will be tightened up and immediately and ruthlessly carried out in order to frighten the like-minded.[32]

Reliable information on the precise number of indictments, trials and defendants dealt with by the *Sondergerichte* before 1933 is difficult to obtain and can be conflicting. Thus according to one unpublished source relating to the courts in Prussia, between 12 August (when they came into operation) and 21 December (when they were rescinded), 16,328 cases were brought before the thirty-nine *Sondergerichte*. However, the number of proceedings actually opened came to less than 10 per cent of that number, and involved some 3,250 defendants. Nearly three-quarters of the total number of cases were in the heavily industrial and urbanised areas of Prussia. Another report published in late November by the Social Democrat weekly, *Vorwärts*, reported for roughly the same period that 306 trials involving 1,439 defendants had taken place before the forty-five *Sondergerichte* operating throughout the Reich.[33] Whatever the actual figure, the courts proved to be a lethal weapon in the hands of the state, especially after January 1933.

In the first weeks and months of Hitler's chancellorship, thousands of opponents were rounded up and brought before the special courts. Official data published in the Reich statistical year books suggest a rise for 1933 (March to December), when 5,365 indictments were brought before the special courts, and of these nearly half were in Prussia.[34] Defendants in many cases had to face the arbitrary and unequal force of the *Sondergerichte*. The position of the prosecution was greatly strengthened at the expense of the defence as a result of a number of innovations 'eliminating formalism' and intending to speed up the process of legal retribution 'with the greatest possible thoroughness and speed, and at the lowest cost'.[35]

Inevitably, such innovations led to a reduction in the safeguards guaranteeing the protection of the defendant. For instance, the pre-trial judicial investigation determining whether or not the charges were justified was dispensed with, as were the opening statements of counsel; the defence was denied access to the charges and lost the power to negotiate the setting of a trial date; a shift towards authoritarian justice was indicated in the removal of the right to be tried by one's peers, leaving judgement in the hands of three professional judges, whose chairman had wide powers including the right to deny defence counsel's submission of evidence to the court; after sentence had been passed there was to be no legal means of appeal; and a retrial could only take place if new facts or evidence were unearthed that convinced the prosecutor of the necessity for a new investigation in the ordinary courts. In short, the role of the trial was to legally *affirm* the guilt of the defendant and to inflict punishment without consideration of mitigating circumstances.[36]

In spite of claims in 1932 that the *Sondergerichte* were necessary to combat political violence of *all* persuasions, they were in fact vehicles for the repression of the left.[37] The author of the *Vorwärts* article cited above marshalled evidence to show how the courts were being used to suppress mostly communists and socialists. The writer showed that of the 1,439 defendants, a total of 914 (or 63.5 per cent) from all parties were found guilty and convicted. But of this number well over half were members of the socialist and communist parties, who also stood a greater chance of conviction; when convicted, they also received sentences which far outstripped those passed against the right. While it is possible that there was little political discrimination in bringing people before the courts, clearly the decisions of the judges displayed a bias against the left. This is a pattern that conforms with Emil Gumbel's findings for the early years of the Republic.[38]

The practice of the Weimar *Sondergerichte* led to widespread concern over the issue of infringements of civil liberties. Nonetheless, this concern was by no means universal, as the heated debate which erupted over the courts in the Prussian State Chamber testifies. On the one hand, the Chamber's working committee on constitutional law, dominated by the centre-right and liberals, acknowledged that the practice of the *Sondergerichte* infringed the basic rights of the individual. Some members stressed, however, that the interests of the state came first. They were prepared to see some regulation of practice but not the removal of the courts. Social Democrats and Communists, on the other hand, wished to see the courts revoked entirely and tabled motions to that effect.[39] The left was too keenly aware of the political bias in the verdicts and called for a reduction in the severity of sentencing. Even the deputies of the NSDAP in the Prussian diet – possibly with the Potempa murderers in mind – complained bitterly about the practice of the courts.[40]

The moderate parties protested against the denial of basic rights and the retrospective application of the *Sondergerichte*'s jurisdiction on political acts before 10 August. The latter feature of the courts threatened the principle of *nulla poena sine lege*, and led most members of the political parties convening in the Prussian State Chamber to support the Catholic Centre Party in its motion calling upon the government to abolish this part of the decree.[41]

The *Sondergerichte* were eventually withdrawn at midnight on 21 December, and unfinished investigations were transferred to the ordinary courts. However, this transfer did not necessarily entail a change in the court personnel dealing with individual cases. Moreover, when the courts were re-introduced in March, a simple transfer back to the *Sondergericht* of case and personnel was effected. The re-introduction of the *Sondergerichte* in March was welcomed by judges and prosecutors, many of whom could now be assured that the most effective instrument was once more at their disposal in their struggle to purge the 'restless spirits' and 'like-minded comrades', as Crohne called them, from the regenerated national community.

IV

The state prosecutor at the special court in Altona listed twenty-one persons for their alleged part in 'Bloody Sunday' in the original indictment sheet drawn up in December 1932, but by the following April this number had decreased to fifteen. The accused came to trial on 8 May. Thirteen of the fifteen defendants came from the same close-knit neighbourhoods of the central Altstadt and fish docks area of the city. Nearly all of them were married with families, and all, except one who was a lodger, had permanent homes.[42] Most were involved with the KPD, either as full-time functionaries or loosely associated with the neighbourhood formations. The same sorts of close residential patterns were in evidence for the twenty-two defendants in a second trial in October the following year.[43] Police interrogations repeatedly showed the clearly important role neighbourhood networks played in providing an informal base upon which to build popular communist-influenced defence organisations, notably the Anti-Fascist Action (Antifa), which had a nominal strength in Altona of nearly two and half thousand by the summer of 1932.[44] Such close communal networks allowed the KPD everywhere to continuously regroup, for they provided its activists with a 'sea' to swim in the face of the severe political clampdown after 1933.[45]

Most of the fifteen men had been detained since 17 July. Some had been detained and subsequently released, and then, on the basis of shaky witness accounts, later re-arrested. Other individuals were picked up as the investigation progressed, sometimes as the result of denunciation or hearsay. In the notable case of nineteen-year-old Bruno Tesch, old scores were clearly being settled. Almost as a matter of policy, testimony exonerating the accused and defence witnesses was disregarded. This manner of loading the prosecution's case against the accused was typical of the way the judiciary was operating against defendants from working-class communities from 1932 and it did not go unnoticed at the time. Rudolf Olden, a prominent lawyer, commented in the left-liberal journal, *Die Weltbühne*: 'It is also important how the conflicting parties are brought before the court. Who sits in the dock and who is allowed to raise their hand as a witness? Often the trial is decided before the charge is even made known, and the verdict is not always just.'[46]

Thirty-five-year-old August Lütgens and thirty-seven-year-old Stanislas Switalla (who was being tried *in absentia*) were charged with overall responsibility; twenty-seven-year-old Walter Möller and twenty-year-old Karl Wolff, both from Hamburg, were accused of being communist gunmen; so too was Bruno Tesch and twenty-five-year-old Peter Wolter from Altona. The remaining defendants were on trial for their role as leaders of house and street cells leading the resistance against the police. Among the charges the men in the first two groups faced were conspiracy to murder, murder, serious tumult and attacks against the state. The others faced charges ranging from accessory to murder and serious tumult to disturbance of the peace.

After an initial investigation led by a county court judge, Dr Hildebrand, a more detailed judicial inquiry by an eleven-man team headed by the state prosecutor in Altona, Dr Behrens, followed. Behrens and his men were appointed to the *Sondergericht* on 12 August. Hildebrand was also assigned to the *Sondergericht* and continued with his pre-trial investigations until April. The judge presiding at the *Sondergericht* was Dr Block (originally appointed on 17 November), assisted by two deputies, one of whom had already been appointed on 14 September.[47]

The trial opened in Altona amidst wide public interest on 8 May and after four weeks concluded on 2 June with death sentences and loss of civil rights in perpetuity for Lütgens, Möller, Tesch and Wolff. Of their co-defendants, six faced sentences of penal servitude or prison totalling forty years and six months and the loss of civil rights for a total period of thirty-four years; three were acquitted, while a fourth had charges dropped under the presidential amnesty of the previous 20 December. These four men were taken into 'protective custody' by Goering's newly created secret state police (*Geheime Staatspolizei* or Gestapo) immediately after the trial.[48]

As we noted above, the procedural construction of the *Sondergerichte* was not designed to uphold the civil liberties of the defendant. Detailed analysis of the surviving police and court records shows that in spite of reservations in some quarters as to the quality of the evidence, Behrens was happy to resort to dubious witnesses, many of whom were political opponents or had a pecuniary interest.[49]

Moreover, he was also prepared to distort the evidence in his effort to substantiate the charge of a communist conspiracy against the NSDAP, police and state. The court was content to connive in this. For instance the *Sondergericht* was unable to prove the direct involvement of Lütgens; nor could it show beyond doubt that Tesch, Wolff and Möller had either held or fired a gun. The witness accounts seriously contradicted one another on particular points, especially those relating to the positions, clothing and physical descriptions of the alleged snipers. Witnesses for the defence were not put under oath, thus rendering their testimonies inadmissible, while evidence that had been previously retracted, and thus was unsafe, found its way back into the court. Key scientific evidence – which now appears to have been fabricated by the police and the state prosecutor's office – and 'expert witnesses' called for the prosecution were allowed to go unchallenged.[50]

However, such anomalies were ignored by the court. Its function was not to dispense justice in the sense of the law, but to reassert the political and social authority believed to have been lost under the Republic. Already, in 1932, the judiciary was becoming increasingly detached from the political constraints imposed by Weimar's constitutional system, which, in spite of the visible erosion of rights, had still been able to offer some safeguards against judicial excesses. After January 1933, the judiciary was able to rely on a more favourable political climate in its efforts to overcome what it perceived as an 'epochal cultural crisis' by dismantling Weimar's 'magna carta of the criminal' and the substitution of a more authoritarian justice.[51]

Henceforward working-class social and political 'criminality' which challenged the basis of the state was to be stopped once and for all through the agency of the *Sondergericht*. During the debate in the Prussian *Staatsrat* over the practice of the courts, members had also expressed concern over prosecutors' offices throughout the Reich resorting to the special courts to try non-political offences. Thus, by the late summer of 1932 at the latest, the distinction between social and political acts was being purposefully blurred and this process was quickened from March 1933, after the introduction of the Law for Combating Malicious Acts. Under this act, political violations and social crimes were dealt with side by side by the special courts solely as a means to strike fear into working-class communities, as Peter Hüttenberger's study of the *Sondergericht* in Munich shows.[52]

Of the three *Sondergerichte* in operation in Schleswig-Holstein from the late summer of 1932, that in Altona was by far the busiest and most draconian in its handling of cases.[53] Under Block's chairmanship, and powered by Behrens' zeal, the special court in Altona before 1933 was more likely than not to find a defendant guilty, and was more inclined to pass sentences of penal servitude than prison, which were invariably more severe and longer than those passed elsewhere.[54] The travesty of justice manifested in the proceedings of the 'Bloody Sunday trial' and the vicious sentences of 2 June, were, therefore, neither anomalous in the tradition of the judiciary at the end of the Weimar Republic, nor were they manifestations of a 'nazified justice'.

The language employed by the court, the prosecutor's office and by other state agencies, from the prison director to the prison social worker, whose reports were so crucial in the clemency procedure from June to the eve of execution, reveals the contours of social prejudice and the degree of antipathy towards a perceived 'communist' working-class community. Their assessments of the condemned men, parroted by the press, were couched in terms of the twin paradigms of the 'slum' and the pseudo-sociological discourse of 'cowardly criminal types' bent on communist subversion.[55]

Lütgens had been born illegitimate into a large family and had received little formal education and, in view of his age, stood beyond redemption. According to Behrens, Lütgens' 'moral inferiority is also revealed by the fact that for years he has left his mother without any news of himself'. Moreover, he had a relationship with a local woman, in spite of having a wife and two children in Russia. He would remain a 'fanatical bolshevik' who would continue to attack the state. The prosecutor therefore energetically opposed clemency.[56] In the case of Tesch, Möller and Wolff, they had grown up in the morally degenerate communist neighbourhoods of Altona and Hamburg. Their lawyer, Harry Soll, wrote to Goering in June pleading clemency on the grounds that 'because of their youth they were unable to escape the influence of their milieu. They were drawn into communist circles through their colleagues at work and friends, and because of their political immaturity, fell under the spell of communist ideas'.[57]

But such arguments cut little ice with the authorities. The police and the prison director saw in Tesch an inveterate 'spirited communist'. His biological father was an unknown Italian, while his mother stemmed from a Croat family – a volatile mix indeed! Wolff and Möller, who had received more positive social and police reports, were nonetheless described respectively as 'troublesome' and of 'little intelligence' and 'too fond of alcohol'. All four were considered to be 'resolute in their views' and 'unrepentant'.[58] Of the fifteen men in the dock in Altona, nine had previous convictions, including two of the condemned men.[59] The language and practice of the judiciary barely disguises the fact that it was not only the fifteen men who stood in the dock, but also the 'ungovernable' working-class community of the Altstadt *per se*, so typical of Germany's many 'little Moscows'.[60]

Given the weakness of communist activists in factories, working-class neighbourhoods remained the chief locus for communist-based resistance both before and after 1933.[61] These neighbourhoods were areas identified with radical or left-wing politics, though these were not necessarily solely defined by the Communist Party. Political and collective consciousness in such communities was forged and underwritten by social and kinship ties, cultural networks and shared material conditions which helped to construct a fairly solid local landscape of 'defensible space'.[62] Examples of this could be found in Berlin's working-class districts of Neukölln, Friedrichshain, Moabit, Prenzlauer Berg, and notably the Köslinerstraße in Wedding, a 'no-go area' to Nazis and the police before 1933; or in Augsburg's working-class suburbs of Oberhausen, Wertach, Pfersee and the Südwestend; or in Nuremberg's St Johannis district. The Schlachthof district in Munich-Central was, like Altona's Altstadt, a large area of mostly poorer working-class households and a communist stronghold. Its numerous taverns were notorious for their 'rough' entertainment and as a sanctuary for local communists. Large parts of the Schlachthof remained 'closed' to outsiders, and its penetration and control by the police and the Nazi state was a slow process after the Nazi *Machtergreifung*.[63]

By making an example of the accused men in the Altona trial, such intransigent working-class communities would be taught a terrible lesson in heeding authority. For this reason alone the *pro forma* plea for clemency was rejected by the provincial chief prosecutor in Kiel, Dr Viktor Sauer. Sauer was no friend of the German working class and had already demonstrated this to great effect.[64] Although he had been appointed by the Nazis in 1933, he himself was not a Nazi. Nevertheless, his reasoning and language cannot be distinguished from that of the young Nazi jurist Roland Freisler, who in 1933 also called for a more authoritarian justice that would not shirk from the extirpation of 'asocial elements'.[65] In Sauer's view:

The survival of the German *Volk* and the state absolutely demands that this enemy be annihilated with all means . . . The hitherto inadequate and thus unsuccessful struggle against communism . . . forces the severest measures, of which only the obliteration of this most bitter and dangerous enemy of the nation can be expected . . . Also, leniency would not be respected by the great majority of the supporters of bolshevism. Instead, it would be inferred as a weakness . . . The carrying out of the punishments would demonstrate indelibly to communist inclined circles the entire gravity of the situation; it would be a lasting warning to them and work as a deterrent.[66]

Lütgens turned Sauer's analysis on its head. On the eve of his execution set for 1 August, he is reputed to have told the prison authorities that 'the government would reprieve him if it felt strong enough, but if it felt weak, it would confirm the verdict and carry it out'.[67]

V

As the KPD was forced into underground activity between late summer 1932 and early 1933, and thus melted into the shadows of the tenements, those charged with defending the authority of the state became less and less able to distinguish between activists and the people of the neighbour-hoods in which they operated. Hence, from the summer of 1932, repression through the courts was directed not at individuals but at communities.[68] At the time of the 'Bloody Sunday' trial the process of asserting authority was still incomplete. In spite of repeated police successes in exposing communist underground networks, popular and semi-organised resistance continued unabated; every time a communist cell was destroyed, another formed to take its place.[69] Thus from the perspective of traditional conservatives such as Viktor Sauer and his masters in the Justice Ministry, and for the Nazi leadership eager to consolidate its position in government, striking terror into the heartlands of the working-class community in order to tame it had become a prerequisite in their bid to reassert their authority.

The eventual success of the judicial campaign to pacify working-class communities can be gauged from an article in an issue of the conservative-nationalist journal, *Die Tat* ('The Deed'), published in November 1933. After a visit to Berlin's 'red' Wedding, Otto Christian Kühbacher, asked 'Where are the people?':

Who knows that in these tenements hundreds of people live, very many in so-called kitchen-apartments [*Kochstuben*]; who knows that from among these people the mass of revolutionary demonstrators had been until now recruited by the Communists; that they used to stand in groups in front of the entrances to the tenements or the taverns discussing noisily or even in anticipation of a call to arms late into the night; whoever knew the Köslinerstraße before 31 January, must now ask: where are the people? They still live there, crammed up to the gables of the many-storeyed houses. Are they still the same or have they become different?[70]

Of course, the people of this community were still the same. But like their counterparts in Altona and elsewhere they no longer ventured beyond its boundaries.[71]

3 The anti-fascist movement in south-east Lancashire, 1933–1940: the divergent experiences of Manchester and Nelson

Neil Barrett

Most of the studies in this collection focus on those countries where fascist movements have made a major impact. This chapter is concerned with the most important British manifestation of fascism, the British Union of Fascists (BUF).[1] I will look at the impact of the BUF, and more importantly the resistance to it, in a single region. Although fascism had a marginal impact in Britain, that is not to say that the anti-fascist struggle here was unimportant. At the least it clearly had an impact at the local level in terms of the maintenance of order, and this was coupled with efforts by certain sections of British society to maintain communal authority, as will be seen in the analysis of Jewish activism below. On a more general level the discussion raises questions about the role and direction of the liberal state in crisis.

Most studies of fascism in Britain understandably emphasise the point that any consideration of the social, economic, political or cultural characteristics of 1930s' Britain shows clearly that it would have been monumentally difficult for a movement of the extreme right to have made significant headway.[2] This is undoubtedly so. Indeed, in political terms alone, one significant consequence of the birth of the National Government in the summer of 1931 was the marginalising of any solutions to the crisis outside a very narrow mainstream.[3]

Such analyses were far from self-evident, however, to those who opposed the BUF. Many were becoming increasingly worried by events both in Germany and Italy, as well as in Spain, where a number of activists had first-hand experience of fighting alongside the increasingly beleaguered republican forces.[4]

Most of the fairly small number of studies of anti-BUF activity have rightly concluded that the storm centre of such activism was the East End of London. As a result, they have tended to overlook other foci of opposition to the movement outside the capital. The importance of Lancashire as a potentially fertile recruiting ground was not lost on the BUF, however, and by 1934 the north-west of England was attracting considerable interest. By the following year it was rumoured that the BUF was considering moving its national headquarters from London to Manchester, which had just replaced Preston as 'Northern Command Centre'.[5] Although nothing actually came of this, Manchester did become the Northern Area Headquarters for the whole of the north of the country with the reorganisation of the movement in 1936 into two zones, north and south.[6]

The vicissitudes of the county's major industry, cotton textiles, most notably after the slump of the early 1930s, provided the cause which the BUF believed would attract considerable support. This particularly acute crisis was undoubtedly a major reason for the numerous concerted efforts by the BUF to attract support from among impoverished cotton operatives, working or otherwise. Webber notes that the BUF had 40,000 members nationally in 1934, some 5,000 in Lancashire alone (although by late 1935 this figure had fallen to 1,500).[7] It was not until late 1938 and early 1939 that national membership numbers returned to their 1934 levels as the BUF endeavoured, with some success, to appeal to growing anti-war sentiment. Membership in Lancashire had recovered somewhat earlier, reaching 2,000 members by the end of 1936; and by September 1939, membership in the county once again reached its mid 1934 high point, bringing it into line with the national trend.

I want to examine in detail the responses to the growth of the BUF in two parts of Lancashire: Manchester and Nelson. The former, the principal city of the region, was and remains a major urban centre with a long tradition of political activism. In the 1930s the Communist Party of Great Britain (CPGB) was an important force on the left locally. Its presence owed a great deal to its influence in the engineering industry, which was significant within the local economy, and to the intense activism of specific sections of the Jewish community. The CPGB led the fight against the BUF in Manchester and its satellite towns, though it was far from the only player in the field. It was particularly adept at making use of numerous formal and informal channels which either already existed or were created in an attempt to block BUF efforts to establish a significant bridgehead in the area.

Nelson is an interesting counterpoint to Manchester. It too had a radical tradition, and was known locally by the sobriquet 'Little Moscow'. The town had not existed before 1870. Yet by 1890 there was a settlement large enough to warrant borough status, which brought democratisation of its institutions; and the town continued to grow rapidly up to 1914.[8] Its population increased from 5,589 in 1871 to 32,713 by 1901. Nelson attracted radicals, often ostracised in their own localities because of their views, who mixed with those attracted to the area by relatively high wage rates: non-conformists drawn from the land or from worked-out lead mines in Swaledale, Wharfedale and Wensleydale in neighbouring Yorkshire. A smaller number of immigrants came from Cornwall. The Fowlers note that the most popular church in Preston was Salem, part of the radical Methodist Independent Connection, with its tradition of chapel democracy, self-government and education, temperance and political activism.[9] The prominent Nelson Independent Labour Party (ILP) activist, Stan Iveson, remembering the Carradice brothers (also prominent in the local ILP), remarked that the family had been driven out of Malham in north Yorkshire by the local squire, who had objected to their radical beliefs and their Methodism, which had clashed with his own Anglican Tory outlook.[10]

In Manchester anti-fascist activism was characterised by three salient and often connected features. Firstly, there was direct confrontation with the BUF on the streets. This was closely connected to Jewish activism, most notably through the Young Communist League (YCL), and was spearheaded by its Cheetham branch, known as the Challenge Club. The club took its name from the YCL newspaper and with a membership estimated at between 150 and 200 was one of the largest YCL branches in the country. The Challenge Club was formed in Cheetham in late 1933, over a disused garage. Most Challenge Club members were Jewish.[11] It provided a place for the YCL to meet, and a gym and cycling club operated from the premises. Food was also collected for Spain, and a number of members fought there for the Republican cause. Outdoor meetings were also arranged at the local 'Speakers' Corner' on Marshall Croft. All this activism stood in marked contrast to the apparent inertia of the Jewish elite in the city, and indeed nationally, challenging the usual perception of the persistence of communal authority within the Jewish community. Secondly, the anti-fascist movement used more traditional political channels, often in an attempt to get BUF meetings banned. Such methods were used despite the mistrust of significant sections on the left of the National Government, which was often perceived, at the very least, as having fascist potential. Thirdly, and despite the reservations of the national Labour Party, there was within the Manchester left clear cross-party activism in opposition to the BUF.

The first BUF meeting of note in the city took place on 12 March 1933 at the Free Trade Hall. Those newspapers which covered the event largely concerned themselves with the violence which attended it. The

Manchester Guardian reported that some 130 BUF stewards had been on duty and that the numerous hecklers had been very harshly dealt with, despite the pleas of Sir Oswald Mosley that they should be allowed to ask their questions.[12] As one questioner was felled by a blow from a rubber truncheon, the mood of the audience became markedly more hostile and fights broke out in the body of the hall, accompanied by shouts of 'Down with fascism!' and the singing of *The Red Flag*. It was also reported that order was not restored until six policemen entered the hall and escorted the BUF stewards outside. Thus, from the outset in Manchester, there was a conscious policy of denying the BUF the opportunity to get its message across, and a willingness, when the situation demanded it, to confront the Blackshirts physically. The BUF never shook off the reputation of being a movement which had few qualms about the use of violence, and this made an appeal to a wider audience all the more difficult.[13]

Just over eighteen months later it was reported that six anti-fascist activists had been ejected from a BUF meeting, again at the Free Trade Hall.[14] Probably the most vociferous was Evelyn Taylor, who was arrested and fined because of her activities. She appealed against the conviction, but her appeal was rejected by the Recorder of Manchester, Sir Walter Greaves Lord, who concluded: 'I think people are a little apt to think that under the idea of free speech there exists a free and unlimited right of interruption, which carried to its complete conclusion would make free speech quite impossible and would destroy one of the very greatest liberties we possess.' For her part Taylor showed no contrition, saying that she had not come to hear Mosley speak and was determined that no one else should.[15] The outrage of the liberal establishment at the tactics of sections of the left in attempting to deny the BUF what might now be termed 'the oxygen of publicity' is clearly visible from the statement of the Recorder of Manchester. For these people, such activities struck at the heart of liberal democracy and represented a clear flouting of established societal norms. Yet many anti-fascist activists were of the opinion that free speech was not a licence to say whatever one wanted, an attitude which, as in the case of Taylor, might bring them on occasion into sharp conflict with the authorities.

The ability of the anti-fascist movement in Manchester to mobilise a large number of followers was clearly evident in the aftermath of a BUF meeting at Hulme Town Hall, close to the city centre, at the end of June 1936. As Mosley left the building, *The Times* estimated that between two and three thousand persons rushed his car, booing and shouting.[16] The police were called to escort his car to the nearby BUF local headquarters. However, it was at this point that the disorder reached its climax, as an extremely hostile crowd gathered outside, windows were broken, and the fascist flag was torn down. Nellie Driver, a prominent BUF member from Nelson attended this meeting and was also present inside the headquarters. In her view the people of Hulme were receptive to Mosley, and it was only the action of drunken 'Reds' that had inflamed them, especially after it was rumoured that BUF men had trampled to death a three-year-old boy. Indeed, Driver concluded, 'the local inhabitants were highly indignant at the invasion of all these troublemakers'.[17] After a night of violence, order returned only slowly, though the *Manchester Guardian* concluded that the crowd had been so numerous that, had it wanted, it could have caused far greater damage.[18] It appeared to Jewish activists in the Challenge Club that the leaders of their community, in so far as they recognised a threat from fascism at all, simply hoped that the BUF would disappear. For example, Bernard Rothman, a well-known Jewish activist at the time, believes that the Jewish elite in the city were of the opinion that challenges to the BUF only encouraged the movement. Another activist, Lily Wilde, concludes that community leaders merely buried their heads in the sand, hoping the problem would go away.[19] Certainly, until the middle of 1936 the Jewish elite – above all the Board of Deputies of British Jews (BoD) and its Manchester arm, the Council of Manchester and Salford Jews (CMSJ) – saw the BUF as a relatively minor threat. Yet at a meeting at Belle Vue in September 1934, Mosley clearly showed his awareness of where the most vociferous opponents of the BUF were in Manchester, and his anti-semitism, when he remarked: 'Look at the mobilisation of Jews from Cheetham Hill Road' and 'what they call the will of the people today is nothing but the organised corruption of the press, cinema and Parliament, which is called democracy, but which is ruled by alien Jewish finance – the same finance which has hired alien mobs to yell here tonight'.[20]

The tardiness of the communal elite to recognise the threat of the BUF appears in some measure to be because the threat was well removed from their everyday existence. Most, if not all, lived well away from the less salubrious Jewish areas, in what their poorer co-religionists saw as gilded ghettos. The BUF chose to confront Manchester Jewry in Cheetham which, by the 1930s, was very much a poor Jewish enclave.[21] The bulk of the Jewish population still lived to the north of the city centre, though there was a small but growing community about four or five miles to the south. As their social position improved, many Jews in the northern enclave moved away from Cheetham to the more prosperous suburbs of Prestwich and Whitefield.

The Jewish elite began to take more heed of the threat from the BUF around 1936, albeit in a rather modest and short-lived way. Any understanding of this involves some awareness of the internal dynamics of the Jewish community. The Jewish elite continued to exercise social control over the wider Jewish community in a way that had long ceased to exist in British society more generally. This authority at the local level was mediated through the CMSJ, which had control over important aspects of communal life, such as food production and burial. Bill Williams argues that this was important because the Jewish middle class, and particularly its leading social figures, continued to play a vital role in attempting to integrate newcomers into the social, economic, political and cultural ways of the host community.[22] This can be seen as an implicit bargain struck between the local Jewish elite and their Gentile counterparts; the benefit for the former was their wider acceptance by local polite society.

However, certain sections of the community, and especially more recent Jewish immigrants, retained a proletarian distinctiveness. This seems to have been largely a function of their concentration in the garment trades, which were notorious for poor wages and seasonal work, coupled with left-wing traditions which a number had brought with them from eastern Europe. These factors served to keep significant numbers of left-inclined activists outside the influence of the Jewish elite. Some of these people, and especially those associated with, or sympathetic to, the CPGB, were very active in the two main unions linked to the garment trades in the area: the Tailor and Garment Workers' Union and the Waterproof Garment Workers' Union. These unions certainly provided another social support network for poorer Jews, serving to reinforce a sense of separation from the wider community. Writing about such people in 1939, the president of the BoD, Neville Laski (elder brother of the left-wing intellectual, Harold Laski), denigrated those who had fled the pogroms of eastern Europe in earlier times as 'ignorant and uncultured, many without a trade and speaking no language save Yiddish'. He contrasted such immigrants with those fleeing Nazi tyranny, most of whom, he noted approvingly, were professional types.[23]

As the anti-semitism of the BUF became more marked, even the BoD and its local agencies found it difficult to ignore. Thus, the BoD nationally and the CMSJ in Manchester took a number of steps both to monitor the activities of the BUF and to work behind the scenes to counter anti-semitic propaganda. These steps included the setting up of Vigilance Committees and the use of notable speakers, both Jewish and Gentile, to put the case for Anglo-Jewry using texts prepared by the BoD. Their behind-the-scenes activities, however, gave credence to the claims of anti-fascist activists that they were more concerned with image than with the realities of the situation as they affected working-class Jews.

This view does seem to contain a good deal of truth. For example, many of the main functions of the Vigilance Committee was to guard against anti-social behaviour by members of the community, which it was thought might bring the Jewish people into disfavour.[24] For Jewish anti-fascist activists, this line only served to strengthen the hand of their detractors, as it seemed to suggest that their community needed to be closely monitored to ensure their behaviour as model citizens. In 1938 the Executive Committee of the CMSJ rejected overtures from the Northern Council against Fascism (NCAF) for co-operative ventures, probably because the radicalism of the NCAF unnerved them, but also because it was beyond the control of the local Jewish elite, which made it doubly dangerous.[25] The Jewish elite seems to have been more concerned with the form of anti-fascist activity than with its effectiveness. This, it appears, was a function of its leading communal role. There seems to be little doubt that the leaders of the Jewish community in Manchester accepted, not without sorrow, that there were radical and vociferous sections of the community outside their sphere of influence, and were determined that there should be no further defections over the question of the BUF and anti-semitism. This appearance of activism lent greater authority to the appeal to those over whom they retained some influence to remain calm, and to resist the confrontational activism of some of their co-religionists. The link to the national body, the BoD, through the Laski connection was one which the CMSJ courted assiduously. Neville Laski corresponded frequently with the Home Office, and was undoubtedly aware of the view of the Chief Constable of Manchester, who noted that 'from our experience a good deal of the trouble which develops can be attributed to the action of certain Communist Jews in the crowd'. He added that of five persons arrested at Marshall Croft in Cheetham on 20 November 1936, three were of 'Jewish persuasion and well-known Communists'. He must have been even more worried by the report that Jewish ex-servicemen in Manchester were becoming concerned about BUF slanders against their community, and were determined to respond: exactly the kind of confrontation the communal leadership was endeavouring to avoid. However, Laski was able to use his influence to placate this influential strand of local Jewish opinion.[26]

Outright physical confrontation with the BUF was far from the only weapon in the armoury of the anti-fascist movement in Manchester. This is clear from the agitation against the BUF meeting at Belle Vue, on the south-eastern outskirts of the city, at the end of September 1934. Opposition to this big set-piece event began to be marshalled several weeks in advance. This activism operated at both local and national levels. Locally, the Manchester Anti-Fascist Campaign Committee was distributing leaflets outside factory gates by the beginning of September, urging that Belle Vue be turned into 'a workers' stronghold' and concluding that 'a powerful demonstration of working-class solidarity will best ensure the fascists that violence will not be tolerated'.[27] A resolution from the First Manchester Branch of the Amalgamated Engineering Union (AEU), proposed by Benny Rothman and carried unanimously, supported 'the counter demonstration to Mosley's Blackshirts and call[ed] on its members to rally to Belle Vue . . . in opposition to the Fascists'.[28] By contrast, a few days earlier, the Manchester and Salford Trades Council had rejected a resolution to consider organising a well-disciplined procession 'in order that Manchester may demonstrate its opposition to fascism'.[29] Many delegates had been critical of this decision and of the concomitant failure to forge links with the CPGB. However, the left in Manchester did not, by and large, display the petty sectarianism evident elsewhere.

Anti-fascist activism was also clearly apparent outside the confines of the labour movement, and concerted efforts were made to prevent this particular BUF meeting taking place. Writing on behalf of the CPGB in Manchester, Maurice Levine called on the Watch Committee not to 'allow the extremely provocative demonstration which aims at terror against the working class by organised brutality'.[30] Opposition did not only come from the more extreme left. The *Manchester Guardian* reported that 'a number of well-known Manchester men and women of various shades of opinion and connected with various organisations and societies protested to the Manchester Watch Committee their

abhorrence of Blackshirt hooliganism and terrorism. We recall the scenes of March 1933 in the Manchester Free Trade Hall, the brutal and outrageous acts committed at Olympia and the inhuman brutality and mass murder in Germany and Austria – not forgetting the vicious and shameful wave of anti-Semitism let loose by fascism, which has meant disaster for the Jewish people.[31]

One of those present was Joseph Toole, who had been Labour MP for South Salford in the first Labour administration and also between 1929 and 1931. At this time he was a member of Labour's National Executive Committee. He was something of an outspoken maverick, and fiercely anti-communist. In 1933 he had attempted to persuade Manchester City Council to ban the wearing of uniforms by political groups, arguing that 'Fascists are persuading thoughtless people that great social changes are wrought by wearing black shirts and parading the streets with foolish gestures.'[32]

The Chief Constable of Manchester, John Maxwell, made it clear that he would not ban the BUF event, and was not even prepared to permit a counter-march by anti-fascists. John Strachey, who had thrown himself wholeheartedly into the anti-fascist crusade after his split with Mosley, concluded that the latter decision constituted 'a fundamental interference with the rights of the subject'. He went on: 'and it is vitally important that we should assert our rights in this matter because these are being nibbled away one by one. This is, by itself, one of the expressions of bit by bit fascism.'[33]

The view that the state was either openly fascist, or at least had fascist potential, was one which informed many left-wing analyses of the growth of fascism in Britain. Stafford Cripps, for example, a leading light on the parliamentary left, concluded in a Socialist League pamphlet: 'There can be little doubt that we have definitely moved along the path towards the Corporate State, not only in actual legislation and method of government, but above all in the psychology and ideology of our rulers.'[34]

A deputation, consisting of representatives from anti-fascist groups in Manchester and the Council for Civil Liberties, was received at the Home Office by a junior minister, Captain Crookshank (Conservative MP for Gainsborough). Permission to see the Home Secretary had been refused. This followed a letter to the Home Secretary, detailing objections to the decision of the Chief Constable. It concluded that:

> The Chief Constable stated that he could not discriminate between a fascist military parade and an organised peaceful demonstration of Manchester citizens. We cannot recognise that there is any parallel between these forms of demonstration . . . The ban on the anti-fascist demonstration threatens to establish a dangerous precedent. Actually the Chief Constable of Manchester in banning the counter-demonstration is resorting to methods which are more akin to the practice and policy of fascism elsewhere.[35]

In the event, a counter-march did take place, and the *New Leader*, the organ of the ILP, claimed that some 5,000 anti-fascists had opposed a mere 1,000 Blackshirts.[36] Under the headline 'Drowned out in Manchester', the *Daily Worker*, the newspaper of the CPGB, asserted that Mosley had been 'swamped in a sea of working-class activity'.[37]

The use of formal political channels, coupled with co-operation on the left in the city, was to be observed again in 1937, when the anti-fascist movement endeavoured to prevent the BUF from holding a meeting in Cheetham Town Hall. They had been unsuccessful on two occasions in the previous year, when the Manchester Corporation Town Hall Committee, which was responsible for the letting of municipal buildings, held firmly to the view that they ought not to act, as free speech was a vital constituent of British life.[38] However, this did not deter anti-fascist activists, especially the North Manchester Co-ordinating Committee Against Fascism (the North Manchester arm of the NCAF). At a meeting convened on 27 January 1937 it resolved that:

The North Manchester Co-ordinating Committee representing thirty organisations with a membership of 15,000 declares that deliberate provocation on the
part of Mosley's Fascists is being carried a stage further by their unwarranted and
unwanted visit to Cheetham Town Hall this Saturday night. There can be no
possibility of there being any basis for fascism in our area, and we strongly
denounce this further threat to the public peace. We feel confident that the
authorities would not permit the use of a Corporation Hall by the Fascists had all
the representative bodies immediately expressed their emphatic disapproval. We
call upon the Chief Constable, Watch Committee, Town Halls Committee, and
the Lord Mayor, to immediately withdraw permission for the meeting, and, in
future, that any application by the British Union of Fascists for a hall shall not be
entertained by the Committee responsible for the letting of public halls.[39]

Although they again proved unsuccessful in their endeavours, it is interesting to note the variety of the groups affiliated to the NCAF which had
been set up by the Manchester Exchange division of the Labour Party in
May 1936.[40] Numerous organisations were represented, including
Trades' Councils, Co-operative Societies and branches of the League of
Nations Union. Their diversity refutes the frequent assertion that anti-
fascist bodies were seldom more than CPGB fronts, and gives an insight
into the political unity in the city on this matter. The letter to the Watch
Committees was on headed paper and listed the panoply of well-known
individuals who supported the NCAF as well as the numerous affiliated
bodies. The named individuals included Victor Gollancz, C. E. M. Joad,
Harold Laski, D. N. Pritt, Eleanor Rathbone and Bertrand Russell.
Affiliated organisations included local union branches such as the Transport and General Workers' Union and the local branch of the Amalgamated Union of Upholsterers. Several friendly societies also lent their
support, as did the local branch of the national Zionist organisation,
Poale Zion. Political groups included the Prestwich branch of the Labour
Party, the Manchester Young Liberal Association, the North Salford and
Cheetham Labour League of Youth, the Cheetham and Crumpsall
branches of the YCL, and the Manchester Workers' Circle.

Relations between left-wing groups in the city certainly had their ups
and downs in the 1930s. At critical moments, however, there does seem
to have been closer unity than the national Labour Party in particular
would have liked, as it attempted to purge its ranks of communist activists
and resist the blandishments of the CPGB for close co-operation or the
re-affiliation of the latter to the former. In 1934, at a rally in Platt Fields
against both the growth of fascism and the Incitement to Disaffection Bill,
the communist Willie Gallacher appeared alongside the Labour Party's
Arthur Greenwood and Aneurin Bevan, and prominent local figures such
as the historian A. J. P. Taylor, then teaching at the university, and
Stanley Mossop, Bishop of Manchester.[41]

Whereas anti-fascism in Manchester was characterised by confrontational activism, the focus of concern in Nelson was the local response to the BUF campaign in the cotton towns. In Nelson, too, there was a keen interest in international affairs. Local activists on the left seem to have been well informed about the increasingly disturbing events on the continent, and made an explicit link between those developments and the home-grown variety of fascism.[42]

The BUF launched its first of many cotton campaigns at the Floral Hall in Southport in July 1934.[43] Here Mosley repeated his four-point plan for Lancashire, first enunciated over a year earlier. This, it was estimated, would either create or save some 65,000 textiles jobs. Very briefly, the plan sought to exclude all foreign textiles from Crown Colonies, remove Indian tariff barriers, exclude Japan from the market and compel Indian mill owners to rebuild the slums of the East and give their workers a decent life. How these points were to be achieved can only be speculated upon, but a letter to the *Cotton Factory Times* concluded caustically: 'Sir Oswald is going to protect the Empire. He has promised to put you on the same footing as your Italian and German counterparts. What more can you ask him for? Hail Mosley – the man with a mission.'[44]

Such ambitious claims might not, of themselves, have constituted too much of a threat to the political equilibrium in the cotton towns, but coupled with the long-term problems in the cotton industry, which had been in sharp decline since the short-lived post-war boom, they were something of a challenge. Margaret McCarthy, the Accrington communist, recalled that roughly two-thirds of the CPGB membership in the town had gone over to the local branch of the BUF.[45] Over a decade the BUF published a number of pamphlets which exposed the nature of the downturn in the cotton industry. These pamphlets included titles such as: *Cotton, India and You, Lancashire Betrayed, Is Lancashire Doomed?, Mosley's Cotton Policy* and *Cotton: Socialists and Communists Exposed*. They reiterated the four points outlined above and also claimed a connection between the interests of international finance, which was perceived to be dominated by Jews, and the decline of the cotton industry, most notably in relation to the Indian market.[46]

The decline of the cotton industry was exacerbated by the slump after 1929. In Nelson, which had been less hard-hit than most other cotton towns during the 1920s because of its relative independence of the Indian market, unemployment rose from 6 per cent in 1929 (below the national average) to 25 per cent in 1931 (well above the national average), before falling back to around 12 per cent in 1936 and 1937 (about the same as the national average).[47] The BUF saw such vicissitudes as a perfect opportunity. Lancashire was characterised by one of the party's leading polemicists as 'the best potential soil for revolutionary action, a derelict county, which the government obstinately refuses to regard as a depressed area'.[48]

Anti-fascist activists in Nelson, it seems, took BUF propaganda about the cotton industry seriously. Len Dole remembers that, though many in Nelson were emphatically opposed to the BUF, nevertheless anti-fascist activists were concerned that BUF proposals for cotton ought not to be peremptorily dismissed.[49] This policy, it was felt, would better serve to limit any appeal the BUF might have. This was especially true during the Red Rose League campaign in the latter part of the decade. This organisation, whose meetings began with the ritual burning of a Japanese shirt, was extremely active in the cotton towns. It was not, however, simply a BUF front, though its activism did complement the drive by that movement for greater penetration in the area. This has been confirmed by a former member of the BUF, G. P. Sutherst, who became Assistant District Leader in Middleton.[50] He had close links with H. Y. Robinson, who funded the Red Rose League, and recalls that it was particularly successful in Blackburn, Burnley and Nelson, where he well remembers the activism of Nellie Driver. Sutherst recalls that money flowed in from cotton owners in particular, and although he asserts Robinson was never a member of the BUF, the complementary nature of the two movements was readily discernible. Mosley addressed a business lunch arranged by the League in Manchester on 20 September 1938. The Special Branch noted that some 140 persons were present 'all of whom represented substantial interests'.[51]

Counter-meetings were often arranged by anti-fascists for the same night as BUF meetings in Nelson. Nellie Driver recalls that 'it was a source of wonder to visiting city officials to see the *Daily Worker* and *Action* sellers stood peaceably side by side in the streets, without even a fight ensuing'.[52] Prominent local fascists were known by most of their opponents, and one of the latter, Bill Whittaker, recalls Nellie Driver as he sold the *Daily Worker* outside Woolworth's in Nelson. She used to go inside the store, quickly re-emerge, give a fascist salute and say 'Heil Hitler!' For Whittaker this was more a cause for humour than rancour.[53] Such encounters were in stark contrast to the violence in Manchester.

Mosley visited the town twice, in 1938 and 1939. During the first visit the local Tory newspaper, the *Nelson Leader*, described the meeting as well attended and orderly.[54] In an article in the rival *Nelson Gazette*, entitled 'Swift only to Destroy', Sidney Silverman, the Labour MP for Nelson and Colne, noted the fair reception afforded Mosley, though he went on to chide the BUF as anti-democratic, intolerant and alien to British culture, explicitly linking it with its continental counterparts.[55]

Mosley visited the town again early in 1939, and once again seems to have been given a fair hearing. The left in Nelson appears to have continued to uphold the liberal principle of free speech, which may have been reinforced by Nelson's strong radical traditions. There may also have been a desire that Mosley should not appear a martyr, suggesting possible solutions to the ills of the dominant local industry, but being denied the chance to speak because of the actions of a vociferous and powerful minority. Speaking for the left, Silverman rubbished BUF plans for cotton and asserted that the main reason for its interest in the town was because 'there are a lot of businessmen (so-called; they are really disgruntled Tories) who are near fascism in Nelson. The Conservative Party seethes with them.'[56]

Liddington estimates that in 1935 the BUF had around a hundred members in Nelson and Colne, though this figure conflicts markedly with a Special Branch report of the following year, which put the number of active members at only two.[57] Nellie Driver, undoubtedly one of the two the Special Branch had noted, estimated in an interview recorded in 1978 that the CPGB locally was around a hundred strong in the 1930s, a figure not disputed by activists.[58]

The local Labour Party had initially been cool towards the call for united front activity. It had received an invitation from the local United Front Committee on War and Fascism to attend a meeting, but had not responded.[59] The local party's opposition remained steadfast during the following year, though one of its leading figures, Selina Cooper, spoke at a 'No More War' conference organised in the town. Some eighty people attended the conference from a wide range of organisations. Speakers included Dan Carradice of the ILP, Richard Bland, a Methodist minister and representative of the League of Nations movement, and Elizabeth Stanworth for the CPGB. Indeed, Liddington notes the close and fairly amicable relations which existed between the Labour Party and the CPGB in Nelson, concluding that 'in tolerant constituencies like Nelson and Colne, Selina Cooper and others were able to work openly with Communists; but officially the Labour Party still preferred to keep them at arm's length'.[60]

In 1936, for example, the local Labour Party voted in favour of CPGB re-affiliation. This would be in 'the best interests of the workers in their desire to obtain a united labour movement against capitalism'.[61] However, this was followed early in 1937 by the narrow defeat of a motion which called upon Labour nationally to bring about a United Front as advocated by the Socialist League.[62]

Two well-known local activists, Gilbert Kinder and Albert Shaw, claim that there existed a *de facto* united front in Nelson in the later 1930s.

Kinder attributes this to the fact that by this time some 1,000 people had been members of the ILP, continuing Nelson's radical tradition.[63] For Albert Shaw, the politicisation of the Nelson Weavers' Association was the key factor in explaining the enduring strength of cross-party links on the left.[64] Differing, or even mutually exclusive political identities could perhaps be contained within a tradition of union radicalism. The membership of the Nelson Weavers' Association declined in the 1930s, falling from 15,000 in 1931 to 11,000 in 1937, but the latter figure was still remarkable, as it represented over one-third of the total population of the town.[65]

All four activists stress the vibrancy of the different sections of the left within the town, the very close links between them, and the way that this closeness could transcend political cleavages. And if we look at the activities of the United Town Peace Council in 1935, not only were all the political parties affiliated, but local churches also joined, as did a number of trade unions, notably the Weavers' Association, women's organisations and the town council, which joined as a body.

It is clear that the experiences of anti-fascists in Manchester and Nelson diverged in a number of ways. The confrontational activism of Manchester certainly extended beyond the Jewish community, but the radicalism of Nelson, and the response to the challenge of the BUF there, represented a more inclusive political tradition, where close co-operation on the left was the rule, not the exception. This inclusive political tradition made a resort to violence less likely, and made the left both more sure of itself and better able to deal with the challenge the BUF presented in the depressed cotton towns of the 1930s.

Questions of community identities loom large in this analysis. This is perhaps best illustrated by a comparison between the non-confrontational responses of the left in Nelson and the militant activism of sections of the Jewish community in Cheetham. The dominant tradition in Nelson was an inclusive one, able to incorporate a number of divergent themes within a fluid world-view. By contrast, Jewish anti-fascist activists were overwhelmingly drawn from a subordinate tradition, one which the mainstream had endeavoured to marginalise. As a consequence, it might therefore be concluded that the activism evident in Cheetham was not only a function of the challenge of the BUF, but also a conscious reaction to the apparent indifference of the communal elite to the more generalised plight of their poorer co-religionists, especially those who remained outside the purview of communal norms of authority and control. The response in Cheetham was not replicated across the city – far from it – and the confrontation in Manchester ought therefore to be understood in terms of the local community rather than the city as a whole.

Clearly, one of the major differences here is that between the politics of a city labour movement and that of a small town, but it is not merely a question of the relative size of the communities. Anti-fascist activists in Manchester were forced to develop a number of strategies to combat the BUF, both on the ground and at a more elite level of political action. There was a complex mosaic of numerous and often divergent traditions in the city. In Nelson the Weavers' Association dominated politics and rendered the differences that arose from the relative size of the two communities all the more striking. The Nelson Weavers' Association bound together the left-wing traditions in the town, and this meant that it was possible for a number of divergent identities to be contained within a dominant tradition. In Cheetham, anti-fascist activism was often no more than a function of a distinct but subordinate identity: Jewish, working-class, usually left-leaning, often communist. But, most importantly, Jewish anti-fascism in Cheetham was estranged from the dominating influence of the Jewish community leadership; it was the assertive response of a cornered community defending itself, by physical force if necessary.

4   Spain 1936. Resistance and revolution: the flaws in the Front

Helen Graham

> during a revolution . . . when events move swiftly, a weak party can quickly grow into a mighty one provided it lucidly understands the course of the revolution . . . But such a party must be available prior to the revolution in as much as the process of educating the cadres requires a considerable period of time and the revolution does not afford this time.[1]

The military coup of July 1936 against the progressive, reformist Second Spanish Republic precipitated a movement of popular resistance in which could be glimpsed the revolutionary potential of the social base of Spain's Popular Front (the centre-left electoral coalition victorious at the polls in February 1936). These radical energies would dissipate and the revolutionary attempt fail largely through the internal insufficiencies and inconsistencies of the groups constituting the radical left. But it was nevertheless the driving energy of that popular response which salvaged the reformist Republic, allowing the state to be reconstituted and a three-year war effort to be sustained in desperate conditions. This chapter will suggest some structural and conjunctural reasons why a revolutionary option failed to cohere as a basis for the Republican war effort. In the process it will also seek to indicate how we might go about unpacking the components of 'Republican disunity' – often referred to as if it were the product of pure ideological voluntarism and a 'monolithic' explanation for defeat. In fact, Republican divisions (both between elements of the radical left and between it and the proponents of the reformist Popular Front) need to be set in a longer time frame and in the context of a left which had always been highly fragmented – politically, socially and culturally – as a consequence of Spain's particular process of uneven development.

With the military rebellion of 18 July 1936, the Republican state imploded. The cohesion of the army was shattered, and with it the

Republic's conventional defence structures. The force of the blast also disorientated the Popular Front alliance, temporarily eclipsing republican, socialist and communist party and union leaderships. From the epicentre of this state crisis of unprecedented proportions the fault-lines ran out, separating islands of local or regional resistance. In addition, powerful centrifugal forces, the product of Spain's particularly uneven process of socio-economic development, defined and dynamised a movement of local, popular, and in places revolutionary, resistance to the rebel officers and their civilian supporters.

The core of the workers' committees and militia that made up the emergency structures of defence, communication and supply was constituted predominantly of the party and trade union members whom one might call the mobilised mass base of the Popular Front. They were vital to Republican survival through the 'July Days'. Between the Front's February 1936 election victory and the July coup, the radical extra-parliamentary potential of this movement had been viewed with great unease by the republican and socialist party political leaderships. These had a much more limited interpretation of the Front as a uniquely parliamentary strategy to achieve legislative reform. For them, the Popular Front as a mass mobilised movement had fulfilled its (campaigning) function once the electoral victory of 16 February had been achieved.[2] In spring 1936 the Socialist Party (PSOE) executive had duly opposed its own left's proposal to establish further extra-parliamentary mobilisations.[3] While this initiative withered more from the socialist left's own political indecisiveness and organisational incapacity than from its opponents' efforts, elsewhere, most notably in Asturias – where the socialist left was not strong – the Popular Front after February 1936 maintained the dynamic of popular mobilisation which had originated with the amnesty campaign for the prisoners of the October rising in 1934.

In Asturias, after the February 1936 elections, local Popular Front committees (some even newly created after the polls) showed their potential for becoming independent vehicles to press working-class demands. This politics of constant plebiscite asserted local institutions over the central state and obviously ran counter to republican and socialist leaders' determination to 'contain' the Front within parliamentary channels and to assert the power of central government. In Asturias there was popular mobilisation to demand the immediate reinstatement of workers dismissed for political reasons (including party or union membership) after the Asturian rising; compensation for the victims of the post-October repression; direct action (such as boycotts) against local figures implicated in these; urgent practical measures against unemployment and the acceleration of social reform.[4]

The parliamentary Frontists had to deal with even more radical forms of direct action too: there were land occupations in the spring and summer of 1936 in various parts of the rural south – an area dominated by large landed estates and semi-permanent class warfare whose social and economic systems epitomised Spain's chronic underdevelopment. For the essentially social democratic PSOE, and even more so for Spain's liberal republicans, the very idea of extra-parliamentary Popular Frontism was unwelcome, while for many republicans the land seizures seemed to indicate the revolution-in-waiting. All in all, the mass mobilising potential of radical Frontism was interpreted by parliamentary socialist and republican leaderships alike as the unwelcome intrusion of external European tensions into the domestic political arena. Yet the military coup created the conditions which made it necessary. The *ad hoc* structures of emergency defence and rearguard organisation created by popular mobilisation were all that stood between the Republic and defeat at rebel hands.

Hundreds of Popular Front committees of varied political hue were formed in the wake of the coup. Their political complexion depended on the relative strength and, crucially, access to arms of socialists, anarchists, republicans and communists and also on the balance between union and party forces within a given locality. (Union predominance sometimes led to committees being termed 'of syndical unity'.) These men and women were the shock troops of the Republic. In photographs and documentary footage they are depicted behind the barricades, in street fighting and storming rebel barracks – most famously in Madrid (Montaña) and Barcelona (Atarazanas). But no less crucial were the behind-the-scenes activities of food supply and other tasks of infrastructural organisation on the civilian front. Given the sheer numbers they mobilised, the unions (UGT and CNT) were particularly important, both on the front line and in the rear where they provided alternative communication lines, primarily through the railway and transport unions. This was vital since the state's communication channels had fractured or vanished with the coup. The ministries and many *diputaciones* (seats of provincial government) and *ayuntamientos* (seats of municipal administration) stood empty. In many areas of urban Republican Spain (with the notable exception of the Basque Country) proletarian militia controlled the streets (in Barcelona the anarcho-syndicalist CNT confused this with the possession of state power). And it was here, in the big cities and towns, where the crucial early battles were fought to define the geography of the Republican zone.

This picture of energy, enthusiastic improvisation and heterogeneity captures both the left's strength and its weakness. For most rank-and-file participants, initial mobilisation 'to defend the Republic' was spurred by the possibility of changing and controlling the immediate, lived environment, delivering what was perceived as the 'unfulfilled promise' of 1931, the year the democratic Republic was founded. We should recognise, then, that the collectivist social and economic reorganisation, commonly described as the popular revolution, was rooted in the local, in an underdeveloped state which did not yet have an entirely unified, interdependent economy: it reflected working-class and popular identification with *patria chica:* the lived unit of existence whether variably village, neighbourhood, town or city. This process of, as it were, invertebrate localist collectivisation was able to occur in parts of the Republican zone precisely because of the space opened up by state paralysis.[5] One of its most visible symptoms was the absence of owners and managers which, in turn, often made collectivisation the only means of securing the production and distribution functions essential to maintaining the emergency structures of popular defence. Thus the abeyance of the state (which was not, however, the same as its destruction) made the collectivist process termed the popular revolution both possible and necessary.

The silence and vacuum at the centre of the Republican polity in the months after the July coup were the result of the collapse of the republican-socialist alliance on which the reforming Republic had been based since its birth in 1931. Internal divisions and difficulties in the Spanish social democratic movement were part of the problem.[6] But most evidently it was about the crisis of historic Spanish republicanism, whose latent divisions were ripped wide open by the coup. This exposed political ambiguities which substantially undermined it as a force within the Republican camp. In the conservative Catholic interior (Old Castile) significant commercial and agrarian sectors of the republican base – smallholders, tenant farmers, traders, small entrepreneurs, landlords, shopkeepers, etc. – sided with the rebels. Here the peasant farmers were among the first to enlist. Elsewhere the allegiance of middle-class sectors was less clear-cut. Spain's middle classes were extremely fragmented and regionally specific in terms of their economic interests, social and political outlook and culture.[7] They did not necessarily identify in positive terms with a rebel cause perceived to be dominated by a Castilian military elite. Potentially at least some of these social groups could previously have been incorporated into the 'Republican nation' if the centre-left had addressed policies to meet some of their concerns between 1931 and 1933.[8] As, for a variety of reasons, this had not happened, these groups came to feel increasingly vulnerable and alienated. When land seizures and strikes took place in the 'hot' spring and summer of 1936 they were seen as harbingers of social disintegration and prompted a panic among the middle classes.[9] So when the coup occurred many in what became

Republican territory, while not actively pro-rebel, lacked confidence in the Republic's ability to guarantee a social order conducive to their interests.

If the atomisation of republicanism was a significant factor in state dysfunction after 18 July then, conversely, as the infrastructure of government crumbled under the impact of the coup, the republican political class also lost its means of exercising power. Republicanism had no large-scale independent organisational existence as the socialist movement did, and in the 1930s its political presence had been at the level of local or national government and in the state bureaucracy. The ambiguities of republicanism, its collapse and crisis all fuelled the attempt by the interim government of centre-right republican Martínez Barrio to mediate settlement with the military rebels during 18–19 July. This was not only in vain as the rebels were not prepared to negotiate, but also further undermined republican credibility in the eyes of the popular forces resisting the military onslaught. The political class of Spanish republicanism was thus marginalised within the Republican polity which meant the pre-war Popular Front of republican-socialist coalition was extinct, killed off by the coup.

Moreover, during July and August 1936 it was not at all clear to liberal-left supporters of an inter-class Popular Front that it could be reconstituted at all. At the time it looked as if the liberal democratic Republican order might instead be transformed as the energy and radical potential (radical above all in its direct, *participatory* quality) of the popular resistance movement was translated into state or political power. Many workers, irrespective of their specific political or syndical affiliation, wished to abolish the basic institutions of the existing socio-economic order and transcend capitalist property relations. But the potential of what was undeniably a profound *social* movement among significant sectors of the organised proletariat could not be realised because it could find no *political* channels into which to flow.[10] The axial organisation in any radical political front would necessarily have been, by dint of its sheer size, the anarcho-syndicalist labour union, the CNT. Yet it had no blueprint for articulating an alternative structure of political power. The ideological and organisational implications of its historic anti-statism would mean that the social transformations of the early months would have no opportunity to cohere politically.

Meanwhile, the local roots of the resistance movement, which privileged communities over the state, were coming rapidly to disadvantage the Republic in the changing, and largely externally determined, conditions of the conflict. German and Italian aid to the rebels tipped the balance of power inside Spain within the first month of conflict. Until then, the Republican militia had faced provincial garrison revolts, which they had defeated in more than enough cases to ensure that the rebellion would have been extinguished. But once the Army of Africa (troops from Spanish Morocco) landed on the mainland – airlifted by German planes at the end of July and equipped with the military hardware of the rebels' fascist backers – then the militia were in the main unequal to the new task.[11] The insurgent generals had set a new agenda. The military coup was escalating into full-scale civil war. If the Republic was to survive, in whatever form, its political leaders had to put an army into the field. In order to do this, there was a need to articulate an integrated, *national* defence which, in turn, presupposed the reconstruction of some kind of central state apparatus. Whoever controlled this would of course crucially influence the future political shape, economic policy and social–cultural values of the Republic.

By the beginning of September 1936 state-building had shifted to the top of the Republican agenda. The sheer imperative of Republican survival had much to do with this. August had seen a steady rebel advance through the rural south leaving massacres and mass terror in its wake, most notably at Badajoz on 14 August. Once Talavera, the last important centre on the southern advance to Madrid, had fallen on 3 September, the capital itself was directly under threat. All state-building requires a political blueprint. What needs to be explained is why the decision was made to reconstruct and consolidate the *liberal democratic* state. In short, it was because inter-class, parliamentary Popular Frontism remained the least weak of the political options available as a basis for the Republican war effort. This 'least weak' status was not the result of anything sufficiently well defined that it could be called a concerted Frontist strategy. Indeed republican and party leaderships remained in considerable disarray for most of 1936.[12] To explain the resurgence of a liberal democratic Frontist alliance we must look to two other factors.

The first of these is what could be called the 'geo-political' impact of the military coup on the balance of social forces inside Republican Spain. The division of territory resulting from the coup did not, as is well known, neatly separate the rebel and Republican electoral and social constituencies from each other. In fact, for the Republicans particularly, the coup made the question of alliance building even more problematic. The wartime Republic was left without a large part of the pro-collectivist, landless, rural proletariat of the south, which had been felled by the advancing Army of Africa as it waged its war of agrarian counter-reform. Yet it still retained the smallholding peasantry of the north-east who favoured not collectivisation but *reparto* (the distribution of land to individual small peasant proprietors). The Republic also had the bulk of the urban middle classes who looked to it to provide certain guarantees of social order based on a respect for private property. Within the Republican zone, then, a revolutionary transformation of the social and economic order was by no means the clear or dominant option and it was certainly one which, if pursued, would make the commitment of the liberal bourgeoisie to the war effort highly problematic.

An appreciation of these domestic factors naturally reinforced the determination of those who wanted to reconstitute the Popular Front on a new base. While this choice reflected their pre-war political preference for the nascent liberal democratic order of 1931, it was also driven by republican, socialist and communist assessments of the international scene. The Popular Frontists became convinced at the outset of the war that Republican victory would require the active support of Britain and France and therefore a domestic political configuration attractive to the liberal democracies. While the political conclusions of Popular Front supporters were not necessarily the only defensible ones to be drawn from contemplating the fragmented constellation of social forces in the Republican zone, a more radical option would have required a cohesive revolutionary coalition.

This brings us to the second factor explaining the re-emergence of the Popular Front: namely that the radical left possessed neither a strategy for political revolution, nor the organisational structures which could have articulated power throughout Republican territory. It could not, in the event, challenge the liberal republicans and social democratic left, weak and atomised though these forces were in the wake of the coup.[13] Pre-existing ideological and organisational cleavages and structural tensions within the left also exercised a centrifugal force after the coup, ruling out any possibility of a common blueprint for a radical workers' alliance which could have met the challenge of channelling and structuring the radical transformatory potential of the popular defence. Yet without assuming political power, the left would soon discover that it had no means of defending the social and economic changes of the early months.

Of the groups committed to the defence and consolidation of the collectivist social order, the most important in terms of experience of militancy and organisational weight was obviously the libertarian movement (CNT-FAI and the anarchist youth organisation). But rather than constructing a radical coalition, it is well known that the CNT collaborated in governments, namely those of the *Generalitat* (Catalan autonomous government) between September 1936 and May 1937; and the Republican administrations headed by veteran socialist union leader Francisco Largo Caballero between November 1936 and May 1937 whose major objective was the reconstruction of the liberal democratic state

The situation in which the CNT found itself in the summer of 1936 has been explained in retrospect, both by anarcho-syndicalist veterans and historians alike, in terms of a legendary 'dilemma': either seize power and abandon the 'fundamental anti-statist principles' of the libertarian movement, or remain true to these and see the revolution defeated by its political opponents.[14] According to this version, the CNT opted for political power and the movement was destroyed. It is of course understandable that anarchist militants, surveying the wreckage of Republican hopes and very often the blighting of much of their own adult lives, spent in poverty, prison, in hiding or in exile, should gravitate retrospectively towards an explanation of anarchist eclipse which is ultimately consolatory: the root cause of disaster, it is implied, was deviation from core anarchist values. But the notion of a binary choice is misleading. In 1936 the CNT, rather than opting for political power, discovered that its historical experience had left it bereft of the necessary organisational structures or political strategy to do so. Collaboration in the Catalan and national Republican governments, rather than signifying a political option, was the consequence of the libertarian movement's lack of one.

The months from September to November 1936, in fact, saw the crystalisation of a crisis which had been visible inside the CNT since the emergence of the Second Republic in 1931. As a parliamentary and pluralist regime, the Republic saw the opening up for the first time of political channels as a way for the Spanish working class to improve its conditions by means of social reform. This gave rise to a polemic inside the anarchist movement, with some sectors arguing that it was time to abandon anti-parliamentarianism and compete in the political arena with the PSOE and its union, the UGT. Failure to revise libertarian ideology and praxis, they warned, would leave the CNT's rank and file exposed in the new political environment. This would ultimately erode its base as members were attracted to the perceived benefits of its socialist rival as a union associated with state power. These fears were given more substance by the UGT's track record of trying to use its leverage within the state labour bureaucracy to marginalise the CNT and absorb its membership. Under the Republic, the UGT was trying to replicate the monopoly it had enjoyed during the Primo de Rivera dictatorship between 1923 and 1930. In the opinion of the reformers in the CNT, their own purist wing, by refusing to sanction the organisation's political engagement, was only helping the UGT leadership achieve its ends at the cost of the welfare and rights of the CNT's own base.[15] These differences were part of the conflict inside the CNT which fed the 1932–3 *treintista* split, when a number of pro-reform union federations in Catalonia and Valencia left the CNT. Some, in Catalonia, were never to return.[16]

The impact of the reformers' arguments on the CNT as a whole was limited, however, by the way in which other CNT-identified social constituencies experienced the Republican years 'on the ground'. Historically, the CNT, as an immensely heterogeneous movement both in terms of ideology and (regionally specific) practice, had always been the conduit for the most politically excluded and economically dispossessed social groups. These were people who continued to be marginalised under the Second Republic which, from its birth in 1931, they experienced not as the republicans' 'ideal' but as continued economic hardship and political repression when they protested about their plight. The incidents at Castilblanco and Arnedo (December 1931 and January 1932 respectively) and Casas Viejas (January 1933) are only the most well known of many incidents involving violent Republican state repression against workers. Moreover, one should also consider the rent strike experience in 1931, and the cumulative impact of certain pieces of legislation, notably the highly repressive Law for the Defence of the Republic (promulgated in October 1931) which, it could be argued, virtually criminalised the CNT.[17]

The period from 1931 to 1936 saw a paradoxical combination of trends: as the CNT experienced a decline in membership,[18] so the organisation's general mobilising capacity increased as unemployment began to bite. This hit unskilled and marginal sectors very hard indeed and there was no safety net as the socialists' plans for social security legislation were shipwrecked on the joint rocks of treasury impoverishment and the republican-socialist coalition's lack of any overall fiscal strategy. The exhaustion of the public works budget before the particularly hard winter of 1932–3 explains much of the turmoil of that year.

High unemployment levels also massively embittered the CNT's battle against the UGT's bid to control the labour market. Strike demands in 1932 and 1933 (with over half of the strikes occurring in the agricultural and building sectors) reflected this situation: there should be no further reduction of the working day, a rota system should be implemented to ration work, and a quota established to ensure the unemployed were hired.[19] There was virtual open warfare over control of the labour arbitration machinery (*Jurados Mixtos*) dominated by the UGT from its position in the Labour Ministry (1931–33). The CNT's September 1933 construction strike was primarily aimed at gaining union recognition and equal bargaining rights by breaking the UGT's monopoly on hiring at new construction sites, and in the agricultural sector there was constant conflict from 1931 to 1933 between socialist and anarcho-syndicalist unions over the functioning of the *Jurados*.[20] This antagonism had much in common with that between the SPD and KPD under Weimar. The KPD, like the CNT, increasingly identified with and mobilised those politically and economically excluded from the Republican order – the unskilled, unemployed, migrants, the marginal – while significant sectors of the UGT's base, like the SPD's, were skilled and employed.[21]

In general terms both the Law for the Defence of the Republic and the Law of Associations (April 1932) also favoured the UGT and those skilled sectors of the workforce encadred in it which could operate via official state channels, while it penalised and often persecuted the rest of the left – whether anarchist, anarcho-syndicalist or communist. Militants were detained and union premises closed. On innumerable occasions, in city and countryside, the Republic showed itself to be 'the Republic of order' in its violent response to worker demands. Thus Republican policies exacerbated social and economic tensions consequent on the depression, and in the process reinforced the anarchist-purist critique of the Second Republic as merely 'the continuation of the old regime' under a democratic facade.

In May 1936 the CNT's Zaragoza congress would endorse the purist anti-parliamentary line, while also endorsing the re-incorporation of those union federations which had left in 1932–3. But the circle could not be squared: in real terms the CNT's internal conflict was by no means resolved when the war erupted. Indeed one of the consequences of the Zaragoza congress was that some of the most prominent *treintista* union federations in Catalonia, which had left the CNT in 1932–3, would end up joining the Catalan UGT in the summer of 1936. To understand the origins of this conflict, which exploded under the Republic, we need to look back beyond the 1930s to uncover a different pre-history for the CNT: one which charts the rejection of insurrectionism and the evolution of political, integrationist currents in the organisation.[22] The more we know about the nature of these cleavages, the more difficult it is to justify referring to the CNT on the eve of the civil war as a single organisation identified with an anti-parliamentary, revolutionary ideology and praxis.

Even more fundamentally, the discussion about whether the CNT might have 'turned ideology on its head' in July and August 1936 and gone after power omits a vital consideration. As libertarian ideology had crucially shaped its organisational form (i.e. that of its unions), to date the CNT simply did not possess unified, integrated structures into which to decant that power. As the course of strikes earlier in the 1930s had indicated, the CNT did not even have the organisational means to communicate with its constituent unions.[23] Indeed, when the war broke out the CNT was still in the relatively early stages of transforming its unions into vertical, industrial ones. So even if the CNT had had a political project, it still had no organisational apparatus for co-ordinating the war effort throughout Republican territory.[24] It was precisely to address this kind of structural problem and the need for co-ordination that a body like the Consejo de Aragon would emerge at the beginning of the war in a region which formed part of the CNT's heartland.

In a sense, then, the CNT's identification with localist popular resistance needs to be problematised far more than it has been. Such an identification undoubtedly points to the libertarians' superior understanding of the dynamics of popular mobilisation, and of its value as a liberating, socially and culturally transformative *process* – as compared to the Popular Frontist concentration on the end result. But the CNT's identification with community rather than state, and its canonisation of the popular defence, also obscures serious ideological and strategic flaws; this was the materialisation of a crisis which had been threatening since 1931, and which made it impossible for the libertarian movement to challenge the Popular Front agenda of reconstructing bourgeois state power.

In view of the CNT's own organisational limitations, the chances of establishing a Republic-wide radical alternative to the Popular Front thus depended on the ability of purist anarchists to forge links with other groups. While the non-Stalinist communist POUM (Partido Obrero de Unificación Marxista) shared similar radical goals, and indeed was possessed of a significantly more sophisticated understanding of political power, it was numerically exiguous and geographically circumscribed: confined to the industrial north-east, and mainly in the provincial towns of Barcelona's industrial belt rather than in the capital city itself.[25] The viability of a radical alliance was thus really dependent on agreement between the CNT and the left socialist-led union the UGT as the two labour giants. But there were several major, and as it turned out insuperable, obstacles to its realisation.

Most fundamentally, the attitude of the UGT executive to the state constituted the major stumbling block. It had criticised the slowness of Republican reform in the pre-war period and blocked PSOE participation in government after the February 1936 elections for fear of the damage that association with failed reform could wreak on socialist credibility and, most particularly, on their own union membership figures. But, in fact, the UGT's left socialist executive continued to share with the Popular Frontist Socialist Party leadership a very singular view of the movement's 'manifest destiny'. According to this view, the PSOE–UGT alliance would inherit the state and convert its existing institutions to socialism from within. This shared internal political culture had been reinforced by the UGT's 'insider status' between 1931 and 1933, when Largo Caballero had been minister of labour and socialist union cadres had exercised state power as bureaucrats running the *Jurados Mixtos*.[26] The notorious verbal revolutionism of UGT general secretary Largo Caballero in the last two years of the pre-war Republic (1934–36) had been a precarious strategy, intended to placate radical and discontented members of his own union, in particular the southern landless, while also curtailing the right's pretensions to immobilise reform further. Moreover, the socialist left implicitly defined the revolution as a quasi-mystical event requiring no practical preparation, and thus no organisational risk for the UGT. This appeared to serve the union leadership's primary drive to organisational consolidation very well. For this was a major tacit objective of its conquest of state power. In a sense it was this conception of how the revolution would occur (as a spontaneous rising should the military dare to oppose the popular will) which 'legitimised' the singular inaction of the socialist left and UGT national leaderships in the spring of 1936. Although the conspiracy in the garrisons was an open secret, all militia organisation and training in the tense summer of 1936 was done on the basis of local party and union cells. There was no overall national co-ordination even within the socialist movement, and, of course, none between the organisations of the left. Absorbed by its own political balancing act and mesmerised by republican crisis, the socialist left, with its eyes on state power, was caught off guard by the coup.

The implicit statism of the UGT leadership meant that it was as profoundly traumatised by the events of July and August 1936 as its party counterparts. For the coup's disintegrative impact took its toll on the UGT's organisational hierarchy as much as on state and political party structures. Neither Largo Caballero nor the rest of the UGT national executive had any intention of championing a decentralised social radicalism which it had not initiated and which had significantly undermined its own control of the UGT. It was symptomatic of the new collective order born of state fragmentation that local union committees were acting autonomously even when they claimed a UGT denomination. And it is in this context that one must understand the UGT leadership's energetic and persistent championing of the nationalisation of industry. Certainly there were cogent reasons for this in terms of articulating an integrated national war effort. But an equally crucial agenda was ensuring the survival of the UGT itself and the recovery of leadership control.[27] The entire historical experience of the UGT, above all the increasing identification with state power in the 1920s and early 1930s, informed Largo Caballero's wartime decisions. On 4 September 1936 he accepted the post of prime minister and thereafter expended his energy in bringing the

CNT into government as a means of controlling it rather than pursuing a separate political coalition between the two union federations. In fact, such a coalition on the left had probably already been blocked for good by 1934, when Largo Caballero vetoed UGT participation in the Workers' Alliance (Alianza Obrera). This was originally an initiative of the Catalonia-based left communist BOC (Bloc Obrer i Camperol), one of the forerunners of the POUM, which intended to use it as a vehicle for activism outside Catalonia.[28] But precisely because the Alliance was envisaged as an inter-organisational structure, it could have offered a real opportunity for the left to consolidate and to co-ordinate its action, had it been realised. First, by de-marginalising the BOC's Catalan leadership, it might have influenced the mainstream PSOE and UGT into developing a more sophisticated theoretical reading of the Second Republic. But if this is a somewhat problematic proposition, at the very least a functioning Workers' Alliance could have provided the crucial national co-ordination lacking on the left in the spring and early summer of 1936. And nor was it only the invertebrate nature of the CNT's organisation which made this a costly failure. For the UGT itself had significant structural weaknesses too. While its national leadership in Madrid could, in normal times, communicate relatively easily with all parts of the organisation, internal regional and provincial articulation simply did not exist in many areas.[29] This also meant that lateral communication between the different provincial and regional organisations was impossible or very rudimentary. Thus we can appreciate the material impediments to realising a radical, union-based alternative state structure in the summer of 1936. Moreover, as the quote which began this article suggests, once the war had erupted it was too late to elaborate a blueprint or build cadres to defend it. All revolutions seriously erode the cadres and organisations which make them. The essential – if not necessarily sufficient – precondition of success, then, is that both the strategy and the experienced cadres be in place beforehand.

But even to begin to argue for the potential of the Workers' Alliance in this respect would require us to indicate a sea change in the attitude of the socialist left leadership of the UGT. Yet this group had no more interest in an alliance with the CNT in 1936 than it had in 1934. Quite the contrary, since with the gathering crisis of republicanism the socialist left envisaged the PSOE as on the threshold of occupying state power alone in the spring of 1936. By then, moreover, UGT-CNT grass roots relations were themselves deteriorating under the impact of economic crisis and this made an inter-union alliance an even more remote possibility.

By the spring of 1936 conflict between the CNT and UGT memberships was particularly evident in Madrid, where the CNT had begun to mobilise in what was traditionally a UGT stronghold. The increasing appeal of the CNT's mass mobilisation and direct action tactics over the arbitration-based unionism of the UGT was a consequence of demographic and industrial changes in the capital combined with the economic crisis of the 1930s. The CNT was particularly strong among the large numbers of unskilled building labourers who, attracted by the boom in the industry, had flocked to Madrid to work on construction sites during the 1920s. Their situation had worsened as the industry, faced with the effects of recession, began to cut back. With no security or bargaining power, confrontational tactics and strike action were increasingly the only options available to these unskilled workers.[30] The UGT leadership, wary of the increasing number of CNT-backed strikes, which it saw as a threat to its own control in the capital, was seeking to reimpose the 1931–33 arbitration machinery of the *Jurados Mixtos*.[31] But this in fact only served to exacerbate the inter-union conflict. In April 1936 the UGT's fears of loss of control seemed confirmed when, on the fifth anniversary of the Republic, many of its members, ignoring the opposition of both socialist and communist leaderships, joined the general strike declared by the CNT. The UGT press accused the CNT, tellingly, of fomenting 'rebellion against the state', while the CNT press responded by renewing its criticism of socialist collaborationism. Largo Caballero was the 'old corrupt collaborationist socialist', kow-towing to the state as he had in the 1920s during the Primo de Rivera dictatorship and now advising republican ministers on how to 'handle' strikes in return for favoured status and renewed state privileges for the UGT.

The inter-union conflict sharpened still further with the Madrid construction strike which began in June 1936 and was still unresolved at the time of the coup.[32] On 11 July the UGT (through its newspaper *Claridad*) called for a return to work, 'for the sake of the Popular Front, for the consolidation of . . . victory over the bosses'. This was met by another scathing attack from the CNT. More significantly, a sizeable percentage of the UGT base in the capital (24 per cent) was also hostile to a return to work and sided with the CNT.[33]

In other cities too there were violent confrontations between the rank and files of the two 'sister' unions. There was a particularly savage clientelistic membership war being waged on the Barcelona waterfront between the socialist and anarchist dock workers' unions.[34] Members were of course important in their own right, but the particular violence (and resulting fatalities) of the dispute was because work, an increasingly scarce commodity in the depression, was allocated according to union size. This other kind of war, into which the July military coup and ensuing civil war erupted, brings home the extent to which the material effects of economic crisis drove a wedge between the social constituencies of the left. The cumulative effect of such clashes in both urban and rural Republican Spain obviously created a legacy of distrust which eroded the political space for a substantive agreement between the UGT and the CNT.[35]

In the light of this situation, the lack of real political and strategic unity which undermined the left from the outset of the war is scarcely surprising. While there were instances of syndical unity – solidarity forged in the heat of militia defence and perpetuated in various local committees – the underlying picture is more complex. Many analyses to date have operated explicitly or implicitly on the assumption that the military coup itself, in constituting an overwhelming external threat to the Republic, somehow erased the pre-war dynamic of inter-left relations with all their tensions, hostilities and contradictions. In fact, though the coup fractured organisational structures, it left intact memories of conflict and deeper-rooted patterns of collective political behaviour and social identity. In consequence, the political unity around which the left's entire discourse was built in the 1930s proved remarkably hard to achieve, even minimally, in practice.

To understand the relationship between the forces of the left during the war, and the political evolution of the Republican zone, we must look back to the pre-war Republic, to its social as well as its political history. Ultimately too, the cleavages of the 1930s need to be seen in relation to Spain's acutely uneven development over the long term, which had produced an internally variegated labour movement. The different ways in which work and the state were experienced socially shaped, over time, this ideological and organisational heterogeneity. (And here one refers not only to the clearly different practices of Spain's anarcho-syndicalist and social democratic organisations but also to the competing perspectives *within* each.) So many of the political tensions, and the strategic and tactical divisions were the product of this diversity; that is, of the way in which it shaped different constituencies' experience and expectations of the Republic from 1931 onwards. Of course it is true that the war exacerbated tensions and determined the ways in which existing crises were manifest. But underlying these we have a left which, throughout its whole existence, had been highly fissiparous.

In the spring of 1937 both the socialist left and the CNT would be exposed to the consequences of their political contradictions, and failure to conclude an alliance between 1934 and 1936. Largo Caballero, as titular head of the left, found himself without any solid political base; and, faced by the united opposition of his parliamentary socialist, communist and republican cabinet colleagues, was obliged to resign the premiership.[36] He had been ousted not by a Stalinist plot, as he and his supporters insisted, but as the result of the left's own internal political inconsistencies and strategic failure. The socialist left leadership had not understood the dynamics of the July Days and, in any case, had one foot in the statist Popular Front camp – betokening significant political confusion. The CNT for its part did not have the organisational capacity to articulate the social revolution politically. The radical minority in the UGT to whom it might have appealed for support[37] had never occupied the primary leadership positions in the union hierarchy. Moreover, the loss of large parts of the rural south to the military rebels in the first months of the war had swept away many of the landless labourers who might otherwise have provided the social support base for a more radical, collectivist political option in the Republican zone. Beyond this, as we have seen, there existed between both union movements at the popular level differences of culture and practice which generated significant mutual hostility.

In such circumstances it was scarcely surprising that the Popular Front, as the least weak option, was reconstructed as the basis of the Republican war effort. It would be different from the pre-war Front, however, in that the crisis of republicanism required its construction on a new axis. Instead of a republican-socialist alliance, the wartime front was to be erected on the basis of one between the PSOE and the Spanish Communist Party (PCE). The lightning ascendancy of the PCE, a tiny, marginal party before 1936, to become a political force of the first magnitude in the wartime Republic has to be understood in terms of the internationalisation of the Spanish conflict and the growing importance of Soviet aid. But this is far from the whole story. We can also trace a domestic political continuity in the functions fulfilled by the PCE during the civil war. Most obviously, the party assumed the mantle of progressive republicanism, acquiring a significant base among the middle classes in the Republican zone, and especially among those professional sectors linked to state employment. But, more importantly, the PCE was functioning as a conduit, bringing the previously unmobilised, both middle and working class, to the state. In general this can be seen as part of a modernisation process speeded up by the war itself. Of particular importance was the PCE's mobilisation of youth in the United Socialist Youth (JSU) and its associate bodies. As a result, the PCE was creating within its own organisational structure a model for the inter-class alliance sought by republicans and socialists since 1931 as the social base of a reforming regime.[38]

The PCE could not, of course, solve the significant ideological and policy contradictions inherent in such an alliance in a country with levels of development as disparate as Spain's. However, its discipline ('democratic centralism') did allow it to avoid the organisational fragmentation sustained by both the socialist and republican movements as a result of these contradictions. The PCE's important medium-term aim was to contain these contradictions, by balancing policies and by careful propaganda work, in order to keep the Popular Front alliance together for the duration of the war. This we could term the functionality of democratic centralism.

Not least because of the PCE's role, the reconstituted wartime Popular Front was able to go some distance in 1937 and 1938 towards articulating the political power and state infrastructure crucial to a sustained defence against the military rebels and their German and Italian fascist backers. But unlike the exponents of radical Frontism, the Popular Front's leaders and strategists never really appreciated the importance of the original links between community and popular mobilisation. This would be illustrated by the May Days crisis of 1937, the dynamics of which went much deeper than an 'imported' Stalinist witch-hunt. Nor did the liberal democratic Popular Frontists understand how to address the distinct meanings which the Republic's different social constituencies continued to attribute to 'resisting fascism'. The Popular Front failed to develop discourses and strategies for mobilisation which could have better sustained popular morale and even perhaps have begun transforming these disparate constituencies into the Republican nation.

Within the Popular Front it was the PCE which came closest to appreciating the importance of such strategic propaganda work and indeed attempted to implement it. However, the PCE's aggressive recruitment methods, its sectarianism and its outright persecution of other groups on the left (most notoriously the POUM) undermined its own medium-term political goals by alienating the rest of the Republican front. This we could call the dysfunctionality of Stalinism. In the end, then, the Popular Front's own shortcomings made it the maximum reflector of the social and political fragmentation which had defeated the radical left.

5 The Blueshirts in the Irish Free State, 1932–1935: the nature of socialist republican and governmental opposition

Mike Cronin

The popular historical mind in Ireland has firmly identified the Blueshirts as the embodiment of the Free State's experiment with fascism.[1] In February 1932 when the Army Comrades Association was formed (the Blueshirts had four 'official' titles: name changes were prompted by internal reorganisation or government bans), only the *Irish Independent* saw fit to give notice of the event.[2] The period from 1932 to 1935 transformed the Blueshirts from their origins as a fledgling ex-servicemen's organisation into a major force in Free State politics; and one which challenged the authority of de Valera's Fianna Fail government, and caused such violent opposition from socialist republican forces that some observers feared a return to the animosity of the civil war of 1922 and 1923.

From the foundation of the Irish Free State in 1922 until the general election of 1932, the victors of the civil war, the pro-Treaty party Cumann na nGaedheal, had dominated Irish politics. This was due not only to electoral victory, but also because of the abstentionist line taken by Eamonn de Valera's Sinn Fein. In 1927, following the murder of the defence minister, Kevin O'Higgins, by members of the Irish Republican Army (IRA), the attendance of Sinn Fein in the Dail was demanded by the prime minister W. T. Cosgrave. Sinn Fein split over the issue. Some preferred to remain abstentionist, but the majority followed de Valera in taking up their seats under a new name, Fianna Fail. The perception among Cumann na nGaedheal supporters, which stemmed from the civil war period, was that Fianna Fail was dominated by gunmen and criminals who could not be trusted in democratic politics. During the 1920s Cumann na nGaedheal had done an impressive job in establishing the mechanisms of state: there was an unarmed police force, a politically neutral army, and a functioning legal, judicial and governmental system. However, by the end of 1931 problems still remained for the Cumman na nGaedheal administration. Relations with the church were increasingly strained; opposition from republican groups, although muted, was still evident; most importantly, the Free State was still linked to Britain under the conditions of the Anglo-Irish Treaty as they had stood in 1922. There had been no movement on the question of the border, land annuity payments, the oath of allegiance to the crown or the presence of a governor-general in Dublin Castle. It was in this climate that the 1932 election took place. Fianna Fail, after a successful campaign based on the message 'On to the Republic', were able, with support from the Labour Party, to form a government. The feelings of mutual suspicion plaguing the years 1932 to 1935, which would give impetus to the Blueshirts and their opponents, were evident among 'respectable' politicians at the first meeting of the new Dail. 'On the Fianna Fail side, there were rumours that elements in Cumann na nGaedheal would not allow them to take office. Accordingly as the Fianna Fail deputies filed into the government benches, almost every man of them carried a revolver.'[3] Despite the high levels of mutual suspicion, it seemed perversely natural for the Irish that a party which had previously refused to accept the legitimacy of the Free State had, within ten years, won plurality support at a general election; stranger still that the previous government, which had defeated de Valera and his followers in a civil war, should allow them to take office. Despite the transition from legitimate Cumann na nGaedheal government to a Fianna Fail government perceived as gunmen and degenerates, the peaceful parliamentary acceptance of the will of the people in 1932 demonstrates the uniqueness of the Irish situation in a European context. Although Ireland was a country recently freed from colonial rule and war, had pressing border problems, was dominated by a dogmatic and traditionalist church, and was incompletely modernised both socially and economically, the mechanisms of democracy were accepted. All this was achieved, not in the absence of fascist extremism, but in the very face of it. Throughout the years 1932 to 1935, the Blueshirts received a level of domestic political respectability that people such as the Mosleyites in Britain and the Rexists in Belgium could have only dreamed of.

The aim of this chapter is to explain the background of the Blueshirt movement, their socialist republican opponents, and the ideological and physical battles which the two fought. This struggle was played out against the backdrop of a new state establishing itself and its democratic traditions, aware not only of contemporary European events and ideas, but still locked into the animosities and thinking of recent Irish history. The overall picture is often intricate, sometimes confused. Essentially, the fascistised aims of the more outlandish Blueshirts, despite any successes which they may have potentially had, were resisted from within their own community and by those in authority, as well as by their ideological opponents.

The air of mutual political suspicion and the impending victory of Fianna Fail at the polls led to the formation of the Army Comrades Association a week before the election in February 1932. The Association was primarily an ex-servicemen's organisation, and was originally concerned only with the threat which a Fianna Fail government would pose to the pension and job rights of former members of the Free State army. The first few months of the movement's existence were remarkably dull – although they did well in recruiting members (by October 1932 the membership had reached 8,337).[4] Despite the Association's insistence that it was a non-political body, ex-Free State army men were, by definition, likely to be supporters of Cumann na nGaedheal. In August 1932 this link was formalised when a new president was elected. Dr. T. F. O'Higgins was a serving Cumman na nGaedheal Dail member and the brother of the murdered defence minister, Kevin O'Higgins. Understandably he had a total loathing for Fianna Fail and the IRA, and would stand firm in opposition against them.[5] Under O'Higgins' leadership the Association became increasingly politicised. Association members formed the body-guard at Cumann na nGaedheal meetings on a regular basis in an attempt to stop attacks on speakers by Fianna Fail and the IRA. The whole area of freedom of speech become highly political. O'Higgins stated in August 1932: 'We shall deem it our bounden duty to resist any counter attempts to interfere with free speech or the free expression of opposition . . . should any Irishman come to harm as a result of "traitor pointing"' the consequence may be a deplorable condition of reprisal and counter reprisal.'[6] This was followed by warnings that the Fianna Fail administration would oversee the introduction of communism into Ireland, and a general barrage of criticism of their method of government – especially attacks on those civil servants and government officials whom Fianna Fail viewed as loyal to the former Cumann na nGaedheal administration. Throughout the summer of 1932 the links between the Association and Cumann na nGaedheal became increasingly obvious. Most leading Cumann na nGaedheal frontbenchers joined the Association. It was in this climate that the Association was seen as a threat by their opponents. The *Irish Press* announced that the Association was unwanted,[7] *An Pho-blacht* the Sinn Fein newspaper denounced it as a new fascist force aiming for a military dictatorship and the continuation of the imperialistic domination by Britain,[8] and the government began surveillance to ascertain the numerical and armed strength of the movement.[9]

Fianna Fail called a snap election in January 1933 in which it increased its majority. During the election there were countless violent scenes as Association members fought with supporters of Fianna Fail and the IRA. More significantly, five leading members of the Association stood as Cumann na nGaedheal candidates. The election brought to an end any question that the Association's aims were merely apolitical. The victory for Fianna Fail appeared to members of the Association as a victory for thuggery, intimidation and communism which would lead to a destruction of the values which the majority had fought for in the War of Independence and the civil war.

A month after the election the Association adopted the blue shirt, and ensured their place in Irish political mythology. The same month also saw the most important development for the Blueshirts. De Valera sacked the Commissioner of the Police, General Eoin O'Duffy. O'Duffy had been appointed by the Cumann na nGaedheal administration in 1922, and had always been considered by his opponents as a Cumann na nGaedheal loyalist. There were attacks on O'Duffy's political credentials in both *An Phoblacht* and the *Irish Press* in the weeks leading to his dismissal. For the Blueshirts and political opponents of Fianna Fail the sacking of O'Duffy was symptomatic of all that was wrong in the Free State: the government was being dictated to by the IRA.

In July, when O'Duffy had returned from a holiday in Italy, where he met Mussolini and had become completely enamoured of the benefits of the fascist regime and the social teachings of Pope Pius XI, he was invited to lead the Blueshirts. O'Duffy accepted the post, renaming the Blueshirts the National Guard, and, with the help of several leading thinkers from University College Dublin and University College Cork,[10] he presented a manifesto that proposed radical changes for the movement and for Ireland.[11] The radical changes included the opening of the Blueshirts to everyone, even women and children; the adoption of a corporate and vocational policy modelled on that outlined by Pope Pius XI; the reorganisation of the electoral and parliamentary systems, and complete opposition to the policies of Fianna Fail, the activities of the IRA and the spread of communism.[12]

O'Duffy's leadership and the reorganisation of the Blueshirts were hugely successful. By March 1934 membership had leapt to 37,937.[13] Like many leaders of European fascist or fascist-styled parties during the 1930s, O'Duffy showed signs of egomania. He vigorously promoted the importance of himself and the movement as saviours of Ireland. In August 1933 he planned to parade 20,000 Blueshirts round Dublin as a commemoration of the lives of the fallen Cumann na nGaedheal heroes Michael Collins, Arthur Griffith and Kevin O'Higgins. There was talk of a Mussolini-style 'March on Rome' which even the London *Times* reported.[14] The 'March on Dublin' never happened. De Valera banned it, and recruited ex-IRA men into a new police force, the 'Broy Harriers', in an attempt to stop anyone trying to defy the ban. The atmosphere of mutual antagonism which surrounded such an open display of Blueshirt strength led to extreme measures being taken by the IRA. One ex-Blueshirt recounts how he was detailed to storm a house in Merrion Square overlooking the march route and disarm an IRA machine-gunner, whose task was to fire on the march creating total mayhem.[15] For the IRA, the government's action in banning the march and the reaction of the people of Dublin merely underlined the untenability of fascism as an Irish political ethos. *An Phoblacht* commented:

Forbidden to hold a general parade by the law which his gun-thugs enforced when the coercion act was first established, forbidden by the bishops to shelter within the sanctuary of churches, Duffy is faced with defeat.
  Last Sunday the people of Dublin showed their anger at even the appearance of one Blueshirt. Men and women of Dublin thronged in the streets to vent their pent-up passions on the British-boosted, British-subsidised fascists. The strengthened cordons of police saved the Blueshirts from the people. They escaped to their headquarters with their ears ringing with hoarse shouts of 'Arbour Hill' and 'Seventy-seven'.
  Duffy says that he will endeavour to hold meetings throughout the country. Again he will fail. There is but one course open to the humiliated would-be dictator. The Blueshirts must become one with the faithless futile treachery of the pitiful past.[16]

O'Duffy had suffered a defeat. His potential as a threat to the state had been tested by de Valera and, under great pressure from his constitutional partners inside Cumann na nGaedheal, he had erred on the side of caution. The ban on the march was followed by a government proscription of the National Guard, since the movement was now seen as an increasing threat to the stability of the nation. The effect of the ban was to further the suspicion of the de Valera government amongst its opponents. Following on from the dismissal of a trustworthy and long-serving police commissioner, here was the banning of a political opponent. The net result of the ban was a total realignment of all the major Fianna Fail opponents. Cumann na nGaedheal, the small Centre Party and the Blueshirts joined together to form the United Ireland Party, more commonly known as Fine Gael. The Blueshirts, despite not having any members sitting in the Dail, took one-third of the places on the party's committee, and O'Duffy was appointed president.

  From their new power base at the head of the main opposition party the Blueshirts went from strength to strength. New members and extra funding flooded into the movement, and the whole issue of shirt-wearing became increasingly respectable. Both in the Senate and the Dail, members of Fine Gael were to be seen wearing their blue shirts. The liturgical trappings of Irish fascism had made their appearance in the bastion of Free State democracy.

Yet even at this early stage the demise of the Blueshirts as a political force was in sight. Despite the popular backing which Fine Gael received, there were grave misgivings within the party over the direction O'Duffy and the Blueshirts were taking. Once in a position to dictate the running of a large political machine, O'Duffy and sections of the Blueshirt hierarchy lurched further to the right as the intellectuals from Cork and Dublin increasingly gained a foothold. The thinking among Blueshirt leaders was that the defeat of Fianna Fail could no longer be achieved by traditional political opposition, but required the wholesale restructuring of Irish society. The language from Fine Gael platforms and publications concentrated increasingly on the corporate state and the reorganisation of the economy and politics, and less on a criticism of the domestic policy of Fianna Fail. The move to fascist forms of thinking was highlighted by the opposition press. After the Ard Fheis (the Sinn Fein party conference) at which O'Duffy outlined his corporate programme, the *Irish Worker's Voice* under the headline 'Fascists drop all masks' stated:

The 'democratic' masks were flung off and fascism's face nakedly revealed when British imperialist storm troopers met at the first Blueshirt convention last week. According to O'Duffy, capitalism's decline and the workers' challenge to the robber system can no longer be met by 'democracy'. Fascist terror, concentration camps and murder are necessary to hold the masses in subjection. 'Let us not make an idol of Parliament' says O'Duffy. The challenge of this fascist gang must be met by united resistance of the worker and farmer masses irrelevant of divisions.[17]

By November 1934 O'Duffy was gone. He had been forced to resign after he spoke of his plans to forcibly invade Northern Ireland with an army of Blueshirts in an attempt to recapture the province from Britain, and backed a Blueshirt campaign of unlawfulness which was attempting to end Fianna Fail's policy of land and cattle seizures during the economic war. The extreme politics which O'Duffy was presenting were at odds with the wishes of the Cumann na nGaedheal and Centre Party elements within Fine Gael (many of whom had been involved in the struggle to form the democratic Free State), and also opposed by many rank-and-file Blueshirts. They were only interested in domestic concerns, and did not care for the language of corporatism and vocationalism which O'Duffy and his advisors were lifting from contemporary European thinkers. Despite forming a rallying point for the opponents of Fianna Fail, O'Duffy had introduced ideas which were considered alien and dangerous by pursuing a form of thinking which was generally perceived as fascist both by his supporters and his opponents. The Irish nation had not fought against the British and engaged in a civil war to see their sacrifices washed away by O'Duffy's poor attempts to imitate Mussolini or Salazar.

The opposition which signalled the demise of the Blueshirts came from three main sources. Firstly, there was the resistance to O'Duffy's fledgling fascism from members of his own party, which has been described above. Secondly, there was opposition from the broad left and republican movements, which were in a confused state of flux in the 1930s (and are referred to here as the socialist republicans). The third strand of opposition came in the form of legal restrictions imposed by the Fianna Fail government.

Socialist and republican opposition came from a number of quarters, including the IRA, the Republican Congress, the Labour Party, the Irish Communist Party, various trade unions, and a profusion of leftist workers' groups.[18] The resistance to the Blueshirts provided by such groups was highly vocal and is important because it was opposition to the Blueshirts as a fascist group. Whereas the government and internal opponents within Fine Gael saw fascist traits or quasi-fascist traits, the republican socialists made a blank ideological judgement: anyone wearing a blue shirt was a fascist.

Since 1927 the cause of republicanism had been legitimated by the entry of Fianna Fail into the Dail. As a result, Sinn Fein and the IRA, which had refused to enter the Dail, had been left without a firm agenda. In 1931, the search for a new direction had been led by the formation of a new group, Saor Eire. Saor Eire was based on a mixture of traditional thirty-two-county republicanism and a broad left ideology of social equality and social reconstruction. In the early 1930s the Catholic church was obsessed with a fear of communism. The bishops decided that Saor Eire was a front for a communist group and denounced it in a joint pastoral. The Cumann na nGaedheal government, wary of the importance of church support as the election neared, responded to the bishop's pastoral by banning Saor Eire. The first attempt to construct a new agenda for the socialist republican movement had failed before it had begun.

The arrival of the Blueshirts on the political scene gave all the different socialist and republican groups a common purpose. It was a movement and an ideology which they could attack with the broad support of the Fianna Fail administration. The IRA opposed the Blueshirts in the way they knew best: with a mixture of denunciations and intimidation. They played old cards by linking the Blueshirts with a traditional British imperialist plot to control Ireland, as well as new cards such as the threat of fascism. In 1933 the IRA dismissed the Blueshirts as a viable political force and warned: 'the White Army is an armed organisation aiming to provoke civil war in Ireland, and with England's help prevent loyal Irishmen from using England's difficulties to Ireland's advantage. Toleration is therefore unthinkable. Every man should have the right to arm for freedom. No man should have the right to arm for England here.'[19] The actual resistance to the Blueshirts took the form of physical attacks. These ranged from the rumoured attack on the Blueshirt march, to attacks on lone Blueshirt members walking home. Government papers relating to the Blueshirts released in 1993 list over 300 incidents of Blueshirt–IRA-related violence.[20] The effect of the IRA resistance was to raise the political temperature, thereby increasing the pressure which the Fianna Fail government put on the Blueshirts. It also served to make the Blueshirts increasingly active. The movement had always claimed that it was a non-violent organisation which would only ever defend itself and never go on the offensive. Throughout 1934, however, there is increasing evidence that the Blueshirts, in an attempt to counter IRA hostility, did take the offensive and instigated attacks themselves.[21]

   The Irish left campaigned vigorously against the Blueshirts, often in conjunction with the IRA. There was a great deal of cross-over in personnel: men such as Peadar O'Donnell and Frank Ryan, for example, who had been mainstays of the IRA since the War of Independence, moved from a largely republican position to a predominantly socialist one. A major force in the struggle was the Republican Congress, formed in 1934 by the same group of people who had started Saor Eire. Essentially the Republican Congress was a breakaway group from Sinn Fein and the IRA which felt that the socialist message was not strong enough in those organisations. Countless internal arguments over the direction of the Congress, its message and ideology, meant that the group was never likely to be strong and coherent; and, indeed, it lasted barely a year before it dissolved into chaos and argument over the workers' struggle, leftist ideology and the future of the republic. During its brief existence, the Blueshirts provided it with a focus.[22] The Congress saw itself as a potential mass movement and the only viable defence against the imperialist fascist challenge. Through its organ, *Republican Congress*, it rallied its supporters with rhetoric-laden pleas:

Above all else, an organ of mass struggle against fascism, that must be the plea of every committee working towards the Republican Congress. Only one power can withstand the imperialist attack now developing in this formation, and that power is the sound common sense of the great mass of the people. Only one power can keep the anger against fascism from degenerating into mere squabbles, and that is solidly formed mass opposition conscious of its tasks. The danger is not that fascism could get the backing of a deep section of the Irish people: its naked imperialism prevents that.[23]

The Republican Congress was fully aware of the links between Fine Gael and the Blueshirts, and was open in its condemnation of the links between a supposedly democratic party and an openly fascist group: 'In Southern Ireland the pro-British capitalist and Rancher interests [politically represented by the Cosgrave Party] are organising a fascist [Blueshirt] party to hold that portion of the country for the British Empire.'[24] Above all else the Republican Congress was looking to form a rallying point for anti-Blueshirt feeling. In their different publications leading supporters of Congress, such as George Gilmore, openly criticised the IRA and the Fianna Fail government for failing to provide a lead for the people who were frightened by the Blueshirt menace. The aim of Congress was to provide a central lead:

Here was a situation crying out for action – on the one side a determined attempt by the British and their supporters to clamp down upon Ireland the straight jacket of Fascist dictatorship. On the other side an increasing spirit of republicanism amongst the people generally, expressing itself in spontaneous popular uprisings and counter demonstrations at Blueshirt meetings, but looking in vain for a lead against the growing menace of Imperialist fascism.[25]

The leftist groups in Irish politics could never be successful in their own right. They were deeply divided and ultimately preached a message as alien to the Irish people as that of fascism. What they did manage to do was provide another centre of opposition to the Blueshirts. However short-lived their existence and unity, the constant rhetoric of groups such as the Republican Congress served to increase the awareness of the danger that certain elements in the Blueshirts were posing to the future political stability of the Free State. The most poignant plea against the evils of fascism came in May 1934 when the Blueshirts were at their strongest. Although in retrospect the plea looks over-zealous, it ran alongside a story covering the Nazi suppression of German workers' rights. In this respect the Republican Congress was opposing what it saw as a very real danger.

Nobody believes that the imperialists could achieve a majority of the people in the South, but if they get power while the masses are asleep they will hold power through their dictatorship. Irish capitalists see this attack developing and they call for the defence of their parliament. Now what interests have the masses in this fight? This is the fascist menace in an attempt at dictatorship by the most reactionary interests in the nation. Their rule would put back history. It would be brutal beyond words. It would degrade workers into almost unimaginable conditions of slavery. It would mean the slaughter of working class fighters. It would mean the tightening of chains of Empire on this nation. The fight against fascism however cannot be a defensive one. Fascism can only be battered down if the full weight of the working class and small farmers is hurled against it. And this is precisely why Fianna Fail cannot fight against it.[26]

Throughout their three-year existence the Blueshirts were firmly opposed by the Fianna Fail government. Just as the Blueshirts saw the government as an unprincipled collection of gunmen, the government in turn saw the Blueshirts as a dangerous collection of zealots and cranks; and, more specifically, as the last attempt by the allies of the defeated Cumann na nGaedheal administration to salvage political power. De Valera seemed to fear that the Blueshirts would unsettle the continued stability which he intended to bring to the Irish Free State. And he was especially concerned about their moves towards fascism.

It is for this reason that nearly every legislative device available was used against the Blueshirts. The process began in early 1932 when the Fianna Fail cabinet, fresh from their election victory, placed the newly formed Army Comrades Association under surveillance. The aim of this surveillance was to ascertain the numerical strength of the movement and any arms supplies which they held. The detailed eighteen-page report also included accounts of speeches given at local branch meetings, and any attacks made on the Fianna Fail government by members or speakers.[27] It is interesting to note that the whole report was compiled and overseen by the then Commissioner of Police, General Eoin O'Duffy! The surveillance of the Blueshirts continued throughout their entire existence. On two separate occasions during 1934 Blueshirt headquarters in Merrion Square were raided by the Garda, as were the addresses of the Blueshirt executive. Accompanying the surveillance of the Blueshirts were the legal moves to inhibit the movement. In 1933 legislation was brought in that demanded the surrender of all firearms held by individuals. This created great confusion and annoyance. Since the murder of Kevin O'Higgins in 1927 all Cumann na nGaedheal ministers had been allowed to carry arms to protect themselves from assassination attempts. The removal of these weapons was seen as a threat to the ex-ministers. The feeling of fear was inflated when it emerged that the only people who reported having their firearms removed by the Garda were Cumann na nGaedheal or Blueshirt members. There is no evidence to suggest that either Fianna Fail or IRA supporters had their weapons removed.[28] The legislation effectively left the Blueshirts an unarmed force, while their opponents in the IRA remained armed. This delighted the IRA: 'The members of the new imperial force – renegades from the republican movement, ex-members of the forces which betrayed the republic in 1922 and executors of comrades who upheld it – have cried out in fear because they have been deprived of the guns which gave them false courage'.[29] Not only was the government responding to the threat from the Blueshirts, but in doing so it was seen by the IRA as giving respectability to their own cause and their methods of political operation.

A great bone of contention for Fianna Fail during their years of opposition had been Cumann na nGaedheal's use of Article 2A of the constitution and the Military Tribunal to clamp down on the IRA and left-wing organisations such as Saor Eire. These methods allowed for arrest and imprisonment without charge, and more frequently trial before a military, not civil court. The use of these tactics was seen as oppressive, and the annulment of Article 2A was one of Fianna Fail's first acts in government. The ever-increasing threat from the Blueshirts during the early 1930s, and the fact that the movement was resorting to violence and lawlessness, prompted Fianna Fail to re-introduce Article 2A. In 1934 the Military Tribunal sat for nearly 200 days, and heard over 1,000 cases. The outcome of these cases saw 304 Blueshirts imprisoned compared to only thirty-eight known IRA men.[30] The Tribunal was used as a highly effective means of removing leading Blueshirts from the streets. By the end of 1934 six of the twelve-man Blueshirt executive were imprisoned. These included the highly influential Commandant Cronin, Commander Dennis Quish, Captain Padraig Quinn and Lieutenant Patrick Quinlan – not only important figures for the movement nationally, but also hugely popular figures with large localised power bases.

The government tried two other tactics to stall the Blueshirts as a popular mass movement. First they tried to ban the movement outright. This happened on 23 August 1933 when the government banned the National Guard, and again on 10 December 1933 when the Young Ireland Association was proscribed. The success of these bans is difficult to gauge, as the Blueshirts always re-formed in a different guise. By December 1933 the movement had realised that the government would repeatedly attempt to ban the organisation, no matter what its name. For this reason the formation of the League of Youth on 14 December 1933 was accompanied by a legal petition requesting the High Court to judge on the legality of the organisation. While the judgement was taking place the Blueshirts were immune from governmental ban. The judgement was not completed until 1937 when the ruling was in favour of the Blueshirts. By then, however, the Blueshirts had ceased to exist in any form. The short-term nature of the bans which the Blueshirts so easily out-manoeuvred was highlighted by their ideological opponents. The small workers' movement led by James Larkin Jnr replied to the December 1933 ban by stating:

O'Duffy's employers – the bankers and ranchers, the men of property, the allies of England – have not been defeated by the ban. They are intensifying their plunder of the working people. They are building up their legal constitutional party and under its cover are organising their armed yeomanry. They possess all the wealth and influence of the country; they have the British behind them and the key positions from the Civil Service to the Free State Army are in their hands.[31]

The final tactic was equally unsuccessful. Following the precedent set in other European countries, including Britain, the Irish government attempted to introduce a ban on the wearing of uniforms. The debate on the Wearing of Uniforms Bill in the Dail was steeped in European parallels and fears that the Blueshirts could somehow become a force as threatening as the Nazi Brownshirts or the Italian Blackshirts. The Fianna Fail minister Seán Lemass stated that:

as a post-war development there has been a tendency in many countries towards the militarisation of politics, which it is very necessary to arrest if democratic institutions are going to be preserved. We can see in many European countries this development of politics at its various stages; its incipient stages, its half-developed stages, and its completed stage. The proposed legislation would retard these developments in Ireland.[32]

The debate raged around the issue of the Blueshirts' supposed fascism, and there were many impassioned speeches by Fine Gael deputies, including John A. Costello's famous statement that, 'the Blackshirts were victorious in Italy, and the Hitler shirts were victorious in Germany, as, assuredly, in spite of this Bill and in spite of the Public Safety Act, the Blueshirts will be victorious in the Free State'.[33] The bill was passed in the Dail, but rejected in the Senate, which refused to give it a second reading. This meant that the legislation was kept off the statute book for eighteen months. As with the challenge to the banning of the Blueshirts, the Uniforms Bill was rendered superfluous because of the demise of the movement.

The Fianna Fail government used all the legislative machinery which they had at hand in an attempt to defeat the Blueshirts. Their motivation was two-fold. First was the fear of a potentially fascist movement, and second was the fear of a political opponent which might threaten Fianna Fail supremacy. In effect, the government's attempts at banning the movement were largely unsuccessful. The Blueshirts managed to manoeuvre round most of the legislation, and in the process may have even gained a degree of extra support. What the government's attacks on the Blueshirts did achieve was the formalisation of opposition to Ireland's fledgling fascism. The stamp of democratic authority on a process of resistance which had started within the Blueshirts' own ranks, and had been furthered by socialist republicans, formalised an umbrella of opposition which would condemn the movement to failure.

The Irish civil war had been fought over the issue of the Anglo-Irish Treaty. Those on the pro-Treaty side who would later form the Cumann na nGaedheal government argued that the Treaty offered the best way forward in eventually securing a full, united Irish republic. They firmly believed that in 1921 the British government would not and, in the face of Unionist opposition, could not offer a full republic. They argued that the Free State, the Boundary Commission, and other devices put in place by the Treaty could be used to secure a republic over a period of years as both Britain and the Unionists were convinced that Irish aims were not hostile or derogatory to the status of either party. The anti-Treaty side argued against this rationale. They insisted that it was the republic or nothing. Continued war against the British was preferable to the acceptance of defeat which the Treaty signalled.[34]

The Cumann na nGaedheal administration during the 1920s did much to establish Ireland as a functioning state, but failed to advance the cause of the republic. After the split between the forces of Sinn Fein and Fianna Fail in 1927, and the acceptance by Fianna Fail of the democratic process, republicanism as personified by the anti-Treaty forces had a place in the Dail. In the elections of both 1931 and 1932 Fianna Fail campaigned hard on the issue of the republic, and were openly critical of Cumann na nGaedheal's failures. The ploy was a political success, and once in power Fianna Fail set about attacking the mechanisms of British rule which survived in the Free State. De Valera was central to the success of this project; his republican views were combined with a firm sense of political realism and a Machiavellian attitude to politics and diplomatic negotiation.[35]

Despite constant criticism from Sinn Fein and the IRA, de Valera had by 1937 achieved a remarkable amount. Cumann na nGaedheal's argument had always been that you could never force the British or Unionist hand. Everything that could be achieved had to be done through negotiation and agreement. De Valera and Fianna Fail flew in the face of this logic. All the attacks on British power came unilaterally and without prior negotiation. In the first two years of office de Valera removed the symbols of British power from the Free State. The oath of allegiance sworn by members of the Dail to the British crown, which had been a constant source of conflict during the Treaty negotiations, was removed. Next, the British governor-general in Dublin Castle was sent home and replaced by an Irishman whose powers of office were withdrawn. The most important battle was in the area of finance. Under the Treaty the Free State had to pay the British government land annuities to compensate for land lost as a result of independence. De Valera refused to pay these and the situation quickly deteriorated into a tariff war. The Anglo-Irish economic war lasted from 1932 until 1935 and ended with a partial victory for de Valera. More importantly it signalled Fianna Fail's determination to fight any injustices which they felt existed, rather than merely negotiating. By 1937 de Valera had achieved his ultimate victory: the remaining Irish ports under British control were returned, and a new constitution formalised the establishment of the Irish republic.

What de Valera and Fianna Fail fundamentally achieved in the first half of the 1930s was the governmental institutionalising of republicanism. This was despite criticism from Sinn Fein and the IRA who saw themselves as the only true republicans, and intense opposition from the Blueshirts who believed that such a sustained attack on the relationship with Britain was damaging to Ireland's future. However, by pursuing such policies in the face of the opposition, de Valera was able to steal the ground from both political extremes present in the Free State. Most importantly, de Valera showed that changes in direction could be made by the Irish government using the existing system. Despite the problems which hampered Irish development as a modern European nation economically and socially during the 1930s and beyond, the mechanisms of power did not need altering. De Valera successfully used the existing political framework, despite demands from the Blueshirts for a corporate state, and pleas from the socialist republicans for a leftist workers' republic, as the only ways to save Ireland from its real and imagined perils. By placing his faith in Irish parliamentary democracy, only a decade old and still establishing itself, de Valera achieved the formalisation of the republic; but more importantly he was able to resist the threat of far-right extremism. The decade-old system which the Free State had borrowed from its former imperial oppressors served them well; for Ireland, despite huge upheavals and changes, there would be no Weimaresque collapse of democratic structures when fascism threatened.

The debate which rages over the very definitions and common experiences of interwar fascism is not only highly charged but has also produced a mass of work.[36] To try and locate the Blueshirts in any definitional framework would take more space than is available here.[37]

During the 1930s Ireland shared with many continental states the 'pre-conditions' for a fascist movement: the presence of extreme nationalism; opposition to the presence of communism, real or imagined; opposition to liberal democracy as a defunct system; hatred of racial minorities within the state; an irredentist ethos; and impending economic collapse. Irish nationalism had a long pedigree and was still a potent force in the Free State. The presence of the Catholic church as one of the main mouthpieces of political, moral and social thought in Ireland meant that the 'godless' ideology of communism was high on the agenda of contem-

porary evils. Several groups within the state had their reasons for opposing the parliamentary system as it stood; some viewed it as British, while
others felt it irrelevant to the Irish situation. Irredentism was, and still is, a
characteristic of Irish politics: without a resolution of the Northern question, the issue will always remain part of basic political ideology. The
prospect of economic collapse was very real for Ireland in the 1930s;
although the damage caused by the world depression was limited, the
Anglo-Irish war brought into sharp focus the whole future of the Irish
economy, dominated as it was by agriculture in an industrial world. The
only common feature of fascism which was not present was some form of
racism (although certain intellectuals such as Arthur Griffith and Maud
Gonne did pay lip service to anti-semitism).

    This did not necessarily mean that the Free State was ripe for fascism.
Such a comparison with Europe is simplistic without reference to the
specifically Irish context. If the key pre-conditions for fascism are re-
viewed from an Irish perspective the situation looks altogether different.
Nationalism in Ireland has a long and distinguished history, the struggle
for nation status stretching back over three hundred years. As a result,
nationalism had to be the central message of any Irish political party, and
during the 1930s it is de Valera, not the Blueshirts, who successfully
converted this into political practice by establishing the republic. The fear
of communism, a monster created solely by the Catholic hierarchy in
Ireland, was seized on by all the main political parties. Cumann na
nGaedheal banned the fledgling Saor Eire, not because that party was a
threat to the state, but because church support was central to the success
of any political party. All the main parties, the Blueshirts and Fianna Fail
included, were compelled to echo the church's warnings about communism. The question of the usefulness of parliamentary democracy, seized
upon by the Blueshirts as an issue, is again duplicated by other political
groups. The socialist republicans expressed nationalist and leftist doubts
as to the viability of the system as it stood, while Fianna Fail not only
altered the status of the parliament's upper house in 1937, but also
brought together a committee to investigate the relevance of corporate
re-organisation to Irish politics.[38] As with nationalism, the issue of irredentism was central to any strand of political belief: whether it was mere
lip service, or an outrageous plan such as O'Duffy's to recapture the North
by force, the question of the six Northern Counties could not be ignored
by politicians of any party. The question of impending economic collapse
is more difficult to deal with. Blueshirts would argue that any impending
collapse was brought about by de Valera's economic war with Britain – a
war which he started. De Valera on the other hand, would argue that the
war was started specifically to pre-empt any economic collapse.[39]

Although the soil for a fascist challenge was potentially fertile in Ireland, there was little room for its growth. The major constitutional parties already held that ground. Ideas, issues and problems which formed the basis of the fascist pantheon elsewhere in Europe were standard political practice. The Irish Free State was very much in the mould of others being established in contemporary Europe and, as elsewhere, extremist politics did emerge during the 1930s. Certain Blueshirts undeniably toyed with fascist ideas, and did dream that the 48,000 shirted members would help create a reborn Irish nation. Equally, the socialist republicans gave an Irish voice to various forms of contemporary socialist and communist thinking. However, because the usual pre-conditions for the rise of fascism could also be exploited by Fianna Fail and countless other groups in the Free State, the Blueshirts had no free political ground to capture.

The Blueshirts had limited electoral success only when they addressed local 'bread-and-butter' issues, as they did in the south-west. Provincial Blueshirt leaders such as Commandant Cronin from Co. Cork and Captain Dennis Quinn from Co. Limerick spoke of nothing else. They did not talk about corporatism; they talked instead of farming, the economic war, the need to halt emigration and migration – fundamentally, the need to protect a way of life. It was around these issues, the stuff of real-life politics, that the Blueshirts found the backbone of their support in the rural counties. The importance of domestic concerns over fascist ideology as a means of acquiring popular support was borne out in 1935 when O'Duffy formed his openly fascist National Corporate Party (NCP). The NCP looked constantly to Europe and talked only of reconstruction; it did not dabble in day-to-day domestic issues. Despite his claims that such a party would attract a comparable membership to that of the Blueshirts, the lack of a domestic agenda and the party's open fascism meant that its membership peaked at eighty. Fascism was an untenable ideology in Ireland.

A casual observer looking at the state of Irish politics in the 1930s may see echoes of a European pattern. The Blueshirts appeared as a fascist-styled movement, opposed by the socialist republicans, and this gave the appearance of an ideological battle raging in one of the new nation states thrown up after the upheavals of the First World War. There is an element of truth in this view. The Blueshirts, nevertheless, were a product of an Irish situation. Elements within Cumann na nGaedheal were looking for the best possible way to fight against the domination of Fianna Fail. The state of uncertainty within that group, and a lack of firm direction, meant that a number of rogue thinkers and political egomaniacs could come to dominate the main opposition. From this position of dominance they were able to propagate ideas drawn from contemporary European thinking and present a fascistic programme for Ireland. Despite the excitement which this process gave to the political scene, and the support which it provided for the Blueshirts and Fine Gael, such ideas could only exist in the short term.

Such outlandish ideas were opposed from within by rank-and-file Blueshirts who were primarily concerned with the best way of solving domestically relevant problems. The leaders of Fine Gael, from whom the Blueshirts gained so much respectability, also resisted. For men such as W. T. Cosgrave, who had spent ten years establishing a democratic state, it was preferable to see de Valera in power than risk the onslaught of fascism. As Frank MacDermot (the leader of the Centre Party in the Fine Gael coalition) wrote to O'Duffy in July 1934: 'the time has come when I feel obliged to make a more formal protest than I have yet done against the tendency of certain speakers and writers of our party to attack the Parliamentary system of Government, and to imply that it is official policy to replace it by a Blueshirt ascendancy modelled on fascism'.[40] The party, as well as the rank and file were not prepared to accept fascism.

Externally the Blueshirts were resisted by the socialist republicans who, despite their lack of unity, presented a strong and highly vocal front against an attack on the notion of the republic, and the values of the worker and small farmer. Most importantly, all the strands of opposition and resistance were given the stamp of authority by the government. Fianna Fail, motivated as it was by notions of self-preservation and a deep distrust of 'foreign' ideologies, blocked the Blueshirts at every turn.

The experience of the Blueshirts and the opposition to them must be seen in the context of a nation struggling to modernise and develop on countless fronts in politics, economics and social policy. What is evident from the behaviour of all those who opposed the Blueshirts and the fascistic rhetoric of its leaders in Dublin, is that the struggle for parliamentary, democratic and national freedom would not be given up to an ideology that had no relevance to Ireland.

6 Town councils of the Nord and Pas-de-Calais region: local power, French power, German power

Yves Le Maner

Translated from the French by Sarah Kane

There is no doubt that an attachment to one's village or town is one of the primary factors which makes up the collective consciousness and one's sense of national identity, a factor which is all the more prominent in border regions. In 1939 two million people lived in the *département* of the Nord in 669 communes, while in the *département* of the Pas-de-Calais, 1,800,000 people lived in over 905 communes. The region seemed to have two faces: a densely populated urbanised core comprising 197 communes in the Nord and 108 in the Pas-de-Calais, bordered by rural areas where 50 per cent of communes in the Nord and 80 per cent of communes in the Pas-de-Calais had fewer than 1,000 inhabitants. If one adds the very clear distinction between the 'classic' sociologically differentiated principal towns of each *arrondissement* – Arras, Boulogne, Dunkirk, Valenciennes, Douai – and the towns which had grown up around the textile and mining industries, such as the suburbs of Lille, one begins to get a picture of the great diversities within the region.[1]

In both these *départements*, the sense of belonging to a local community has, until very recently, prevailed over the sense of regional identity. This parochial loyalty was strengthened by the trials of the First World War, when the Nord, and to a lesser extent the Pas-de-Calais, experienced their first long period of occupation, the aftermath of which had a profound effect on the collective memory.[2]

This first period of occupation raised the mayor to the rank of 'great notable of the people'. It also favoured the emergence of new men – notables more in terms of ability than in terms of status – who, after the elections of 1919, embarked on long careers in local government which would bring them up against their second ordeal of occupation twenty years later. Thus, in 1939, the communes of the Nord and the Pas-de-Calais were run by town councils made up of older men, most of them war veterans, characterised by their hatred of the 'Boche' both as soldiers and as occupiers.[3] This was especially true for the mayors: more than half of those in the Pas-de-Calais had reached the age of sixty and a fifth were over the age of seventy in 1940.[4]

Sociologically, the mayors reflected the divisions of the region: dynamic landowner–farmers in the countryside, 'rural bourgeois' in the principal towns of the cantons, and trade unionist, socialist and co-operative movement officials in the working-class areas.[5] Indeed, results of the council elections in 1935 had revealed a sharp division along geographical lines: a solid core of the right and of 'moderates' in the rural areas of the west and south of the Pas-de-Calais; isolated radicals in the traditional towns of Arras, Valenciennes, Boulogne and in the semi-rural and semi-industrial areas of the Avesnois and the Cambrésis; powerful socialist strongholds around Lille, in the Cambrésis and in the west of the Bassin Minier of the Pas-de-Calais (for instance in Lens and Bruay); and communist bridgeheads in the Bassin Minier, notably between Douai and Valenciennes.[6]

This chapter focuses on the power dynamics between the various governing bodies during the occupation of 1940–44. In the following account, local government is usually identified with the sole person of the mayor, and this itself is a reflection of the stature which the position assumed in wartime. After the trauma of the summer of 1940, when a number of local notables failed as leaders, those mayors remaining in post represented for several months the only indigenous power in the Prohibited Zone. Over time, they became the target of indirect, high-level political battles between the German authorities and those of Vichy France. To what extent did the power of the notables suffer in this precarious situation? In what sense – and for how long – did the occupation modify relations between notables and the local population, and change fundamental political attitudes? These are the major questions this chapter seeks to address.

The mobilisation had very little impact on town councillors on account of their very high average age – in the Pas-de-Calais less than 10 per cent of the mayors were called up. Also, a circular of 2 September 1939, empowering prefects to appoint representatives in order to make up for the loss of those who had been called up, was not implemented in the Nord and the Pas-de-Calais. Nevertheless, the war had immediate consequences for the smooth running of local government because a number of town clerks were mobilised and this resulted in a considerable increase in work for the mayors. As a result, municipal services fell into a disorganised state.

The decree of 26 September 1939 (which came into force on 12 October) left a profound mark on local politics. The decree contained a number of measures aimed at reinforcing the authority of the prefect over town councils 'for the duration of the war', including the right to suspend the council or the mayor, and the right to designate a councillor whatever his rank in the hierarchy to replace a dismissed mayor (Art. 3, 4 and 5). The resulting 'administrative supervision signifies the subordination of local authorities to the central power'. At the same time the decree was to ensure the maintenance of order and the 'battle against subversive machinations'.

This decree was rapidly implemented in the Nord and Pas-de-Calais: the suspension of communist town councils was essentially effective as from 3 October. No indulgence was shown to councillors who had broken with the PCF (Parti Communiste Français). There were many of them in the two northern *départements* and all were relieved of their duties.[7] Between October and December, the prefects installed eleven special delegations in the Pas-de-Calais and thirty-seven in the Nord without encountering any major difficulties: from the URD (the right-wing conservative party) to the socialists, an all-pervasive sense of national unity existed and political 'partnerships' were created which would have been considered impossible a few months before. The prefectural administration had nevertheless tried to designate members of the SFIO (Section Française de l'Internationale Ouvrière) as a matter of priority so as not to cut themselves off from a working-class community which was on the defensive and weakened by the sudden collapse of the PCF, particularly in the Bassin Minier (Pas-de-Calais).[8]

In certain important instances, however, the powerful mining companies had succeeded in imposing their own men (for instance, at Liévin and Sallaumines). It should be noted that in a number of communes, particularly in the west of the Bassin Minier, the socialist sections had anticipated these prefectural measures and driven out of the town hall those communist councillors elected on the lists of the Popular Front; thus at Maisnil-les-Ruitz, the communist mayor had been forced to resign on 29 August. After the dissolutions, the socialists then went on to purge communist militants who held junior positions in the town councils. This happened, for instance, at Divion, where on 29 October the communist councillors were forcibly expelled. In Calais, the majority on the council ousted the twelve communists who had remained faithful to their party. Thus, the socialists had taken advantage of the 'phoney war' to conduct a tough anti-communist offensive.

Unlike that of 1914, the invasion of 1940 was characterised by the mass exodus of notables. The origins of this decision to flee are still obscure. Naturally the mayors had been informed during the 'phoney war' of the measures they needed to take in the event of invasion, and, in particular, of the procedures for withdrawal into the 'interior zone'. Yet the suddenness of the German assault meant that the prefectural authorities were unable to issue coherent instructions in time. After the event, some mayors made a case for 'ministerial instructions concerning the withdrawal of mobilisable men'.[9] But it seems that in the vast majority of cases, orders were not given, or if they were, only after the mayors had fled. The existence or absence of evacuation orders remained, moreover, a contentious subject between the prefectural administration and several of the mayors.[10]

With the exception of a few known cases of evacuation by order of the military authorities (French authorities in the Avesnois; German in the region of Houdain and around Dunkirk), it seems that the vast exodus in the Nord and Pas-de-Calais was largely instigated by the notables. Sometimes they were directly responsible, as when they acted out of concern to protect those citizens living in areas exposed to bombardment, but most often they were indirectly responsible, by setting an example which others then followed.[11] Such was the case in Sauchy-Lestrée, where the flight of the mayor and the majority of the eleven councillors in May brought about the departure of almost the entire population.

In a very large number of cases, the notables completely abandoned their citizens. Thus, at Arras, the town council fled 'before the order for evacuation was given and at a time when the prefectural administration had given the order to stay put'; this was the day before a dreadful bombardment left 200 civilians dead. It was the notables of the large towns particularly who abandoned their people. Besides Arras, the towns of Lille, Douai, Valenciennes, Roubaix and Tourcoing found themselves bereft of their mayors when the Germans arrived.[12] No one political grouping had a monopoly on cowardice: the mayor of Valenciennes, a radical and former under-secretary of state for war, was among the first to leave; in the suburbs of Lille, many SFIO mayors also abandoned their fellow citizens. The departure of numerous notables and the disintegration of the police force created a power vacuum.

By falling short of their primary duty to protect the property of the community, these deserting mayors lost all popular authority. It was equally clear that the rapid establishment of the 'Prohibited Zone' and the drawing up of the 'frontier of the Somme' prevented for several months the return of 'evacuees' anxious to get back home. It was only from the end of September 1940 that the first town councillors received authorisations to return.[13] Most of them found that their property had been looted by local people. This led to resignations and some very serious internal disputes, for example at Boyelles, an *arrondissement* of Arras. Moreover they had to face up to unfavourable public opinion, and, showered with sarcastic remarks, they were even sometimes forced to resign by their deputies who had stayed put and had taken over the duties of mayor during that terrible summer. For example, at Mazingarbe and at Hersin-Coupigny councillors who had remained in their posts had, in the absence of prefectural authority, taken it upon themselves to suspend or 'dismiss' the runaway mayor. Some mayors chose not to come back at all.[14]

The collapse of the state apparatus – particularly evident in the Pas-de-Calais where the prefect Rochard was dismissed on 9 August – took place in an atmosphere of fear, panic and demoralisation brought about by the invasion and subsequent defeat. The effect of this was the complete isolation of the people, and the commune became for several long weeks the only French administrative structure able to function in the Prohibited Zone. The absence of supervisory authorities induced those councillors still in post to form 'war committees'. In numerous communes, where the numbers of council staff had been severely reduced, citizens from all walks of life took the initiative and set up coherent groups outside prefectural control. This movement was particularly widespread in the *département* of the Nord, where the shock-waves had been most severe and the defections most numerous.

In certain communes of the Douaisis or the Valenciennois, communist ex-councillors profited from the debacle by taking the place of fleeing councillors and by forming war committees, for instance at Anzin, Denain, Avesnes-le-Sec, Douchy and Wallers. Some of these initiatives continued for several weeks – indeed several months – to the great annoyance of the sub-prefects, who were concerned by the late and feeble reaction of the German authorities. The Germans, it seemed, erred through ignorance, or rather were satisfied with the behaviour of these special teams, whom they judged to be 'serious and effective'.[15] On 22 August, sixty-four town councils in the Nord were officially 'withdrawn' and replaced for the most part by war committees.[16] Similarly, in Avesnes, one of the hardest hit *arrondissements*, only a third of the twenty-seven larger communes still had functioning town councils in December.

The invasion was so rapid and German efforts so concentrated on the war with Britain that the German military authorities were now obliged to improvise: how should they 'digest' the reality of the occupation of the Nord and Pas-de-Calais? In order to make up for the mass flight of notables, they designated on the spot a large number of 'acting mayors', most of them selected from among the town councillors who had stayed behind.[17] This practice was to continue until mid June. After that date, the French authorities themselves were involved in the process.[18]

The military administration, having established itself, proceeded to carry out a small-scale purge. Those to fall victim were the few Jewish notables and, in particular, the oldest mayors.[19] The desire to recruit younger people into the municipal corps was particularly evident in the large working-class communes, especially in the Bassin Minier, under the influence of assertive young *Wehrmacht* officers. At Hénin-Liétard, the mayor, described as 'tired and worn', had to resign in August; at Loos-en-Gohelle, the seventy-two-year-old mayor was forced to resign on the grounds that he was 'too old and ineffectual'. The latter case highlights the complex motivations behind this 'rejuvenation' of the municipal corps. The prerogative of appointing a mayor, in theory at least, belonged to the French administration. Now on 13 October 1940, the *Standort-kommandantur* of Loos designated a 'commissarial-mayor' selected from the council.[20] The following day, a junior officer called the councillors together to inform them of this decision, and had it registered in the minutes book and then approved by a vote before publicising it.

This incident might have been trivial had it not raised fundamental questions of sovereignty and authority. The prefect of the Pas-de-Calais protested vehemently, and appointed as quickly as possible, by decree, a new mayor, whom he also picked from the ranks of the councillors. As soon as this mayor was officially invested, he had to face the threats of the *Standortkommandantur*, who demanded his resignation while 'promising him the firing squad in the event of a refusal'. For several weeks the Germans refused to have dealings with him and stuck by their own mayor, a move which drove the special commissioner of Lens to declare: 'In short it appears that there are two communal authorities or mayors in Loos-en-Gohelle, one of them recognised by and operating in the interests of the French Administration and the other designated by and working for the German military authority.'[21]

An identical situation arose in the neighbouring commune of Hersin-Coupigny after the Germans had directly dismissed the president of the war committee on suspicion of a number of shady dealings. This provoked the blind rage of the sub-prefect of Béthune who wrote: 'as a result of this affair, I believe that the following question must be clearly resolved: whose responsibility is it to appoint a mayor? Is it the responsibility of the prefect in accordance with the clauses of the decree of 26 September 1939 or is it the responsibility of the German Military Administration?'[22]

The question was entirely justified. Indeed, while the *Kommandanturen* were taking more and more initiatives, French administrators noted with some concern that new measures had been enforced throughout the Prohibited Zone: evacuated mayors' requests to return were systematically refused; mayors had been forced to sign a declaration of loyalty (July 1940); and the prefects had been told that they had to inform the Senior Counsellors of the Military Administration of any changes in the town councils.[23]

Moreover, it seemed clear that the Germans wanted to concentrate all responsibilities on the sole person of the mayor, while ignoring totally the existence of the town councillors. The 'taking hostage' of mayors in this way was methodical, coldly calculated and systematic. Thus, in the autumn of 1940, the Germans began a strategy of 'weakening' the notables which was to last many months. The mayor was made responsible for discipline in the population and could be taken into custody for several hours, or even days, for the slightest incident (damaged telephone wires or graffiti chalked on walls, for example). They were also subjected to heavy fines.

The Germans' fear of a power vacuum during the first few weeks of the invasion also took hold of the French administration itself. The prefectural administration was only just in place by September. The sub-prefects tried to resume contacts with the mayors as quickly as possible. A first series of inspections conducted by French civil servants accompanied by German officers had already taken place from mid June in the suburbs of Lille.[24] A second more thorough series was organised under the same conditions during the first two weeks of September.

At the end of September the accounts were done: few mayors were prisoners of war (only 18 out of 905 in the Pas-de-Calais), but many were evacuees, for whom going back would not be easy. Unobtrusively, the prefects appointed the deputies who had proved themselves in May, and tried to check the flood of resignations occasioned by the increased difficulty of the mayor's role. Aware of the dangers of annexation, Vichy tried to preserve the cohesion of town councils in the Prohibited Zone and to reinforce the mayors' authority in order to maintain the relationship between local people and the political institutions of the state. Every request to resign met with a categorical refusal on the part of the prefects: it was necessary to keep experienced men in post so as to allow communal administrations, which had been severely tested by the call-up of numerous town clerks, to function normally, and so not to add to the deterioration of popular morale.[25]

Above all, the town councils became a symbolic battlefield, not only between the Germans and the French authorities, but between the different representatives of the French administration. At Tourcoing in August 1940, for example, the German *Kommandantur* had imprisoned the mayor appointed by the prefect and reinstated Salembien, who had been dismissed by the Vichy authorities for fleeing in May 1940.[26] The prefects made brutal attacks on the few town councillors who played the German card against the French administration. Thus, at Sains-en-Gohelle, a large mining commune in the Pas-de-Calais,[27] the socialist mayor who had requisitioned premises belonging to 'les Mines' in order to store the property of refugees, was suspended by the prefect for abuse of power on 3 September 1940. He then lodged an appeal with the *Kreiskommandantur* of Béthune. The prefect stood by his decision and clarified the matter for the benefit of the Military Counsellor of Arras:

> on account of the loyal and proper collaboration which exists between our two administrations, this affair ought not to grow into an incident; some clarification however seems to be necessary. It is in fact imperative that the decisions of the French administrative authority are respected by those who are put in charge of implementing them . . . The example of Mr Dupuich might be followed soon enough by other mayors, who, for the most diverse reasons would not hesitate to appeal to the German military authorities against the orders which they receive from the sub-prefecture and the prefecture; if this were to happen, it would be to the very great detriment of the people whom we govern . . . What I am most concerned to do, you understand, is to take action against the deficient mayors as I am duty bound to do.

This apparently naive plea expressed implicitly the isolation of the prefects of the Prohibited Zone.

German intervention in communal affairs reached its greatest intensity in the period which stretched more or less from autumn 1940 to the miners' strike of June 1941. The failure of 'Operation Sea Lion' meant that the provisional administrative arrangement was brought to an end and the conditions of occupation in the Prohibited Zone made permanent.[28] A flood of new responsibilities, often presented in a humiliating fashion, rained down on the communes during the winter of 1940–1. This was particularly the case for the lengthy process of planning the billeting arrangements for the considerable German military presence, especially in the coastal 'Red Zone'.[29] Frequent calls to appear before the *Kommandantur* wounded the councillors' pride. Their authority was undermined by certain elements of the population who would go directly to the 'authorities of occupation'. In the Bassin Minier, the Germans mockingly observed the housewives' protests against the mayors which they knew full well had been organised by the clandestine PCF.

The fastening of an undoubted financial millstone around the communes' necks, arising from the occupation costs, was coupled with heavy taxation and accompanied by a tight control of their budgets. This increased their dependency upon the Germans, as the following report shows:

The *Militärverwaltung* has instructed that it be shown the budgets of all communes of more than 5,000 inhabitants and that, in the case of smaller communes, samples be submitted for its perusal. This step has been taken on account of the *Militärverwaltung*'s need to supervise the communes' financial situation and their performance for the financial year 1941. As the communes are heavily dependent on state subsidies, the *Militärverwaltung* has been obliged – at the start of its activities – to agree to loans for the communes; it has subsequently proved necessary to verify whether the communes have dutifully performed certain tasks such as finding lodgings for the troops. A need has also arisen to examine whether the budgets include any undesirable expenses, in particular those connected with political organisations, Masonic lodges or other similar schemes, whose support by the communes runs contrary to German interests. This examination by the *Feldkommandantur* has removed the task of approving budgets from the French sphere of duties.[30]

This budgetary control – which was kept up until mid 1941 – was merely one instance of German interference in communal affairs. Political supervision was another. In December 1940, the *Oberfeldkommandantur* (OFK) warned the mayors that 'any attempt to discuss political questions within the town councils is strictly forbidden. Town council meetings have as their aim the discussion of matters specific to the commune and are not forums for political demonstration.'[31] Furthermore the French administration was asked to eliminate as quickly as possible any 'undesirable elements', particularly in the war committees. This was principally a reference to the 'adherents of the radical left', here classed as socialists. More generally the training and competence of the mayors were called into question, as a report drafted by the Counsellors of the Military Administration on 21 November 1940, indicates:

The communal administration is suffering from a shortage of staff. This is due to the fact that some of the staff, particularly the younger ones, are prisoners of war and others have withdrawn into the interior of the country. The mayors, all of them elected, have been put in position not on any neutral basis but by virtue of their membership of certain political parties; frequently they do not answer the necessary criteria ... In all cases, we have brought pressure to bear on the French administration so that they get on with installing suitable mayors. However a number of difficulties still exist for reason of the purely electoral system still in place.[32]

This concern to find some good municipal administrators corresponded with a much greater ambition on the part of the OFK. It was a question of thoroughly 'overhauling' local government, of separating it from its elective roots – in short, of having it taken over by the state. This comes across in the oft-repeated desire to pay the mayors. Already in his report of 30 September 1940, the prefect of the Pas-de-Calais noted the Germans' concern to distance themselves from French legislation: 'The mayors who are denounced or judged to be inadequate are stripped of office by the German authorities. Certain *Kommandanturen* are going to pay the mayors a salary in order to allow them to carry out their municipal duties fully; such is the case at Montreuil-sur-Mer where the town council has received 3,000 francs per month.'[33]

In certain circumstances, the Germans treated the mayors as direct 'functionaries' of the Reich without going through the prefectures: in August and September 1940 they were given responsibility for putting up German road signs. This desire to turn mayors into employees of the state was instantly attacked by the prefects. But the Counsellors of the Military Administration then tried to get round the difficulty by addressing themselves directly to the town clerks without going through the mayor. Thus in December 1940, at the time of the first conscription of labour for Germany, the town clerks of the mining communes were called together and made personally responsible for implementing the measures.[34]

In these conditions it is easy to understand the hopes which the Vichy decree of 21 January 1941 aroused among the officials of the OFK. The decree, complementary to the Vichy municipal law of 16 November 1940,[35] made provision for the establishment of strict rules for the recruitment (either by exam or competition) of town clerks, particularly in communes of over 2,000 inhabitants; and, furthermore, it forbade town clerks to take on other paid work. The Germans were also hopeful that it would depoliticise this rung of local administration.[36] The measure, however, appeared insufficient, leaving the Counsellors of the Military Administration of Lille to redouble their pressure on the prefects on the central question of the mayors' remuneration. On 20 April, now disillusioned, they noted:

Contrary to the evolution of the state sector, the situation in the communes is, despite the changes or appointments to the posts of mayor, a less happy one . . . As in France [*sic*], the bourgeois of the communes are under no obligation to accept a communal post; the prefect often declares, after the dismissal of one mayor or another, that he cannot when all is said and done – or only with great difficulty – find a replacement. On this basis the justified requests of the *Kommandanturen* for the replacement of mayors have to a large extent been deferred. For this reason administrative relations are still unsatisfactory and they will only improve in the long term if we succeed in forming a professional communal service, as has been planned for the town clerks.[37]

The aim was to constitute a municipal corps which was competent, 'apolitical' and 'healthy', which was dependent on the German powers and preferably young. In short, they wanted gradually to 'nazify' the town councils in the Prohibited Zone. This was indeed how the sub-prefect of Béthune had interpreted the situation; walking out, 'profoundly discouraged', from a long meeting with a Counsellor of the Military Administration, he noted that the Germans were dealing all the cards and were deriding the concerns of the Vichy regime.[38]

The German position, at least in outline, was elaborated during the winter of 1940–1 at a time when the 'municipal nazification' was coming up against French inertia. The Vichy municipal law of 16 November 1940 was studied at great length, but the first well-argued analysis was not produced by the OFK until January 1941.[39] The one salient point which emerged from it was that the prefectural authorities needed to obtain the prior consent of the *Militärverwaltung* before making any changes to the town councils. It was then necessary to wait for a very dry memo from OFK 670, dated 1 February 1941, before the implementation of the law could even be contemplated in the Nord and Pas-de-Calais. The memo reiterated the fundamental condition that 'prior German consent must be sought for all appointments and dismissals in communes of over 2,000 inhabitants'. Aware that the Germans had allowed themselves time to think, the prefect of the Nord, Carles, noted: 'I believe that the Germans' resoluteness on this point ought to dissuade one from any attempt to modify the town councils.'[40]

The task of overhauling the municipal corps was tightly controlled, commune by commune, by the emissaries of the OFK, so that by May: 'The changing and replacement of mayors according to the French law of organisation is making gradual progress. The *Kreiskommandanturen* have in all cases supervised the replacement and the reinstatement of mayors and town councillors in such a way that German interests are upheld.'[41] Although the prefects – and to a certain extent Vichy – felt tempted to rebel, this principle went unchallenged, and was reaffirmed once and for all on 2 August 1941 by the German Armistice Commission in Wiesbaden, which stated emphatically:

It is understood that in times of war the occupying power has the right to exercise *all prerogatives deriving from territorial sovereignty* . . . article 3 [of the Armistice treaty] furthermore obliges the French government to inform all French authorities and services that they must submit to the arrangement of the German military administration and must collaborate with them in a proper manner.[42]

The sub-prefect of Béthune began to wonder whether it was necessary to undertake a municipal re-organisation: 'given that in reality it is the German authorities which designate the mayors, I cannot but abdicate responsibility for further choices, in which the Germans will have sole initiative'. This exaggerated the situation. The French administration still held the trump cards and the Military Counsellors were about to abandon their major project of 'nazifying' the town councils. In terms of administration, pragmatism prevailed over ideology.

From the autumn of 1940, the prefects' primary concern was to restore the authority of the state, to try and fill the power vacuum and to demonstrate that the Prohibited Zone was part of the French nation as a whole. On the one hand, this show of strength was for the benefit of local leaders – essentially the mayors – and beyond them the entire distressed and abandoned population; and on the other hand, for the benefit of the Germans.

While waiting for the Germans to make a decision about the law of 16 November 1940, the prefectures set about getting rid of 'abnormal' municipal posts and in particular disbanding the war committees, a measure which met with the approval of the *Militärverwaltung*. The restoration was rapid in the Pas-de-Calais (it was essentially accomplished by January 1941), but was slower in the Nord where such posts and committees were much more numerous. In almost all cases, the reconstituted town councils were composed of ex-councillors and, as such, an attempt was made to respect the political complexion of the communes, including the socialist ones. At the same time, the prefects encouraged initiatives which aimed at reaffirming their annexation to French territory: they favoured in particular the reconstitution, from November 1940, of an 'Association of mayors from the North and East' (thus bringing together the two *départements* of the Prohibited Zone and eight from the Occupied Zone). It was indicative of the times that unity was rediscovered in the face of danger, as mayors of all political persuasions from conservatives to socialists joined together in the management committee.[43]

The law of 16 November 1940 cast doubt over the elective nature of municipal posts in communes of more than 2,000 inhabitants (Art. 2), for which nominations were henceforth to be submitted to the prefect or the minister.[44] All the communes concerned were to be subject to a 're-organisation', each council being 'obliged' from now on to comprise 'a father of a large family, a representative from professional workers' groups, a woman qualified to take care of private charitable societies and aid organisations' (Art. 13). Excluded from this, however, were those who did not inherently possess French nationality and, by implication, Jews (Art. 14).

The conditions for the implementation of the law were defined at length by the 'Peyrouton circular' of 6 January 1941, summarised in a circular from Darlan of 25 February 1941. Peyrouton deferred a decision on the election of town councils of communes under 2,000 inhabitants, which were to continue to be governed by the law of 1884. The core of his circular concerned, of course, the principles which were to govern the famous 're-organisation' of communes of more than 2,000 inhabitants, which effectively sought to 'transform' mayors into government agents, and to reaffirm the imposition of prefectural supervision.[45]

The circular also insisted on 'the necessity . . . of appointing . . . only those of irreproachable morality both in their public and private life, and with an absolute devotion to the politics of the Marshal's government'. And it went on: 'It would be a serious misjudgement of government thought only to call on those labelled "right wing" and who, under the *ancien régime* [*sic*], were described as "reactionaries". As the Marshal of France declared, it is impossible to find in the new order "the features of a sort of *moral order* or a re-run of the events of 1936".'

The law of 16 November 1940 was to remain the cornerstone of municipal organisation until the Liberation. It did, however, undergo certain modifications, common to all of which were the new extensions of prefectural prerogatives. Apart from minor modifications, Vichyist municipal legislation was pragmatic and relatively moderate – qualities which it did not possess in other areas. The Laval circular of 22 June 1942 on the imposition of penalties against town councils is an example of this. While making clear that 'the manifest and sustained hostility to the work of national renewal, sheer bad management and divisions within the assembly which obstruct the smooth running of communal affairs' could not be tolerated, it also conceded that 'Given the difficulties of the task incumbent on the body of municipal magistrates, it is advisable to avoid all measures susceptible of provoking their discouragement or weakening their authority.' And insisting on the need to reinforce the authority of the mayors 'in a period of shortage or of harsh discipline', Laval asked the prefects to use the measures of suspension sparingly: 'written observations or verbal reprimands are preferable in the present circumstances'.

At the most, there were a few repressive drives in January 1942 and February 1943 in the Pas-de-Calais, and a 'round' of dismissals in the Nord in December 1943. Uppermost amongst the reasons for the sanctions were motives of a moral order, linked to the mayor's image of respectability.[46] As for cases of dismissal for political reasons, they were very rare: fifteen in four years for the *départements* of the Pas-de-Calais, a few socialists, a few radicals, but also conservative notables like the *conseiller d'arrondissement* and mayor of Marconnelle, G. Denoyelle (February 1942), or the mayor of Flers, the Baron de Fresnoye (December

1942), who 'held the government responsible for the present situation, saying that its policy of collaboration was the cause of all our ills'.[47] Suspensions, resignations and dismissals in the Pas-de-Calais were thus few: sixteen in 1941 and in 1942, thirteen in 1943 and seven in 1944. The prefects of the Prohibited Zone thus had at their disposal, from February 1941, a legislative apparatus and stable political orders characterised by the pursuit of the status quo.

By mid 1941 in the Prohibited Zone, the French and German powers had traced the limits of sovereignty which were hardly to change until 1944: Vichy bent a little so as to avoid snapping. Thus the vague intention of resisting German orders, contained, for example, in a Darlan circular of 7 June 1941,[48] was quickly abandoned. The situation of the town councils of the Nord and Pas-de-Calais was fixed broadly speaking until the Liberation. Of the 160 communes of the Nord containing between two and ten thousand inhabitants, ninety-one mayors had been retained and sixty-nine appointed (this figure includes a number of presidents of special delegations and deputies who had been acting as mayors since 1940). In the Pas-de-Calais there was even greater stability: eighty-two mayors or presidents of special delegations had been retained out of the 112 communes which had undergone re-organisation (i.e. 73 per cent of cases).[49] Stability had triumphed.

Yet concern for stability must not be allowed to mask the chronological evolution of the prefectures' strategy with regard to the town councils from 1941 to the Liberation. Until the end of 1942, the prefects of the Prohibited Zone lived with the conviction that a large number of mayors might yet rally to Pétain's 'National Revolution'. This illusion reached its highest point on 15 September 1942 when Marshal Pétain received a delegation of mayors from northern France led by Tillie, mayor of Saint-Omer and a National Councillor, amongst whom were mayors of all political hues including the ex-SFIO's Plateel (Hazebrouck), Couteaux (Saint-Amand), Hanotel (Lens).[50] Yet there was particular concern over the response of the ex-SFIO to the collaboration authorities. Nevertheless, Prefect Carles could, until 1943, put forward the town of Roubaix as a model of good management and of sincere collaboration with the administration.[51] But from the winter of 1942–3, the dreams of a great 'rallying to the regime' began to fade and the prefects' tone became harsher.

Unhappy about the direction in which the socialists were moving, the prefects resolved at that point to call upon hard-line Pétainists in order to fill the vacancies in the town councils, notably in the Bassin Minier and the suburbs of Lille. There thus emerged a type of 'new mayor', mostly young and recruited from among the ranks of industrialists, foremen and office workers. Either of PPF (Parti Populaire Français) origin or 'new men', they were technocrats and excellent administrators, like Verley at Dunkirk and Chartiez at Béthune. Yet it was only possible to implement this solution in a few cases for want of qualified and voluntary officials at a time when the war was taking an unfavourable turn for Vichy; and for fear of serious problems should socialist mayors be eliminated *en masse* in the working-class communes (as in the case of Condé-sur-l'Escaut in the Nord, where Carles recognised the impossibility of unseating a notable like Delcourt).[52]

Efforts were made to stray as little as possible from the normality of municipal life. The dissolution of councils and the constitution of special delegations only took place after all the options of reconciliation had been exhausted.[53] Until the Liberation, the prefectures attempted to maintain the stability of the corps of local notables, a principle which they had adopted in the summer of 1940 and which they kept up despite the polymorphic development of anti-authority activity and administrative disobedience.

Thus, at the time of the tours of inspection of the communes, which the prefect of the Nord had delegated Darrouy to carry out in 1942–3, one sensed a feeling of impotence on the part of the administration when faced with the town councils, which were increasingly 'reserved', increasingly sensitive to allied propaganda and increasingly hostile to the occupying force. In his preliminary report,[54] the mayor of Armentières summed up clearly the attitude of the inhabitants of the Prohibited Zone and of a number of notables who from now on followed public opinion: 'The more the government moves towards collaboration with Germany, the more one feels that the population is moving away from it.'

Until the Liberation, the German Military Counsellors continued to keep a very close eye on municipal life.[55] It is possible to detect a slow evolution in the tripartite relationship which breaks down into three stages: until mid 1942, a period of confidence in the actions of the prefectural authorities with regard to the town councils; then, at the end of 1942, a redoubling of pressure in a bid to ensure that more 'collaborationist' town councils were put in place in the large towns; and finally, in mid 1943, a clear deterioration in the relationship with the prefectures and a more systematic recourse to repression, notably in socialist town councils, as confidence gave way to distrust.

There was an initial stiffening in 1942, at a time when the increase in bombings along the coast as well as looting made the situation very bad indeed. One was aware of a drive to encourage mayors, particularly those of large towns, to engage decisively in a process of 'collaboration' with Vichy, and beyond that with Germany, a move which, paradoxically, led to serious tensions with the prefectures. In a note to Regional Prefect Ingrand, the OFK demanded the resignation of the mayors of Lille, Calais, Boulogne and Dunkirk, who were judged to be 'hostile to the collaboration'[56] and freemasons to boot. The prefects were able to justify the retention of municipal officials in three cases, but not in the fourth, namely Boulogne, where the mayor was forced to resign in a hurry, the German request having been accompanied by threats of physical force.

At the same time, the German authorities began to display an increasing irritation towards the socialist town councils which had been retained, suspecting them – correctly – of wanting to 'disengage themselves' and of seeking a clean political slate by engaging in minor political conflicts with the occupying forces. The 'Calonne-Ricouart affair' (Pas-de-Calais) gave the Germans the opportunity to discharge a serious warning.[57] On 25 October 1942, the town council of this large mining commune presented a collective resignation to the prefect, putting forward as a reason their own 'lack of competence', after they had been made to designate from amongst the men of the commune those who should work for the Germans on their immense coastal building sites, a task which had been directly entrusted to them by the OFK (order of 10 October 1942).

This was a socialist town council, installed since 1939 in a communist stronghold. The sub-prefect, fearful that this phenomenon might spread, sought to diffuse the situation. On 21 November, the *Kreiskommandantur* of Béthune accepted the move but the counsellor of the military administration warned dryly: 'Please ensure that this move does not set a precedent and does not turn into a demonstration against the measures taken by the higher authorities'. In fact, the incident had already gone as far as the OFK and had provoked a note to the prefects on 24 November which had the tone of an ultimatum:

The *Oberfeldkommandant* calls attention to the fact that he will not, under any circumstances, be prepared to allow anyone to resign from public office, without adequate motive. In the current climate, it is the particular duty of each person invested with public office to face up to all difficulties with their whole person and with all their energy . . . If someone relinquishes his post without good reason, he contravenes his duties with respect to his motherland. At the same time this attitude must also be seen as a protest against the occupying army if it involves matters which are equally of interest to the occupying forces' administration. I ask you therefore to advise your subordinates, notably the mayors and town councillors, that in future they will also be taken to task by the *Oberfeldkommandantur* if they renounce, without adequate motive, the public office for which they have been given responsibility.[58]

The mayors thus had become in some sense prisoners of their own occupations – permanent hostages.

From this time on, one witnessed a reinforcement of German control over the town councils, a steep increase in the arrests of mayors, and incessant encroachments on the work of the French authorities – factors which led to a clear deterioration in relations with the prefectures at a time when there was a move in Vichy towards a policy of 'franker' collaboration. The leaders of the OFK continued to criticise the 'flabbiness' of the French regional authorities and their inability to check the process of social degeneration. In September 1943, the Germans deplored the paralysis of the French administration in the face of 'intimidation manoeuvres'; in December they complained about the 'increasingly listless' collaboration of the prefectural services.

This situation only provoked the OFK into strengthening their crackdown. This was particularly evident in the Red Zone, where the numerical importance of the troops meant that the communes incurred crippling costs: the slightest protest by the mayors was likened to an act of resistance and led to their arrest, their dismissal and their expulsion from the coastal zone. In the Bassin Minier also, the mayors and the town clerks underwent searches, were summoned to interrogations and could be taken into custody. These arrests were selective and targeted for the most part socialist notables who had become 'suspect': Desclèves at Outreau, Couteaux at Saint-Amand, Beauvillain at Caudry. Both irritated and amused, the sub-prefects were in agreement that these arrests did not at all displease their victims, who used the occasion to restore their political image. Indeed the Germans had understood since the beginning of 1943 that the socialists were in the process of changing course. Thus on 3 March 1943, when the leaders of the OFK were examining the list of *département* councillors, the only rejections concerned socialist mayors, who were labelled as 'Gaullists'.[59]

Only the fear of serious social unrest – particularly after the strike of October 1943 – prevented the Germans from carrying their 'purge' to the limits. They contented themselves with a few tough exemplary sanctions. For instance, in the commune of Colembert in the Pas-de-Calais, the mayor, De Lauristan, was 'persuaded to resign' by the prefect on the orders of the OFK and was imprisoned for having protested against the obligation he had been put under to find accommodation for young French women who were living with German officers (August 1943). A host of measures taken for 'reasons of military security' hit several mayors in the coastal 'Red Zone': such as in the cases of the mayors of Le Touquet (summer 1942), Boulogne (September 1942) and Outreau (March 1943), who were pushed into compulsory resignation and expelled. A particularly brutal case was the so-called Tramecourt affair which ended in the resignation, the arrest (January 1944) and the death in custody of the Viscount of Chabot-Tramecourt, mayor of the commune.

We have so far examined the stakes which municipal power constituted for the French administration and for the Germans, but we must also analyse relations within the commune itself, between the notable and his citizens. The overriding impression is of a crushing burden of work on the mayors. Coupled with their very limited room for manoeuvre, this weakened the position of the notable, who had become both a target of attacks from outside the community and an object of internal discontent. There were two reasons for the increase in administrative work: firstly, the concentration of duties on the sole person of the mayor and, secondly, the accumulation of new responsibilities. By the summer of 1940, municipal power had come almost entirely to be identified with the post of mayor. But many old mayors, at the end of their term, were unable to hand over local power to their heir apparent; thus the body of municipal magistrates, which was already reasonably old before the war, had now aged even more. Several factors conspired to bring about this situation: the absence of a number of town clerks (prisoners, primary school teachers who had transferred, fled or been dismissed), innumerable gaps in the council (as a result of the call-up and the exodus), and the Germans' drive to make the notables the sole resort of responsibility. Thus mayors had to function with an incomplete staff up to the end of the war. A report in May 1943 revealed that out of the 892 councillors present in 1939 in the eighty-three communes of the *arrondissement* of Boulogne, ninety-four were now dead, forty-four were evacuees, thirty-five had resigned, thirteen were prisoners of war and four had been dismissed, resulting in a deficit of 20 per cent.[60]

In other cases, councillors or their deputies had to assume positions for which they did not have the qualifications, or, more frequently, the material means, on account of the unstable socio-economic situation. On the whole, the occupation had a more debilitating effect on those mayors whose incomes were the most modest. Thus the mayor of Favreuil in the Pas-de-Calais, an agricultural worker, had to tender his resignation because 'he could no longer survive'. Such difficulties could also be found in the cities. For example, the mayor of Labourse, a shoemaker, commented in April 1941 that the increase in his workload at the town hall prevented him from working regularly and that the low rate of travel allowance, which remained fixed while prices rocketed, could not compensate for the fall in his income. The result was an increase in personnel work along with an increase in administrative work. Not surprisingly, this situation gave rise to most of the resignation requests in the second half of 1940, at which point the prefect of the Pas-de-Calais remarked that a number of mayors 'were no longer able to manage their own affairs and those of the commune at one and the same time'.[61]

No sooner had the mayors accomplished the exceptional tasks connected with the invasion (the accommodation of refugees, the evaluation of the looting situation, the assessment of bomb damage) than they were bombarded with requests. These requests, originating as much with the prefecture as with the German authorities, became 'normal' occurrences until 1944. The German demands, which varied according to the region and the circumstances of the war, were all equally intensive and urgent in character: general requests imposed by the OFK, but also one-off *diktats* from local potentates and other field commanders on the ground (*Standortkommandaturen*).

The greatest responsibility was undoubtedly that of lodging the troops, in addition to which were the tasks of harnessing the horses, requisitioning fodder and foodstuffs, and guarding telephone wires – the mayor had responsibility for ensuring that the lines were not sabotaged.[62] Such duties had accumulated particularly in the vicinity of the airfields and the 'V' weapons construction sites. But without any doubt it was the job of drawing up the lists of workmen which, morally and politically, was the most difficult to accept. That led to, as we have already seen, a burst of protest in December 1940 when the Germans demanded an initial recruitment of workers for Germany: the town clerks had to designate unmarried workers as a matter of course since the number of volunteers was insufficient.

The pressure exerted by the French administration, if less brutal in form, was no less trying on account of its bureaucratic character. In the working-class communes, the mayors had to cope with a level of social welfare which was 10 per cent greater than before the war, notably in the textile regions which had been profoundly affected by unemployment.[63] In the Bassin Minier, this obligation was only really felt in the second half of 1940, when the allocation of unemployment benefit, drawn from the already hard-hit municipal coffers, put a number of mayors in a difficult position.

But it was in the rural communes that the workload increased the most, in tandem with the management of the distribution of supplies. Like their counterparts in the towns, mayors in the countryside had to ensure the distribution of ration books for food, coal, shoes, and so forth. But they also had to take responsibility for the declaration of cultivated land, the condition of cattle and the supervision of the harvest, theoretically in collaboration with agents from the prefecture. They were expected to intervene in the daily operations of gathering meat, milk and butter. Their role – and thereby also their problems – grew considerably following the miners' strike of October 1943, when the Germans modified the organisation of the distribution of supplies, and gave directly to the mayors some of the duties which until then had devolved to the purchasing commissions of the cantons, including keeping weekly declaratory statements.

If one adds to this the manifold problems linked to the fresh upsurge in looting and Allied carpet-bombing from 1943 – namely rehousing, clearing up, fresh water – then one begins to understand the crushing nature of the responsibilities imposed on the local administrations, many of whom were overtaken by events and incapable of taking important decisions. On top of the German humiliations, there was all the Vichy red tape which greatly irritated a number of mayors who felt as if they were drowning under the weight of futile tasks and were not being supported in difficult situations. Already, in September 1941, the mayor of Thièvres, a small rural commune in the Pas-de-Calais noted: 'Every morning I spend several hours studying the circulars which have come in, annotating them, filing them, and executing a portion of the work which normally falls to the town clerk, who is now overloaded with work.'[64] His counterpart in Eclimeux made known his despondency: 'I no longer want to drown in all this paperwork which arrives incessantly from every quarter. I believe that my duties are becoming the veritable job of an unpaid functionary.'[65] This view was also echoed by the mayor of Achiet-le-Petit: 'Every day, new duties pile up: the cartage of stones, summary statements of the accounts in duplicate, payments for cartage, meetings of every kind, agricultural statistics, requisitions etc.'[66]

The situation was even more serious in the chief towns of the cantons, as is illustrated by the protestation of the mayor of Heuchin (Pas-de-Calais), whose report contained the implicit avowal of 'passive administrative sabotage' on the part of certain councillors:

I am eager to draw your attention to the excessive work demanded of the town councils. Either the latter will be anxious, as I wished it, consciously to satisfy the continual demand for information and statistics which come either from the prefecture or the *Kommandantur* or from the innumerable bodies created with the most diverse names and attributions and then, it will happen as happened to me – resignation on account of overwork; or else they will stop worrying about the precision of the information given out, which might be for them the most sensible approach.[67]

In addition to the physical exhaustion was a moral exhaustion, a result of permanent exposure to criticism, to discontent – individual, collective or organised – and to danger. The discontent on the part of individuals and families resulted from the organisation of the provision of supplies, the distribution of benefits, the drawing up of STO (Service du Travail Obligatoire) lists, all of which rekindled ancient, political and familial resentments. Thus, in November 1943, the mayor of Courcelles-le-Comte complained bitterly about the hostility of a number of inhabitants of the commune after he had drawn up the STO register. In June 1941, the mayor of Ecquemicourt resigned, unable to stand up to the incessant criticisms and complaints from some of his people. Finally, following his dismissal, the mayor of Ablain-Saint-Nazaire concluded, for the benefit of the prefect:

You know the difficulties faced by the mayors in the present circumstances. The measures, all the administrative measures which we are responsible for enforcing (requisitions, various enquiries, regulations etc.) make the mayors unpopular. More so in the country than in the town, the collisions are sometimes violent and the old political or personal hatreds, more so now than before, are tenacious.[68]

The most serious threats, however, came from protests of a political nature, most often organised at the regional level. The campaigns led by the clandestine PCF were by far the toughest and the most numerous, notably in the Bassin Minier, a traditional battleground with the 'reformists' who had become 'social-traitors' in the Party's press. Already, in the summer of 1940, the mayors in post – and more particularly the presidents of special delegations installed in communes conquered by the PCF before the war – were the target of multiple, and often violent protests by housewives and women workers, such as at Méricourt in July 1940, or at Estevelles in January 1941, on the pretext of alleged injustices in the distribution of supplies and the allocation of unemployment benefits.[69] For a long time limited to inflammatory articles in the clandestine press, to slogans chalked on walls or to flysheets, the PCF's campaign took on a more systematic aspect from mid 1943 onwards, with the sending of threatening letters.[70] After the arrest of an underground worker on 14 July 1943, the police discovered a hit list of people to be assassinated in the Bassin Minier: high on the list were a number of mayors. Although they had a wider objective, the numerous attacks on town halls and the burning down of farms operated by the FTPs (Franc-Tireurs et Partisans) – in particular in the Bassin Minier and the Avesnois – were aimed symbolically at the person and the authority of mayors who were considered too close to Vichyist power. The 'Gaullist' campaigns, on the other hand, might have been less brutal (the Lorraine cross in chalk or in paint), but they were geographically more widespread in the rural areas.

Thus, subjected to crushing workloads, assailed by criticism from all sides,[71] the mayors were forced to undergo a change in their power and their image. The first proof of this weakening of the power of the notables can be found in the acknowledgement of a certain physiological exhaustion, which was evidenced by the large number who tendered their resignation. There were 223 cases in the Pas-de Calais in over 905 communes with a very marked concentration between June 1940 and November 1941 (62 per cent of resignations for the whole of the period 1939–44). Among the reasons given, complaints of health and age make up the overwhelming majority (60.2 per cent) and cannot be classed as a smoke-screen masking other reasons. Thus, the mayor of Sains-les-Fressin declared in October 1940:

'I was 70 last August and the hostilities make me feel even older; what's more, two of my children are prisoners of war and I no longer receive news of them . . . The doctor tells me that my migraine is caused by the strain of writing letters.'[72]

In the Pas-de-Calais, 92 mayors out of the 905 in post in December 1939 died during the occupation, with clusters in the winter of 1940–1 and from mid 1943 to the Liberation. In fact 40 per cent of councillors under the age of 60 died, which is abnormal amongst notables, whose life expectancy is very high.

At the heart of the experience of the occupation was the question of defining the nature of municipal power, the relationship between the notable and his community, and the long-term consequences of particular behaviour in times of war. The picture which emerges from an examination of the sources (notably letters of resignation and declarations to the CLLs (Comités Locaux de Libération) in September 1944) is that of civic duty and the responsibility of protecting the community from the demands of the Germans and from Vichy. In order to justify himself at the time of the Liberation, the mayor of Dainville defined his action thus:

In my job as mayor, I have done everything in my power to prevent my people from suffering humiliations and sanctions at the hands of the occupying authorities. I have executed orders as slowly and as negligently as possible. I was called to order and even threatened with imprisonment by the *Feldgendarmerie*. It is through my devotion and vigilance that *nothing serious or painful ever occurred in my commune*.[73]

If such behaviour was relatively straightforward where the occupying army was concerned, it took on a more complex character when it came to the French administration. The example of the supply of provisions in the countryside is instructive in this regard, inasmuch as it was undoubtedly the major worry for the inhabitants of the Prohibited Zone, whether they were consumers or producers. If one excepts the few cases of fraud for personal gain,[74] it is noticeable how frequently the mayors were involved in the collective business of 'negligence in the control of supplies', 'irregularities in distribution', 'non-declaration of threshing', and, above all, 'insufficient declarations'.

The prefects reckoned that the mayors knowingly reduced the quantities declared by the farmers in order to cut down the levies imposed by the Provisions Department. In June 1941, the sub-prefect of Saint-Omer reckoned that the overwhelming majority of the mayors of the canton of Fauquembergues gave false declarations with regard to the collection of butter. He attributed this fact to overwork, but in particular to the mayors' willingness to cheat the authorities in order to protect the material interests of their people.[75]

If the occupation therefore – in the majority of cases – personally exposed mayors to criticism from their people, then it also sometimes reinforced the authority of 'natural notables', especially in the countryside. There is thus a contrast to be drawn between the tacit 'complicity' of the mayor and his fellow citizens in agricultural communes, which were sociologically homogeneous, and the isolation of the notable in working-class communes, which were sociologically more heterogeneous and where class conflicts had hardened on account of the occupation. Herein lies, in all probability, the contrast between the relative stability of municipal power in the countryside of the Nord and the upheaval which was to be registered in many urban and working-class areas in the days after the war.

7 Structures of authority in the Greek resistance, 1941–1944

Mark Mazower

The limitations of a purely political approach to the history of the resistance in Greece have only become apparent with the end of the Cold War. For a long time, historians of both left and right focused on elite politics and saw authority in the main resistance movement, EAM/ELAS (Ethniko Apeleftherotiko Metopo – National Liberation Front/Ethnikos Laikos Apelftherotikos Stratos – Greek People's Liberation Army), as emanating from the top down. The British agent and historian C. M. Woodhouse, in 1948, insisted upon the 'horizontal division' between 'leaders and the led': above the line were the 'politically conscious', below it 'the undifferentiable mass of Greek humanity'.[1] Rarely articulated so clearly, this view has underpinned the research agenda through to the 1980s. But as a sensitive commentator pointed out in a review of Woodhouse's book which most comprehensively synthesised this tradition, *Apple of Discord*, to focus extensively upon politics risked ignoring the social and economic origins of resistance activity, and thereby misunderstanding its nature. It was all too easy to recast the events of a highly fluid and uncertain epoch in terms of the rigid polarities of the subsequent Cold War.[2]

I have attempted elsewhere to adumbrate an alternative approach to the history of EAM/ELAS. In not dissimilar vein, Georgios Margaritis has shown how events which have little to do with party politics – the experience of the Albanian campaign in 1940–41, the collapse of the state, food shortage and black marketeering – led to the tremendous social transformation behind the emergence of mass resistance.[3]

In this chapter I wish to take up the challenge posed by the attack on the old monolithic model of wartime politics and to explore the nature of authority inside Greek resistance. What were the sources of authority in the Greek countryside and to what extent did they collide with one another? If one looks in particular at EAM/ELAS, how far can one talk of some sort of 'democratic centralist' model of political control? The brief, interpretative approach of this chapter can hardly do justice to the ways the situation changed over time, or was different from region to region, and some simplification will inevitably be necessary. Nonetheless, it is hoped that the complex and diverse features of authority in the wartime resistance will be highlighted.

From central authority to EAM/ELAS

Very quickly after the occupation of Greece in April 1941 the quisling government in Athens started to lose its monopoly of force in much of the country. It was not only the Italian, German and Bulgarian forces of occupation which challenged its writ and often acted as rivals for the procurement of food, which had become the government's chief concern. Food scarcity also provoked a serious rise in criminality and brigandage over the first year of occupation – the first signs of what would become a far more critical breakdown of authority. The government's desperate attempts to secure the harvest in the summer of 1942 – its determination to accept no repetition of its disastrous failure the previous year – triggered the first more serious and extensive challenges to its authority.

Two Greek civil servants who fled the country in May 1943 reported that:

the Athens Quisling Government is not in regular and direct contact with all the Greek authorities in the provinces. Hence the latter are removed from the control of the former . . . Most of the civil servants in districts controlled by Greek guerrillas have been also either deposed or replaced by guerrillas or abandoned their posts through fear of Greek guerrillas and the reprisals of the Italians . . . There is complete chaos in the towns temporarily occupied by the Greek guerrillas: they replace the civil authorities by their own nominees in the towns, but as soon as they depart, the old Authorities take over again. The inhabitants thus become divided; there is strife and friction and the administration literally gets dissolved.[4]

As early as the autumn of 1942 organised groups of *andartes* (guerrillas) were preventing civil servants collecting grain or taxes in the mountains of central Greece. Initially they sometimes operated alongside professional brigands who enjoyed the brief return to lawlessness after 1941; but during 1943, as the main resistance organisation EAM/ELAS extended its authority through the provinces, the brigands were disbanded and forced either to return home or to bow to the authority of the organised resistance.

Although EAM/ELAS controlled much of central Greece, a large number of other small resistance groups had also come into existence after the summer of 1942. As they attracted the attention of EAM they were forcibly dissolved and their members were either set free or recruited into the larger 'organisation': the case of Stefanos Sarafis, the eventual military commander of ELAS, is probably the best-known instance of this process. By the summer of 1943 there were only a small number of resistance groups which continued to exist alongside ELAS, most notably Zervas's EDES (Ethnikos Dimokratikos Ellinikos Syndesmos – the National Republican Greek League) in Epiros.

These groups were fundamentally different political entities from EAM/ELAS. They were led in the traditional fashion by a prominent notable (*archigos*), whose authority derived from force of character and reputation. Family ties linked many members, especially among the officers. A patriotic rhetoric which focused upon the traditional obsessions of the pre-war political elite – constitutional change, irredentist claims – constituted their ideology, if that is the right word for the vaguely espoused programmes of post-war renewal which barely betrayed their underlying lack of real interest in such matters. These characteristics set such groups sharply apart from EAM/ELAS with its stress on social reform and ideological propaganda among the rank and file, its self-identification as an 'organisation' based upon social rather than kinship roles, and its deliberately low-profile leadership. Ultimately, these more traditional groupings proved unable to withstand the potent mobilising power of EAM/ELAS; Zervas was the great survivor, and then only thanks to extensive British financial and political support.

The chief question, then, is to explain how EAM/ELAS exerted its authority in the areas under its control. If it did indeed end up constituting a 'state within a state' as both German and British observers attested, what sort of state was it?[5]

The use of violence

The traditional interpretation, shared by both left and right, sees ultimate control in the hands of the KKE (Kommounistiko Komma Ellados – the Communist Party of Greece), exercised through the party's domination of the Central Committee of EAM itself, and through the communist political advisers who operated at all levels in ELAS. Both as a political organisation and as fount of ideological truth, the party is supposed to have successfully centralised power and exerted its own authority behind the facade of EAM/ELAS. There is no doubt that such was the KKE's intention, nor that the centralisation of ELAS forces upon the Pindos range in the spring of 1943 was intended to facilitate greater control from above and to curtail the considerable autonomy which many local units had enjoyed up to that point.

Several caveats must, however, immediately be borne in mind. The first concerns the way information flowed in wartime Greece. Operating in clandestine conditions, amidst the wreckage of a national economy, resistance leaders worked in considerable isolation from one another. Poor roads and mountainous terrain exacerbated this isolation. Confidential messages were carried from one unit to another by runners, who might take many days to reach their destinations. A fast runner from Patras to Kalamata, for example, took around ten days.[6]

Sometimes the pre-war telephone system, now dubiously improved by resistance engineers, was also brought into play, though it was highly insecure. As a result the centralisation of EAM/ELAS remained a relative success that has to be viewed in the context of wartime conditions; it cannot be likened, except perhaps in embryo, to the tight control exercised by post-war communist parties in eastern Europe (much as KKE leaders might have wished for such a thing).

One result of this state of affairs was that resistance leaders in the provinces felt the pull of rival allegiances. On the one hand, Pertouli, or Athens, were far away; the village, on the other hand, was their habitat and source of food and manpower, and what the villagers wanted had to be taken into account. Nor, to put it mildly, did the interests of the villagers converge at all points with those of EAM/ELAS.

Initially, when brigands had terrorised them and stolen their sheep, the villagers had welcomed the advent of EAM/ELAS as a stabilising force. ELAS measures against black marketeers also won the organisation popularity. As 'Free Greece' gradually took shape, however, and the resistance began to make demands of their own, provincial enthusiasm started to wane.[7]

The requisition of crops and animals provided the major point of tension. The *andartes'* hit-and-run tactics against the Axis forces left the villagers exposed to reprisals which left the houses burned and stores plundered. In such circumstances it is not surprising that they started to take a rather cynical view of the *andartes'* heroic claims. One ELAS *kapetan* himself recounts the story of the millowner, an 'old friend of the resistance', who gave refuge to several young *andartes* on the run from the Italians. Having demanded food and wine from him, they settle down by a brook and start to sing resistance songs: 'The cannon thunders in the fields / and thunders in the mountains'. The miller interrupts them: 'Hey boys, the cannon thunders in the fields and thunders in the mountains, but you're here eating my bread and drinking my wine'. By the winter of 1943–4, the villagers in the northern Peloponnese were becoming fed up with the *andartes*, whose morale was dropping fast: 'They are now ill-clad, ill-fed and desperately short of boots', noted one observer.

Discipline which was never good has gone from bad to worse and many cases of looting and common brigandage are now occurring . . . In consequence their morale is low and many want to go home to till their fields and are heartily sick of the whole thing. They dare not desert because they would be shot, but because they do very little fighting and are no longer regarded as heroes by the villagers, the taste has rather gone out of the movement.[8]

A draconian disciplinary code was designed to prevent individual *andartes* plundering from the local population and it clearly had some effect, depending upon the attitude of the *kapetans* in the area. But villagers were little happier being told to hand over their goods without payment 'for the struggle' by some resistance official. The *andartes* soon found that it was essential to impose their authority upon the rural population. In July 1943 a conference was held in Thessaly to discuss this issue. Karageorgis, the senior party representative, told the local *kapetans* to try 'the good, gentle way, justice, love . . . so long as they understand us. After that we have . . .' and he drew a finger across his throat to the amusement of the assembled *andartes*. With such leadership it is not surprising that the behaviour of ELAS should have provoked strongly negative reactions in the villages.[9]

Karageorgis's advice would not have sounded so strange to the *kapetans*. It echoed the very apposite quotation that 'Fear of the Lord is the beginning of wisdom'. What is more it clearly suited the tyrannical strain that was not slow to emerge in some of these men, who now found themselves wielding almost unlimited power. In eastern Thessaly, for example, there was the whimsical *kapetan* Karantonis, a former army officer, 'an enthusiastic type, aggressive and not a very deep thinker', whose propensity for laying down the law to the surrounding villages alarmed some of his fellows. Sevastaki describes him in the village of Tsangli where he commissioned a large house and sat in the living room issuing orders in pure *katharevousa* (educated Greek) and 'sowing fear', in particular among the local Sarakatsani shepherds. Then there was the illiterate *kapetan* Aralis, who threatened the villagers with hanging if they did not provide his men with supplies. Finally one might cite the testimony of Papakonstantinou who ran into problems with villagers who refused to carry a supply of arms on his orders, and was told by his superior that: 'It doesn't matter that you struck them; even if you'd killed one or two, you'd still have been justified.'[10]

Only a small distance separated such attitudes from a much wider use of outright violence and terror. In the increasingly manichean ideology of the war, reluctance to help the *andartes* could be construed as evidence of 'reactionary' sentiments or even 'treachery'. And what made the recourse to violence against the villagers more likely was not only the need to preserve the authority of the *andartes*, but also the latter's readiness to use violence to stamp out all political opposition. The harsh justice meted out to genuine infiltrators working for German espionage was easily extended to other 'suspicious' elements.

The case of Maria Koumbas, a thirty-five-year-old married woman, illustrates the perils that EAM's opponents faced. When the war broke out she was living with her children in Karpenisi while her husband worked in the USA. She had hidden a British soldier from the Germans and acted as a purchasing agent for the British Military Mission. Her sympathies, which she does not seem to have troubled to hide, were strongly pro-Allied. Worse still, she was also a supporter of EDES and joined it in 1942.[11]

All these factors marked her out, and in October 1943, at the time of the fighting between Zervas and ELAS, she and other EDES members in Karpenisi were thrown into jail and their homes were searched. Maria Koumbas was almost immediately released, together with most of her fellow prisoners and she resumed her earlier work. To support her family she traded goods between villages for which she required an ELAS pass.

One morning in March 1944, she was criss-crossing the villages east of Karpenisi with her mule, buying corn to bring to town, when she was unexpectedly stopped by several ELAS *andartes* and detained:

They took me to the telephone office and left me there for an hour . . . Then two different *andartes*, one by the name Vurtselas, from the village of Pleokastro, and one called Panagioti, came and took me to the church. They whipped me with switches and struck me with their fists. They made me deaf in my left ear . . . They kept asking me what the EDES people were doing in Karpenisi, what the EDES people said in their meetings, who they are and where they meet. I told them I did not know anything about these things.

At the headquarters of the local ELAS detachment she was questioned again. Why did she house Englishmen rather than Greeks? Did she not know 'they are our enemies'? Why did she not admit that they were her 'sweethearts'? For three days she was interrogated and tortured in an effort to make her reveal intelligence about EDES. After coming close to death, she spent several days recuperating in the house of a sympathetic ELAS man before returning to Karpenisi.

As a result of such policies, an atmosphere of something close to terror spread over areas like that around Karpenisi, or in the Argolid in the north-eastern Peloponnese. Levadia in the spring of 1944 was reported as being 'in a continual state of anxiety as to what EAM proposes to do either through ELAS or EP, the party police'. Educated people, in particular, were singled out, forced to take part in EAM delegations, or harassed in order to get them to join the 'organisation'.[12]

This political repression was the work of various different components of EAM/ELAS. In some cases it stemmed from orders given by independent *kapetans* or political commissars, as was clearly the case with 'Odysseus' in the distant Evros, or 'Robespierre' in the Valtos region, an area where EDES had roots. But more formal instruments of control were evolving at the same time: the Civil Guard, whose policing operations – not surprisingly in the midst of a total war – slid quickly from 'civil' duties to political repression; above all, the dreaded OPLA (Organosi Perifrourisis tou Laikou Agona – the Organisation for the Protection of the People's Struggle), created as a special security service for high-ranking party cadres, which was by mid 1944 targeting and assassinating political opponents of the KKE, particularly the so-called Trotskyist fraction.

To summarise, then, the authority of EAM/ELAS rested upon the threat of, or use of, violence against fellow Greeks. Instruments of this violence were available to the upper echelons of the 'organisation' through the Civil Guard and OPLA. But they had also emerged at lower levels in more spontaneous and unplanned ways which reflected local initiatives – such as Aris's feared Black-Capped bodyguards or 'Odysseus's 'Death Squad'. The question is to what extent this panoply of political violence represented the fruits of policy formulated at the highest levels of the *andartiko* or how far it was the outgrowth of an increasingly manichean ideology which required no more than the fears and tensions of total war to activate it.

In the absence of careful local studies of the *andartiko*, we are in no position to answer this question definitively. My own view is that the enormous variety of local experiences argues in favour of the second possibility. What makes this still more likely is the evident uncertainty which existed within the leadership of the KKE and EAM/ELAS about the best way forward. Woodhouse himself acknowledges the existence of a serious dispute between 'hawks' and 'doves' over the question of whether or not to 'go it alone'. But the hesitancy within the party emerges even more forcibly in the recollections of Yugoslav partisan officers who noted with some dismay the KKE's reluctance to rely whole-heartedly on the *andartiko*. The result was a policy vacuum at the head of EAM/ELAS. Lack of decisive direction permitted local officials considerable powers of initiative; they would find only through trial and error whether a high level of political terror would be tolerated by the national leadership. Though acting general secretary Siantos does not seem to have been altogether comfortable with Aris's propensity for exemplary violence, he never seems to have asserted his authority against the charismatic 'first *kapetan*'. In Evros, on the other hand, the party leadership was clearly alarmed by Odysseus's campaign of terror, and managed to have him deposed and executed as an 'enemy of the people'. The possibility that the EAM leadership was becoming more repressive over time (hinted at in several memoirs) seems worth pursuing in this context.[13]

Administering the people: resisting the résistance

The passage from occupied territory into Free Greece was dangerous and exhilarating. Petros Roussos, a member of the KKE central committee, had spent two years in the service of EAM in Athens before he made the journey 'into the hills'. As he records in his memoirs, his previous knowledge of the mountains had been limited to an occasional day's hiking around Athens: 'But now the notion of the Mountain acquired a different meaning and other dimensions in our imaginations. A different atmosphere, other emotions awaited us.'[14]

One morning in July 1943 he left Athens, accompanied by the EAM liaison officer who ran the 'channel' out of the capital. Disguised as black marketeers, they took a bus out to a small town beyond Thebes, passing through the notorious road block at Kriekouki, where German sentries checked the traffic heading northwards towards Salonika. Outside Thebes they turned left of the main road, and eventually reached the quiet market town of Domvraina. This was on the edge of Free Greece, less than eighty miles from the centre of Athens.

As they left Domvraina, climbing by mule through the foothills of Mount Helicon, Roussos was astonished by the villages he passed. Familiar with the squalid slums which ringed Athens, he was amazed by the apparently complete isolation of these mountain hamlets. Men from the area had formed some of the very first armed bands; they had been notoriously ill-disciplined, interested in plundering the local shepherds rather than firing upon Italian soldiers. What a contrast, he reflected, with the ELAS detachment now waiting to accompany him on the last leg of his journey: the *andartes*, though equipped with an assortment of different weapons and uniforms, displayed 'perceptible discipline' and military bearing.

Roussos revelled in the romantic euphoria which the mountains aroused in him: 'The wild grandeur of Parnassos inspired awe and respect', he reflected as they trudged across the slopes above the ruins at Delphi.

In the regions we passed the mountain loomed like a massive slab. On other occasions we had seen it at a distance, on journeys we made by car or train. Now we walked it. The dark green firs, and high above them, the gleaming snow. Such places bred fighters for freedom. Invaders would never tread them with impunity. We lay under the oaks, gazing up at the heavens; we could smell the trees, the ferns and the fresh grass. We felt refreshed.[15]

This was the urbanite talking. But Roussos kept his urban outlook in a more important sense too. He was responsible for ideological affairs in the party, and in his view it was the duty of the inhabitants of the modern city to raise up rural Greece and set it on the road to progress. Under the eye of EAM/ELAS, sheep-stealers would be turned into disciplined soldiers, ignorant peasants into enlightened citizens. Not even the backward inhabitants of the mountains, with their harsh accents and strange clothes, would be able to resist the logic of history.

Resist they would, however. The sweeping social reforms which the *andartiko* brought into the mountains, and which constituted for many the most impressive aspect of EAM's rule, elicited mixed feelings and sometimes outright hostility from their supposed beneficiaries. Thus if we are to concern ourselves with the structure of resistance authority, we must look not only at the uses of force, terror and violence, but also at the day-to-day workings of resistance administration and the responses of the villagers. Before the 'enlightenment' and 'direction' of the *andartiko* could lead the country folk to the promised land of 'People's Democracy', EAM's leadership would have to come to terms with this. And having learned to resist the demands of the quisling government in Athens, the farmers must have looked with some mistrust at these powerful newcomers from the capital.

With the growth of EAM/ELAS came a range of administrative reforms – village courts, local self-administration, youth movements, elections with universal suffrage for men *and* women. These new institutions won EAM much respect from observers like Woodhouse and considerable enthusiasm from some sections of rural society: young boys and girls in particular, together with village teachers, doctors and other professionals, seem to have been drawn to the exciting reformist ideals of the *andartiko*. They became one of the chief sources of that undoubtedly genuine enthusiasm for EAM/ELAS which existed in such strange proximity to the fear and terror felt by others.

We should be careful, however, not to confuse reform schemes as they appeared on paper with their performance in reality. Because few participants in village courts could read or write, few accounts of their proceedings have been preserved. 'What were the village courts like?' I asked an elderly *kafeneion* owner in the Peloponnese recently. 'Just a few illiterates playing games', he responded. Hence it is not easy to see exactly how they functioned, or how popular they were. In some areas they clearly were popular: in Mesolonghi, for instance, where the old 'bourgeois' courts continued to operate, peasants turned away from them to the People's Courts.[16]

Probably the majority of court cases involved the traditional subjects of village litigation – animal theft, property and inheritance disputes.

Though swifter than the old days, trials could still drag on. Several sessions of the People's Court in the village of Kislar, near Farsala, had to be devoted to a dispute between two villagers: when Dimitri Gaidartzis claimed that Georgios Frangos had stolen his mule, Marika, Frangos produced a line of witnesses to testify that the animal in question had been brought back from Albania as war booty. (Frangos's case collapsed when his star witness recanted, fearing the consequences of perjury. The mule was provisionally handed over to the local ELAS reserve for safekeeping, and Frangos was ordered to provide the oats and straw it required.)

This was the sort of case which the villagers serving as magistrates in the People's Courts were comfortable dealing with. Not surprisingly, their procedures and conclusions frequently seemed defective to the legal reformers in EAM. They issued sentences for crimes which did not exist on the statute book, but which the local population thought 'right and proper'. They were reluctant to take advantage of certain judicial innovations – public reprimands, for example – at which the villages looked askance. It is also clear that in many courts village women were barred by their menfolk from taking part. They remained shut away at home, and their husbands, fathers or other male relatives represented them in court. Of course, official EAM guidelines for the 'Peoples' Courts' did not discriminate between the sexes in this way. The villagers, however, did not allow their traditions to be swept aside and they kept women out of public affairs as far as possible.

Elsewhere, the courts themselves had only an intermittent and shadowy existence; the local EAM responsible officer, the *ypefthinos*, established the 'general feeling' in the village and sentenced the accused accordingly. By this practice, EAM merely formalised the direct assumption of judicial authority which the first *kapetans* had wielded in such an unabashed form over the submissive and anxious villagers in the spring of 1943.

In the resistance play *O Ypefthinos* (The 'Responsible'), the deeper tension between village mores and eager EAM reformers is carried to centre stage. At one point a senior EAM official, on a visit to the village to see how things are being managed, turns to Kalemis, an elderly villager. 'What exactly do people think, Grandpa?' he asks Kalemis. The old man chooses his words carefully: 'Well, that you are working for a national purpose, and didn't come here to take people's property.' 'Did they tell you', he asks Kalemis, 'that we would abolish private property?' 'Yes', the old man replies, 'and some idiots believed it.' 'And you – tell me the truth – did you think so too?' 'To give you my opinion, comrade', Kalemis replies slowly, 'yes and no – I half-believed it in other words.' At this point the local EAM representative, Panos, intervenes to assure the visitor that Kalemis is now quite clear about the nature of 'the struggle' and has been made *ypefthinos* for maize. It is the turn of the visiting official to be confused. 'How many *ypefthinoi* do you have?' he asks Panos. 'As many as you want', is the reply. 'We've got an *ypefthinos* for billets, for wood, laundry, cleaning, milk for the hospital, for everything.'[17]

A similar catalogue of misunderstandings – deliberate and accidental – between villagers and senior EAM government officials emerges from a rare contemporary analysis of local administration in practice. When Georgios Doxopoulos, an administrative inspector with EAM, travelled round Thessaly he found the country people unable or unwilling to implement EAM's policies. In the town of Nivoliani, for example, the local council had tried to increase revenues by taxing shepherds; however, the shepherds refused to pay and the council ended up contracting a loan from a local money-lender, with the harvest as surety. EAM's coercive powers were clearly limited there. Moreover, villagers did not attend the general assembly unless they had some personal issue to raise. At Kapnista, EAM's instructions concerning the maize were widely ignored. The inhabitants of Koukourava did not – reported Doxopoulos with regret – 'understand clearly the meaning of the principle of self-administration'. In Voulgarini, the various village committees had turned into bitter rivals, each criticising the work of the others. They did not keep written records of their meetings – a common failing – and did not meet regularly. At Neromyloi people were completely baffled by the idea of 'self-administration', even the local council members themselves. They did not understand the purpose of the general assembly, and most left it before it had finished its business.[18]

As the example of the People's Courts showed, a particular area of resistance on the part of the village towards EAM was created by its policies towards women. Many leading progressive intellectuals who gravitated towards EAM/ELAS favoured the equality of the sexes. Not only were women given the vote for the first time (in the 1944 'elections'), but their help was emphatically enlisted in various ways – welfare work, laundry, soup kitchens, nursing and even fighting in special *andarte* units. Resistance propaganda highlighted the need to improve the status of women in Greek society and pamphlets were circulated on topics such as 'The Girl and her Demands'. 'In today's struggle for liberty, the mass participation of the modern girl is especially impressive', claimed one resistance broadsheet. 'In city demonstrations we see her a pioneer, a fighter, courageous and defying death'. This modern girl was fighting for a double victory: 'from the foreign yoke and from the bias and superstition of our country'. At the top of the *andartiko* were prominent role models like Maria Svolos, Chrysa Chadzivasileiou and Rosa Imvriotis.[19] There can be little doubt that many women, particularly younger women, were attracted to the *andartiko* by such attitudes. So much is clear both from personal testimonies and from the pioneering research of Janet Hart. What seems equally likely, however, is that the impact upon traditional opinion in the villages was less positive. The example of women being excluded from the functioning of some People's Courts has already been mentioned. Here is yet another area where we urgently require detailed research: the indications are, however, that the emancipatory gender policies of the *andartiko* provoked a considerable rearguard struggle in the unambiguously patriarchal atmosphere of Greek rural society. The war had turned family relations upside down – forcing women and children into more assertive and public roles. But this very process created a growing demand in some circles for a reassertion of traditional family values. Such a *revanche* – which was *not* confined to men – took place across Europe in the 1940s, and Greece seems unlikely to have offered an exception.[20]

Let us, in conclusion, summarise the main lines of the argument. The idea that democratic centralism provides the best model for understanding the structure of authority in EAM/ELAS must be regarded as a hypothesis – or, better, a Cold War axiom – which requires reconsideration. Power did not simply flow downwards from the upper echelons of the 'organisation'. There can be little doubt that the KKE was the predominant political element in the *andartiko*. But leading KKE cadres were badly split over how to exploit the power of EAM/ELAS and, therefore, over how to act in the territories it claimed to control. Hesitancy and confusion characterise the outlook of men like Siantos, not decisiveness; this created an uncertainty at lower levels which gave *kapetans* and commissars greater room for manoeuvre. What accelerated and accentuated the centrifugal tendencies within the resistance were the very considerable obstacles to easy communication and movement offered by high mountains, hazardous goat tracks in unmapped terrain and constant insecurity.

Detailed studies of life in different localities will be necessary for a more definitive account of resistance authority. Scattered evidence suggests a picture of considerable confusion and complexity. Despite the efforts of ELAS General Headquarters to centralise the movement in the late spring of 1943, local centres of power remained. *Kapetans* continued to enjoy enormous power, as did their political advisers. The use they made of this depended, among other factors, on their character. Some, like Orestes in Evvia, seem to have been easy-going and relatively benevolent, while others resembled Aris and found that the war brought out a strain of sadism and cruelty which they could justify in terms of the needs of the 'struggle'. But their behaviour also depended on less personal factors, most notably the security situation in their area. By 1944, the creation of the Civil Guard and OPLA offered new instruments to resistance officials who wished to take a hard line with their opponents.

As the resistance movement *par excellence*, EAM/ELAS was unwilling to recognise any resistance to itself. Resistance there was, however. In the first place there was substantial political and military opposition from rival groups. ELAS prevented EDES and other resistance movements recruiting where it could, and put known sympathisers under surveillance. What was more, it made life extremely – and increasingly – difficult for members of other political parties in the EAM coalition, and effectively restricted their activity outside Athens. Even a small partner in EAM like the socialist ELD was effectively prevented by the KKE from expanding its activities in the villages.[21]

But there was also a different, less political type of resistance to the 'organisation' which came from sections of the rural population upon which it depended. Starting in many cases from the natural resentment of villagers to any superior authority, this resistance to EAM's requisitioning policies was often a direct descendant of the earlier resistance in 1941–2 to the food procurement policies of the Athens government. By 1944 there were clear signs of EAM's unpopularity among peasantry in the northern Peloponnese and elsewhere.

EAM's dramatic social reforms, which amounted to a revolution in village mores and often reflected the shock of Athenian radicals when confronted with the primitiveness of life in the mountains, also provoked a cautious but tenacious reaction. Local self-administration handed over power to villagers who did not always use it in the ways that EAM's idealistic reformers had anticipated. The modernising aspects of EAM's social policies – notably the egalitarian attitude towards women – clearly shocked many villagers. EAM's opponents spread rumours that it was planning the break-up of the family. This was nonsense, of course, and merely an expression of an antiquated anti-bolshevism. Nevertheless, even Kotzioulas's resistance dramas testify to the uphill struggle which faced young reformers as they tried to change traditional attitudes and mentalities. The village paterfamilias might feel obliged to perform labour service or hand over crops for the 'struggle' but he would not surrender his authority so easily to the *andartes* over his wife and daughters. Hence at this more personal and intimate level, too, we can discern resistance to the resistance which needs to be taken into account before we can evaluate the extent to which life in Free Greece lived up to the claims of EAM propaganda.

8 Nazi Austria: the limits of dissent

Tim Kirk

In February 1939, the security service (SD) of the SS in Vienna presented Josef Bürckel, head of the Nazi administration in Austria, with a report on popular opinion among the working class. It was based on an interview with five former workers' leaders from Vienna's tenth district.[1] The report is striking in its sensitivity to the customs, hierarchies and internal boundaries of working-class communities, and revealing of Nazi attitudes to workers and working-class politics. The men interviewed had been chosen for their credentials as natural leaders. They had been popular trades union officials in the 1920s, elected repeatedly by their workmates to perform a valid role as leaders of their factory community, but had been unpaid union functionaries, and the SD report distinguished them as such from the salaried and ambitious professional politicians of the Social Democratic Workers' Party (Sozialdemokratische Arbeiterpartei, SDAP) These were men who did not discharge their duties for the sake of personal gain or power, but out of a sense of duty.

In addition, their political position, on the anti-Communist right wing of the labour movement, made them precisely the type of worker – 'intelligent' and 'open to discussion' – that the Nazis thought they could win for 'German socialism'. Although they had once been convinced Social Democrats, the report went on, they had been compelled to rethink their politics after the collapse of the party, and were prepared to accept the new political system – provided, understandably, that there were advantages for workers. (They had naturally rejected the Austrofascist regime because it had offered none.) 'They must be won for National Socialism', the report concluded.

The content of this report, and not least its formulaic and euphemistic language, is typical of political intelligence reports on working-class attitudes in Nazi Austria, and reflects the practical application of the Nazis' ideological perspectives and policy strategies in the field of industrial relations and labour politics. The Nazis recognised the historical strength of the Social Democratic labour movement and acknowledged the traditional political loyalties of 'red Vienna', the political nature of class consciousness in the city, and the cohesiveness of working-class communities there. Nazi social ideology, however, foresaw the dissolution of such community loyalties within a 'national community' (*Volksgemeinschaft*) which would transcend existing class boundaries. In this report, as in so many of the commentaries that accompanied the Nazis' political intelligence-gathering, the discussion was of practical ways to begin that process. For, if the Viennese working class was still a self-conscious and cohesive community in 1939, it was one which, after a series of severe political and economic blows, was undergoing a crisis of political commitment. 'National Socialism', it was suggested, could build on the 'enlightened' anti-clericalism and even the 'healthy' anti-semitism of the workers, and should try to draw them into the German Labour Front, which had hitherto remained a little understood – even misunderstood – institution. The process of constructing the 'national community' could begin here, in the workplace, with the integration of leaderless and disorientated industrial workers into a 'factory community' (*Betriebsgemeinschaft*) which would replicate on a smaller scale the corporatist relationships that would characterise the greater 'national community'.

Although the report's assessment was shrewd, however, it was rather optimistic. Austrians, including industrial workers, had initially been enthusiastic about the Anschluß, but much of the early euphoria had already been dissipated, and in the long-term popular opinion in working-class communities was characterised by growing dissatisfaction. Although few were to translate their dissent into action and engage organised resistance against the Nazis, many more made up a constituency of the disaffected around the underground activists. It will be argued below that although the Nazis successfully contained working-class resistance in Austria, they nevertheless failed to integrate the workers into a 'national community', still less mobilise their active support for the regime.

Austrian industrial workers were politically disorientated in 1939. Their position had been weakened by a combination of prolonged economic depression and a decade of political repression. The slump had hit Austria harder than many other European countries, and the deflationary economic policies of Dollfuß and Schuschnigg during the 1930s had ensured that it had lasted longer. The collective strength of the workforce was undermined by widespread impoverishment, brought about by unemployment, short-time working, and depressed wage levels. Greater economic insecurity had had a predictable effect on working-class militancy. Neither a general strike (the labour movement's ultimate political weapon), nor even the threat of local industrial disputes, was a realistic prospect in the early 1930s, still less under the repressive industrial and political regime instituted by the 'Corporate State'. The political crisis which undermined the parliamentary democracy of Austria's First Republic had gathered pace after 1927. In the course of the following seven years, government policy was deliberately confrontational, and beleaguered conservative ministers were increasingly inclined to apply authoritarian solutions to their political problems. As early as 1932 the government began to by-pass parliament and rely on the War Economy Enabling Act of 1917 to pass emergency decrees, a dubious constitutional practice consciously modelled on that of the Brüning government in Germany.[2] Outside parliament units of the Austrofascist *Heimwehr* (effectively the paramilitary wing of the governing Christian Social Party) were not only tolerated by the regular police, but deployed as auxiliaries in order to break strikes, while its Socialist counterpart, the Republican Defence League (Republikaner Schutzbund), was held back by the insistence of SDAP leaders on legality. When Schutzbund members fought back for the first time, the occasion was used to precipitate an armed conflict between workers and state security services. In February 1934 the government forces used heavy artillery to shell the council flats of Vienna, and swiftly routed the small bands of armed workers who held out for a few days in more mountainous parts of the country. The party, the Free Trade Unions, and all other Social Democratic organisations were then suppressed, the leading 'insurgents' were executed, and a series of show trials was held during the subsequent months.[3]

Until the events of 1934, working-class political loyalties had remained remarkably stable. As in other parts of Europe, fascist movements had attracted some electoral support and recruited some working-class members, notably in Upper Styria, where employer pressure, intensive campaigning and neglect by the SDAP national leadership had combined to undermine established political affiliations.[4] But when the Nazi electoral breakthrough came in Austria during the depression of the early 1930s, it was at the expense of the German Nationalist People's Party (Großdeutsche Volkspartei, GDVP), and Christian Social Party. Support for the Social Democrats remained remarkably resilient, but the metropolitan bias of the party was never clearer. Support for the SDAP in Nationalrat (national parliamentary) elections had fallen only very slightly from 42 per cent to 41.1 per cent between 1927 and 1930, while support for the party in local elections in Vienna fell from 60.3 per cent in 1937 to 59 per cent in 1932, at the worst of the depression.[5]

Moreover, if the obvious comparison with Germany is made, the cohesiveness of the Social Democratic working class in Austria up to 1934 is astonishing. The Communist Party (Kommunistische Partei

Österreichs, KPÖ) had never made more than the most marginal inroads into support for the SDAP, and although it now won most of the votes lost by the Social Democrats during the depression, those losses were themselves marginal, and there was nothing like the electoral radicalisation of the German left nor, indeed, of the Austrian right. Electoral support for the Christian Social Party collapsed dramatically between 1930 and 1933, and the GDVP was all but annihilated by the regional election results of 1932. The routes defecting voters took to their eventual destinations were sometimes indirect, and the elections in which their changing allegiances were registered are not strictly comparable, but the overwhelming majority became Nazi supporters.

Nevertheless, the political confidence of the labour movement was badly shaken by the events of 1934. The shock of defeat had exploded a number of myths about the outcome of an eventual confrontation. Rhetorical images of a showdown between left and right had foreseen a revolutionary working class in a position of strength, compelled, reluctantly, to defend the republic by force of arms, and to impose, after victory, a dictatorship of the proletariat on defeated fascist putschists. Instead there had been defeat and humiliation, and there was little eagerness to join battle again for fear of more of the same.

It was in the wake of the February debacle that the fragmentation of the labour movement and the erosion of political loyalties in working-class communities began in earnest. Both the KPÖ and the Revolutionary Socialists (RS), a radical splinter group which immediately distanced itself from the moderate exiled leadership, now attracted significant support. Many committed activists were disaffected and felt alienated from leaders who were perceived to have been overly legalistic, and to have acted too late and too ineffectually.

Fewer moved to the right. Although the government was able to produce one or two defectors for propaganda purposes, the circumstances of the February debacle, and above all the brutality of the methods employed, generated a bitterness which excluded all but a tiny number of defections to the Fatherland Front. More workers defected to the Nazis in the immediate aftermath of the conflict, in many cases apparently for the strategic purpose of gaining access to weapons.[6] Illegal underground activity was not for most workers, however, and it was especially difficult for those with family responsibilities to risk unemployment or imprisonment.

Active political resistance was restricted to a minority, but nobody, either among supporters of the government or among the workers themselves, was under the illusion that anything like national unity, or even a broad consensus behind the government, had emerged from the coup of

1934; it had been specifically anti-socialist and anti-labour both in its conception and in its consequences. Strikes were banned, but the dramatic cuts in wages which employers were now able to enforce were a greater deterrent to industrial action, at least until the later 1930s. Old networks and relationships remained in place both in working-class communities and on the shop floor, and if there was occasionally a *rapprochement* with the fascist 'Unity Union' (Einheitsgewerkschaft, EG) or other institutions of the 'Corporate State', it was in order to win limited concessions from employers. There was a series of short strikes in the metal industry in 1936, for example, when employers refused to accede to demands for payment for the May Day public holiday, a demand that came originally from the EG. [7]

A sufficiently cohesive national labour leadership survived for four years to convene in Floridsdorf on the eve of the German invasion to discuss collaboration with the Schuschnigg regime against the Nazis.[8] The outcome of this belated attempt to create a united patriotic front against Hitler's Germany reveals rather starkly the persistence of underlying political alignments. The meeting resolved to oppose Hitler; Schuschnigg in the end decided otherwise and refused in the meantime to restore to the illegal labour movement the same political rights he had recently conceded to the Nazis. This experience, after four years of clerical-fascist dictatorship, was an important element in shaping the responses of workers to Nazi overtures after the Anschluß.

For the establishment of Nazi rule in Austria took place in a very different context to the Germany of 1933. Whereas in Germany the Nazis' participation in government had been with the consent of leading conservative politicians, power in Austria was seized by force both from without and from within; and although there were many fellow travellers, the country's conservative establishment was effectively dispossessed. Nazi propaganda capitalised on the outsider status of the Austrian Nazis and their 'illegal struggle' against clerical-fascist repression; and as in many parts of eastern Europe they cast themselves as progressive catalysts, modernisers ready to sweep aside clerical and aristocratic reaction. Shared experience of repression, and the Nazis' social conscience were the main constituents of the propaganda directed at workers during the campaign for the Anschluß plebiscite of 10 April 1938, and some cosmetic measures were undertaken to add force to the rhetoric: a few sacked Social Democrats were reinstated and fuel bills were reduced by a few *Groschen*.[9] Circumstances and slogans combined to enable the Nazis to present themselves as an anti-establishment party in Austria. But if Social Democratic workers were 'compelled to rethink their politics by the collapse of the party', as the Nazis asserted, much of that rethinking was in terms of prioritising the clerical right as their first enemy and, in a situation where they had no word or part in the superseding of one fascist regime by another, to allow themselves a little *Schadenfreude* at the expense of their old enemies, and hope their successors might run the economy better.[10]

The economic impact of the Anschluß was not so straightforward, however. The rapid fall in unemployment did not make grateful Nazis of Austrian industrial workers overnight. Its effect was not to put people back in jobs they had lost: in fact more jobs were lost, particularly in the textiles sector, as a consequence of the shift in resources from consumer to production industries.[11] After years of underinvestment Austrian industry was technologically backward and the workforce deskilled. In addition, Austria's reserve of unemployed labour was seen as a resource for the Reich as a whole, and not one which could immediately (or even entirely) be deployed locally in Austria. Many male workers were drafted to Germany, where even unskilled and semi-skilled labour was in short supply, and were housed there in inadequate company barracks. Among such workers, who were often unwillingly separated from their families, morale was low and disaffection often intense.[12] In Austria itself new industrial development was undertaken primarily in Upper Austria (arguably to provide an economic base for the glorious future of Linz),[13] rather than Styria or Vienna. Unskilled workers were recruited from the surrounding countryside, but others came from older industrial areas to take up a new job in Steyr or Linz. No less than for those who were allocated to jobs in the *Altreich* (the Germany of 1937), this meant leaving behind homes, families and friends in established and close-knit communities. Finally, the positive experience of those returning to work was blunted by the effects of an industrial regime harsher than the one they remembered from the 1920s; those who had remained in work (still the majority) noticed the difference immediately. The Gestapo were vigilant in their surveillance of working-class neighbourhoods and industrial workplaces for any sign of industrial activity or industrial unrest, and they were quick to intervene at any sign of trouble; although their role as the patrol officers of the *Volksgemeinschaft* (the 'national community') did not blind them to the chicanery of some 'anti-social' employers, it was generally the activities of suspected Communist agitators or would-be strike leaders that filled the pages of their 'daily reports' of arrests.[14]

The range of options which remained open to those opposing the Nazi dictatorship was narrow. Very few people in Austria (or indeed elsewhere in Europe) became actively involved in an organised underground resistance group. In Austria there was a range of such groups, reflecting the range of ideological orientation and religious belief in the population, but the Nazis were principally preoccupied with the two most important oppositional camps. The first was made up of a loose ideological affiliation of Catholic–Conservative groups associated with the political and clerical elite of the old regime, and the Gestapo in particular was meticulous in recording 'opposition' from this quarter in the early weeks of the new regime. The other was the Austrian Communist Party, whose activities were automatically treated as high treason on account of the party's support for national independence.[15] The unbridgeable political divisions of the First Republic were reflected in the structure of political resistance, however, and it is inappropriate to speak of a national resistance movement in Austria. Although Social Democrats were eventually drawn into belated attempts to construct a national movement at the end of the war, the Communist Party was never welcome in such arrangements, although it had been numerically the most significant resistance organisation in Nazi Austria, and quite clearly dominated all resistance activity on the left up to the end of the war. Indeed, Radomir Lužahas estimated, on the basis of a large sample of active members of all types of underground resistance groups, that almost every Austrian actively resisting the Nazis was affiliated to the KPÖ.[16]

Certainly, the KPÖ was by far the most significant vehicle of active resistance from the working class. Of over a thousand in Luža's sample over three-quarters were involved with the Communist Party. It was also very much an urban, and above all a metropolitan, organisation, although less so than either the much smaller Revolutionary Socialist movement, or traditionalist and legitimist groups. Over half the members of the Communist resistance lived in Vienna, and there were substantial numbers of active Communists in the surrounding Lower Austrian countryside. The only other sizeable movement was in Styria. KPÖ activity in other parts of the country was always minimal. This was made clear in a report on the political activity of the Austrian left in the autumn of 1938, and repeatedly confirmed by successive political intelligence reports from the provinces.[17] Nearly all the Communists in Luža's sample were men, a reflection of the definition of resistance activity rather than the reality of involvement; and the majority had been Social Democrats before 1938. Even after that date some nominally Communist cells were exclusively made up of 'former' Social Democrats who had joined the KPÖ for strategic reasons. Indeed, the heterogeneous political background of the members, and the fact that many had joined for the pragmatic reason that the party was effectively the only resistance movement of the left, no doubt played an important part in the survival of Communist activity through the difficult and ideologically disorientating years of the Hitler–Stalin pact.[18]

After the Anschluß the Communist Party continued by and large to use the same strategies it had deployed against the 'Corporate State'. One of its main objectives was to maintain and expand the clandestine cells and networks of the party, and a great deal of effort was put into the recruitment of members. These then disseminated propaganda either by word of mouth or graffiti, or in flysheets and leaflets distributed in factories and working-class districts. Such activities were risky, and Communist activists were easily detected by the Gestapo. Although there were frequent rounds of arrests, however, and despite a decline in activity after the outbreak of the war, the cadres were repeatedly renewed. It was only towards the end of the war, encouraged by Allied promises to restore Austrian independence, and by Axis military reverses in North Africa, on the eastern front, and in Italy, that groups of armed insurgents were formed in mountainous areas such as the Salzkammergut, Styria and Carinthia.[19] Nevertheless, the discomfort afforded to the regime by these groups was much less than that caused by the Slovene partisans in the newly incorporated border areas of 'Lower Styria' and 'South Carinthia'.[20]

The relationship between the Communist underground movement and the working-class communities it claimed to represent was a complex one. The dramatic growth in party membership after 1934 was not one which sprang from the instinctive political sympathies of Austrian workers but, as we have seen, from a pragmatic and strategic choice taken in the wake of the collapse of the Social Democratic Party; and, indeed, similar conversions took place across Europe as Nazi and anti-Nazi positions polarised. After the war the SDAP, reconstituted as the Socialist Party of Austria (Sozialistische Partei Österreichs, SPÖ) recovered the lost loyalties of its mass membership, while the Communist Party withered away to become as marginal a political force in the Second Republic as it had been in the First. Moreover, whereas the SDAP had always been a mass party, with which the Free Trade Unions had been associated, and whose party card was carried by a third of all Viennese citizens in the late 1920s, the underground Communist Party had always been a minority affair, which never developed a mass base among the working-class communities it claimed as its natural constituency.

This does not mean that underground activists existed apart from the communities in which they lived and worked. Both Communists and Revolutionary Socialists ran fund-raising options, ostensibly in order to provide support for the wives and families of imprisoned or executed comrades. Rote Hilfe and its Socialist counterpart, Sozialistische Arbeiterhilfe, both established during the Austrofascist dictatorship, performed a number of useful functions. Apart from the provision of relief funds for widows and orphans, they constituted the only effective way, other than the contributions of active members, in which funds could be raised from the wider community for resistance organisations. They also performed some of the more political functions of charitable fund-raising. They provided a way in which opponents of the regime who were not actively involved in underground resistance could express solidarity and support; and the collection of relief funds itself functioned as an oblique consciousness-raising exercise. This dimension of the left's fund-raising activity was not lost on the Nazis, not least because donations to their own 'Winter Relief' collections (*Winterhilfswerk*) were held to be expressions of political solidarity, and abstentions a mark of dissent. Levels of popular generosity were monitored by the regime's intelligence agencies.[21] Similarly, both the 'Winter Relief' collections and the pseudo-egalitarian institution of the 'Broth Sunday' (*Eintopfsonntag*) were designed as much as propaganda exercises to raise political awareness of the war as to raise funds or save food.

It is not surprising, then, that the authorities took very seriously the relief funds operated by resistance groups, and made it clear that donations would be treated not as isolated expressions of support, but as membership dues, so that the donor would immediately be guilty of treason. Supporters of the funds were often unaware either of the implications of a donation or of the consequences. In the case of Rote Hilfe, supporters were charged with membership of a treasonous organisation and faced the possibility of a death penalty. Organised resistance was, then, a minority commitment. Nevertheless, its boundaries were rather fluid, and not only in terms of the ambiguous status of relief organisations. Support for underground groups fluctuated, reflecting both the instability of popular attitudes towards the Nazi regime and, up to 1943 at least, a certain resignation about the future. In addition Communist slogans and the rumours generated by the party's 'whispering propaganda' passed into the general vocabulary of dissent. 'Heil Stalin' salutes proved to be an irresistible way for drinkers in working-class bars to provoke infuriated responses from the minor Nazi functionaries of the locality at the end of an evening's drinking. The Gestapo was alert to such provocations, and reluctant to avenge affronted minor Nazis who had been taunted by workers with Communist slogans and old labour-movement songs.[22]

Such incidents reflected a broader body of political dissent in working-class communities which, in the absence of any legitimate public forum, found only informal and ephemeral expression, but was considered no less important for that by the regime. The Gestapo pursued a range of new political offences, from insulting Hitler (*Führerbeleidigung*) and other senior Nazis, to the spreading of rumours, defeatism, the impersonation of party functionaries, and the misuse of party titles, badges and ranks. What they uncovered was a persistent and vocal critique of government policy based on sources ranging from the BBC and Radio Moscow to disinformation from the Communist underground. In the countryside even the predictions of peripatetic soothsayers seem to have constituted a more reliable source of information than the official media for some people. Communities generated their own popular opinion, and had their own sources, from the letters of migrant workers in Germany in 1938 to those from soldiers at the front in the 1940s, and were increasingly sceptical of official perspectives. Not all such talk was a deliberate attempt to undermine the regime, but the minority who sought to do so took advantage of a situation where there was no reliable alternative source of information or opinion to the government media; and powerful bodies of rumour built up, such as the belief that Austrian regiments had been 'sent in first' at the Battle of Stalingrad. Despite reassurances and exhortations from government ministers, the feeling that the war had been lost became as firmly established during the last two years of the war as the belief during the previous three that the German armies were unstoppable, and popular discourse was characterised by rumours of the progress of the Red Army and speculation about what would happen to Austria after the war.

Popular dissent never became political revolt, but this did not mean that industrial workers were unaware of the possibilities open to them. The strength of surviving community ties which persisted in working-class neighbourhoods was reflected in a persistent solidarity in industry. Workers in large factories had almost all belonged to the Free Trade Unions and supported the Social Democratic Party, and neither their fundamental views nor their relationships with workmates changed a great deal. Old shop stewards performed the leadership functions on the shop floor that they had previously fulfilled as union leaders, as the SD report submitted to Bürckel in 1939 made clear. The few marginalised right-wingers remained outsiders even under the new dispensation. The rewards for working-class fascists were no longer as clear as they had been during the depression, when those joining a *Heimwehr* union or Nazi organisation had found it much easier to get a job. The terms of the labour market had been reversed; there was now a shortage of labour, and politics was less important a criterion than skill or competence for employers chasing lucrative arms contracts. Not only that but the workforce was fractious, and although workers could not strike or formally protest, they could make life exasperating for the employer with informal go-slows, the impromptu downing of tools, minor acts of sabotage or judicious absenteeism. Much to the fury of Nazi workers, influence reverted to those old Socialist spokesmen who could speak for the workers and mediate between the workforce and the management.

The frustration felt by Nazi workers whose expected promotions never came, and who perceived themselves to be no less isolated than in the 1920s, was reflected a few months after the Anschluß in complaints to Berlin from an SS *Standartenführer* employed at the Steyrwerke, an old Habsburg arms works at Steyr in Upper Austria. Workers had frequently refused to work, openly insulted party leaders, and provoked friction with SS members.[23]

The workforce of the Steyrwerke had more than doubled between February and July, and the root of the trouble was ascribed to a hundred or so new workers drafted in from Vienna whose arrival had been followed by a wave of graffiti, whispering propaganda, and other signs of political activity. Worst of all, however, was a reversal of the expected patronage:

Prominent Social Democratic leaders, as hard-nosed as they ever were, occupy influential positions, and make sure that their tried and trusted Social Democratic comrades get the best-paid jobs. I am in a position to prove, with totally reliable witnesses, that newly-appointed Marxists, who were unable to get a job in the factory at all for years under the Schuschnigg regime, rise quickly to the best-paid positions, which workers with National Socialist sympathies take a very long time to reach, if at all. But then the head [*Meister*] of the department is an old red bigwig, who makes sure that he is surrounded by his red friends. Life there is made impossible for any National Socialist workers, who are given the worst jobs to do. And these days there are sections of the Steyrwerke where only reds are appointed or tolerated.[24]

Despite such discrimination, Nazi workers were disinclined to break ranks and inform on those workers involved in political activity or 'whispering propaganda', for which nobody had yet been punished. The rhetoric of reconciliation which the Nazis had propagated at the time of the plebiscite, and which the Steyr Nazis themselves had promoted only a few months previously, had been read rather literally, but had been misguided and served only to encourage the arrogance of the 'reds'.[25]

The authorities in Berlin reacted swiftly to the report and brought in the Gestapo from Vienna, who reported similar incidents in all parts of Austria where industry was to be found. The initial euphoria with which the Austrians had greeted the Anschluß had abated considerably, and problems of economic integration with the Reich had given rise to a string of essentially economic grievances which had been translated into political protest. There followed a number of arrests of political activists.[26]

Such crackdowns were no more than exercises in political containment, however, and revealed the limitations of the Nazis' 'national community' propaganda. Labour shortages had given workers a degree of leverage in industrial relations, a problem that remained throughout the war, and was eased only in part by the drafting of thousands of slave labourers from eastern Europe, and attempts to draw women into the labour force; these solutions proved only partially effective and also gave rise to new problems.[27] The government, the arms industry authorities and employers alike were unable to avoid the consequences of the structural changes to the economy that were required by the war effort, and at the same time were compelled to be cautious in demanding self-sacrifice from the workforce. In the Austrian case the situation was exacerbated by the effects of economic reforms (the introduction of the Four Year Plan, and of German income tax, for example) designed to bring the Alpine and Danubian *Gaue* into line with the Reich. Austrians were disappointed to see prices rising to Reich levels much faster than wages, a phenomenon which fuelled latent anti-German sentiment. What had once cost a Schilling now cost a Mark, and workers were demanding that a similar parity be established in their wages. The problem was acknowledged by the authorities, who explained low wage levels in terms of the technical backwardness of Austrian factories compared with those of the Reich. Austrian industry, they argued, was simply less productive.[28]

The dilemma came to a head in the autumn of 1939 with the introduction of the so-called 'War Economy Decree', a measure which abolished bonuses, overtime pay and paid holidays. The effects of these measures in Germany have been well documented.[29] The impact in Austria was no less dramatic. Absenteeism generally, and sickness rates in particular, soared above levels deemed normal or acceptable by the labour authorities or the insurance companies, and productivity levels sank. Such phenomena were essentially problems associated with full employment, and had been a problem in Germany for some three years, along with other labour discipline problems such as strike attempts ('interruptions of work') and inflationary bouts of job-changing. The scale of the problems had been sufficient to convince the regime that a more determined effort to regulate the labour market was necessary.[30] The same slackening of productivity and unusually high levels of absenteeism were quickly replicated in Austria as the labour market underwent an accelerated repeat of the same process. A weekly economic report placed before Reich Commissioner Bürckel in June 1939 estimated a fall in productivity of some 20–30 per cent. The authors of the report suggested a range of possibilities encompassing specific reasons for lower morale and disaffection (the new taxation system) to structural problems affecting productivity, such as the return to employment of less well-qualified and less experienced workers, and increases in the number of hours worked.[31] A further report in August confirmed the trend and argued that the problem had now become a general one.[32]

The problems with absenteeism that came in the wake of the War Economy Decree were of a different order and went beyond the general trend of rising absenteeism. Workers increasingly refused to put in the long hours required, and municipal workers in Vienna complained so vocally about the unforeseen injustices that had arisen, particularly those affecting essential workers in transport and the public utilities, that the municipality made representations to Bürckel. He in turn took up their points with Hitler, supporting his case with references to his political successes in the Saar and in Vienna.[33] Vienna's problems were repeated not only in the Austrian provinces, but throughout the Reich, and after a series of concessions the regime finally withdrew or revised most of the measures before Christmas.

This certainly did not mean that discipline problems were eliminated, and absenteeism in particular caused the loss of 20,000 shifts a day and cost 60,000 Reichmarks.[34] In July 1940 the Defence Economy Inspectorate (*Wehrwirtschaftsinspektion*) in Vienna noted that delays in the construction of a new rolling mill at the Rottenmanner Eisenwerke were a consequence of permanently high rates of sick leave among the workforce.[35] Instances of direct and deliberate sabotage were rarer and were generally traced to Communist activists, or workers with individual grievances against employers, or both. The most common incidents involved train crashes or derailments, the burning of haystacks and damage to industrial machinery. In most cases it was difficult to rule out accidental causes or wear and tear, but the Gestapo kept a record of suspected sabotage. At the beginning of the war suspicious fires and explosions were filed with miscellaneous other events under 'Other';[36] such incidents, however, although relatively few, occurred with such regularity that they were filed separately by 1942, and the Gestapo's initial hesitation to ascribe them to deliberate sabotage was so thoroughly overcome that they were inclined to include practical jokes and general carelessness in this category.[37] Nevertheless, with arrests by the Gestapo running at some 2,000 a month in 1943, there were rarely more than one or two in custody on suspicion of sabotage.

In fact the majority of Gestapo arrests were now for breaches of labour discipline. This category (described variously by different official agencies) covered a wide range of offences from changing one's job without proper authorisation from the appropriate Labour Office to insolence or 'refusals to work'. Defendants charged with such offences frequently had good individual reasons for their behaviour, but an element of disaffection was often to be found behind the generally practical explanations offered.

Significantly, however, the majority of those in custody for breaches of work discipline were foreign workers. As more and more demands were made on industry by the war effort, and more and more men were conscripted, the shortfall in the supply of labour could only be filled by foreign workers, who were shipped up the Danube from the Balkans from the spring of 1941, and then increasingly brought in from the Soviet Union. The impact of such workers, and the hundreds of prisoners of war who joined them, was considerable. Although Vienna had long had a large Czech community, and other minority populations from different parts of the Habsburg empire, the Austrian provinces, with the exception of the ethnically mixed areas of Carinthia and the Burgenland (which had Slovene and Croat minorities respectively) were much more homogeneous. Quite apart from the sexual anxieties, which generated new offences and penalties related to any sort of intercourse with foreigners, the newcomers had an increasingly unsettling effect. The first to arrive were skilled Czech workers, who were deployed in industry, where their political assertiveness was quickly felt, and Polish land workers who were deployed in the countryside. Although foreign workers never became a majority of the workforce, it was not unusual by the later years of the war to find teams of Russians, often women, supervised by a handful of Austrian foremen, and national resistance groups growing up among the different nationalities.

The social composition of working-class communities in Austria also changed in other ways. More women were recruited into industrial work, particularly after the Decree for the Mobilisation of Men and Women for the Defence of the Reich in 1943.[38] The mobilisation of women for war work was, of course, a sensitive issue and, like the employment of foreigners, one that ran counter to the thrust of Nazi ideology. It was particularly sensitive among working-class women, who felt that they were being required to do such work while their middle-class counterparts not only did not work themselves, but kept domestic servants at home as well. Above all, it was felt that women should not be expected to work while their husbands were at the front, particularly if they had children, and women brought before the courts on charges of evading war work frequently pleaded mitigating circumstances due to domestic responsibilities.

Women had also been relatively marginalised by trade unions and the Social Democratic Party and did not respond to authority in the same way as men in matters of industrial discipline. The majority of the older male working class had been schooled by party and union leaders to accept industrial discipline and respond collectively to grievances in an equally disciplined way, and this was reflected in workers' covert collective behaviour during both the Austrofacist and Nazi dictatorships. (This was not always the case, of course, and acts of sabotage were often the result of individual grievances.) Women workers, on the other hand, while less likely to commit acts of industrial sabotage, were also less likely to accept the general terms of industrial discipline. They did not always place paid employment at the head of a list of priorities which might also include domestic responsibilities and child care. More often than not this was simply a matter of unpunctuality or occasional absenteeism – if a child was ill, for example. If such problems could not be resolved satisfactorily on a more or less permanent basis, or if the prospect of industrial work was altogether too daunting, women simply failed to turn up for the jobs they had been allocated. And there was often little attempt to make excuses: in 1943 a young woman in Linz told the authorities she had not turned up for the job allocated her because she did not like it.[39]

Other new members of the workforce were similarly disinclined to accept the priorities of the Nazi war economy. Agricultural workers recruited into unskilled work in industry accepted jobs, but were inclined to return to the land at times of peak demand for agricultural labour. The combination of industrial work (often part-time or temporary) with agricultural work was, of course, well established, and they made no attempt to disguise the reasons for their absenteeism when called to account.[40]

Young people, drafted into employment for the first time, were also inclined to respond poorly to industrial discipline, as were labour conscripts and migrant workers from both Austria and the *Altreich*; like many foreign workers they simply failed to return from holidays with their families. A German stone-mason from the Eisenwerke Oberdonau, for example, left his job and returned home, ostensibly because his wife had just given birth to a seventh child. In the event it transpired that he had found a better job in Munich.[41]

By the last years of the war the composition of the industrial workforce had changed dramatically. The cohesion of established working-class communities, and of the political and trade union networks that had survived on an informal level in the early days of the Nazi regime, were broken down by the influx of new kinds of workers into industry: foreign workers from the occupied east; women; agricultural labourers in areas like Upper Austria, where industry was expanding rapidly; and young people who had no experience of industrial work before the Nazis. Among such workers there was no experience of the industrial disciplines that had prevailed in pre-fascist Austria. Although this made them less solidaristic and unlikely to become involved in Communist Party activities, or in the factory-based resistance cells which had been established in larger companies, their presence in the workforce increased the probability of absenteeism and impromptu stoppages.

The industrial labour problems at the end of the previous war – bread riots, strikes, shop stewards' movements and militant workers' councils – had been very different.[42] And it had been precisely these popular revolts which had informed much of the Nazis' own thinking about industrial relations in wartime. The German right was a prisoner of its own stab-in-the-back mythology which had been used to explain the defeat of the Central Powers in November 1918. They were wary of demanding too much sacrifice from the working class during the Second World War for fear of provoking another November Revolution.[43]

In order to create a 'national community' it was not enough to break up the old organisations of class politics and eliminate the influence of Marxist leaders. The Nazis were quite prepared to use coercive methods in order to suppress labour organisations, but differed from their conservative allies in seeking to go beyond the containment of workers' aspirations. Indeed, what distinguished their policies, and fascist policies generally in this field, was a greater awareness of the inevitability in modern industrial societies of popular pressure for participation in politics. Where conservatives might be content with acquiescence and deference, fascists sought to elicit participation, acclamation and consent, to mobilise support and generate a degree of social consensus. The Nazis sought to foster a 'mass' politics of the right in the same way that labour movements had constructed a 'mass' politics of the left. This would involve a realignment of conservative politics that would unite bourgeois and petty bourgeois interests in a single organisation, and one which would attract broader support from other social groups: peasants especially, and a substantial minority of workers. Conservative politics in Austria had already undergone such a realignment during the 1890s under the influence of Karl Lueger, the anti-semitic mayor of Vienna whom Hitler so much admired.[44] During the First Republic the Austrian right, unlike its German counterpart, was united around, if not entirely within, a single large governing party in the broad coalition of conservative interests represented in Austria's 'bourgeois bloc'. But the Christian Social Party of Ignaz Seipel did not pretend to be a *Volkspartei*, and the governments of the First Republic pursued middle-class interests openly and relentlessly. And the attempts of Dollfuß and Schuschnigg to create an alternative, plebiscitary basis for the post-1934 regime were unconvincing and unsuccessful. They were not so much semi-fascists as failed fascists.

The newly appointed Nazi mayor of Vienna, on the other hand, gave notice in 1938 of the new regime's intention to engage with the left on its own territory: 'I do not believe one can approach the working class . . . with words and speeches. We won't win them over with staged rallies, but only with substantial achievements in reconstruction.'[45]

The Austrian left, in turn, had long recognised the appeal of Nazi populism. So much is clear from Socialist admonitions against defecting to the Nazis in 1934, and in Karl Renter's shrewd observations on the differences between 'clerical' and 'national' fascism in 1938. There was considerable apprehension that the labour movement's own authority in working-class communities was under threat, and this meant that its activities were directed towards the maintenance of community networks, and consciousness-raising through propaganda, recruitment to underground organisations and charity work. These were means of retaining a presence as a political force in working-class communities as much as realistic strategies to undermine or overthrow the regime.

It was a successful strategy in so far as support for the Nazis from working-class communities was largely unforthcoming. Although there was no open rebellion before the Red Army was at the gates of Vienna, and although resistance activism remained a minority affair conducted by a self-renewing political leadership whose precise ideological affiliation was often notional, the Nazis succeeded only in containing working-class opposition and deflecting open rebellion rather than winning positive acceptance of their own political values. Popular opinion in the working-class districts, where secret policemen, intelligence agents and minor party *apparatchiki* regularly eavesdropped on drunken conversations in the hope of finding some truth in wine, was sceptical and truculent rather than approving or acclamatory.[46] Established working-class communities evinced a degree of immunity (*Resistenz*) to nazism which can be directly related to historical associations with the Social Democratic Party and the continuing efforts of underground groups to maintain a political class consciousness. This made possible a structural opposition, or passive resistance, to the regime which went beyond dissent.

9 'Homosexual' men in Vienna, 1938

Hannes Sulzenbacher

One of the first demonstrations of Nazi anti-homosexual politics was the ransacking and destruction of Magnus Hirschfeld's Institute for Sexual Research (Institut für Sexualwissenschaft) in Berlin. Its library was confiscated and a part of it was among the books burnt throughout Germany on 10 May 1933. In the torchlight procession which preceded the burning of the books, a student carried an impaled bust of Hirschfeld which had been taken from the Institute. At the same time all the existing organisations of the First German Homosexual Movement were dissolved.

From the middle of the nineteenth century homosexual men have been confronted with two types of authority: the judicial authority of the police and the courts; and the 'scientific' authority of medicine and psychiatry. Among those exercising the latter type of authority there have been those who have been primarily engaged in assisting the work of the state and judicial authorities, and others who have had the co-operation of homosexuals themselves.

As the work of Michel Foucault and others has shown, the use of the definition 'homosexual' from around 1869 onwards has been inextricably caught up with the attempt to establish control over homosexual desire. 'The noisy entrance of homosexuality into the field of medical investigation' was a consequence of its invention as a clinical condition.[1] Where previously the church and the law had condemned acts of 'sodomy' by those of 'contrary sexuality', medicine and psychiatry now looked for clinical symptoms of homosexuality in the course of a full examination of the body and language of the homosexual.[2]

Medical evidence based on the notion of homosexuality as an essential physical and psychological condition was used not only in the attempt to cure (and consequently eliminate) it, but also as a basis for the exculpation of individuals. Sentencing policy could be influenced by medical

150

arguments, and psychiatric evidence could be used either for or against legal pleas for leniency or exemption from punishment.[3]

As the German sociologist Klaus Müller pointed out in his analysis of 'homosexual biographies and medical pathographies' in the nineteenth century, the process by which homosexuality was established as a medical condition, and a homosexual typology delineated, was supported by the active involvement of homosexual men themselves, whose yearning for identity prompted them to seek an active role in the scientific discussion by relating their confessions to the scientists. According to the feminist historian and sociologist Hanna Hacker, such men did not construct a 'counter-identity' based on 'counter-definitions' within a 'counter-culture'; rather, they strove to create a closely defined sub-culture (*Teilkollektiv*) within the existing boundaries of organised male power, and constructed varying definitions of their own identity which rested on new medical principles and a 'younger' literary discourse.[4] It should, of course, be noted that this attempt to gain equal status in the dialogue with medical authority rarely succeeded, and that the self-definitions and confessions of such men were regarded by the authorities of scientific scholarship as so much source material for the construction of a homosexual symptomology.

The first pioneering figure in the movement against discrimination was the German jurist Karl Heinrich Ulrichs.[5] His theory of the female soul in the male body, and the designation *Urning* constituted the first explanatory psychological model of male love for other men. His twelve works of sexual theory, published between 1864 and 1879, were the first major contribution to the understanding of human sexuality, and to a discipline which recognised the importance of sexuality in determining both private and social behaviour. They were written both for a critical general readership and for those who had a direct interest in the subject; and they were addressed both to *Urninge* and their heterosexual counterparts, or *Dioninge*.[6]

There is little trace of the reception of Ulrichs' work in Austria. His close colleague and fellow campaigner, Karl Maria Kertbeny, a writer and translator who invented the word 'homosexuality', was born in Vienna, but had already left the city by the time he became involved in the campaign.[7] Apart from Ulrichs' influence on a handful of literary works, the only other important influence seems to have been on the work of Richard Krafft-Ebing. The Graz psychiatrist's *Psycopathia sexualis* had enormous influence on the developing study of sexuality both within and beyond German-speaking central Europe.[8] He was a confessor figure to growing numbers of people who identified with his published case histories of *Konträrsexuellen*, and who often appeared in subsequent editions of the expanding work. He was also an active advocate for abolishing judicial punishments for homosexuality, arguing that such behaviour was inborn, and that defendants were acting under the influence of an irresistible force. Krafft-Ebing's concept of the *Konträrsexuelle* was widely accepted as an uncontroversial term, and became synonymous with the term 'homosexual'. As a consequence of their medical objectification *Konträrsexualität* and 'homosexuality' quickly became the 'official' terms during the decades that followed, establishing Krafft-Ebing's sexual theory as the dominant one.

The acceptance of the term 'homosexual' was reinforced by the influence of Magnus Hirschfeld, founder of the 'Scientific-Humanitarian Committee', the most important organisation campaigning for legal rights for homosexuals in central Europe at the turn of the century. His popular reception in Vienna was probably not as great as that of Krafft-Ebing. Nevertheless, his lectures there were packed, and he wrote personally to the *Illustrierte Kriminal-Zeitung*, a scurrilous popular paper published in Vienna, taking the editor to task for the paper's campaign against homosexuals, and enclosing some reading material to give him the opportunity 'to examine the most recent scholarly literature' on the subject.[9] His letter was accompanied by another, from the recently founded Vienna branch of the 'Scientific-Humanitarian Committee', and probably constituted that organisation's only public statement.[10] This letter, too, admonished the editor for the 'stereotypical' use of the word 'pederasty' for homosexuality.

Any educated person, familiar with the results of psychological research in recent years will know that the term pederasty has the specific meaning of love for juveniles, a pathological condition which can also be found in many heterosexuals ... Homosexuality refers to love between two mature adults of the same sex. It is not a pathological disorder, but an innate variant of sexuality which is to be found even among the most robust primitive peoples.[11]

There was a concrete and pragmatic aim to much of the 'emancipatory' discussion of homosexuality: the repeal of the clause in the penal code which criminalised 'indecent acts' between people of the same sex (Paragraph 129 I b). The criminal nature of sexual intercourse between two consenting adult men was doubtful in any case. In the first place it was a crime without a victim; secondly, it was a crime where offender and witness were identical; and thirdly it was difficult for the legislator to show in what way he, or the public, had suffered any harm. Moreover, in those foreign countries which had followed the French penal code, 'sodomy' was not a criminal offence.

And yet there was no public discussion of the abolition of Paragraph 129 I b, and such attempts as there were to initiate such a discussion very quickly ran into the sands. This was the case with the polemics of Karl Kraus in *Die Fackel* between 1904 and 1907, or the 'Out with Paragraph 129 I b' campaign run by the *Kriminal-Zeitung*, a popular newspaper which was by no means free of homophobia itself, but which sought the salvation of 'unfortunate' homosexuals, and the punishment of 'greedy blackmailers'. The traditional form of lobbying, a petition protesting against criminal prosecution supported by a large number of prominent public figures, was never attempted. Although Krafft-Ebing pleaded for the removal of judicial penalties for 'sodomy', he sought to introduce conditions which made such a decision dependent on forensic and psychiatric examination. Petitions were submitted, but almost all of those which the state archival authorities of the time considered worth preserving were the pleas or confessions of individuals, four of which were anonymous. None of them was granted.

Paragraph 129 I b of the Austrian legal code was wider than the corresponding clause in German law, Paragraph 175. It remained unchanged from 1852 to 1971 and was not restricted to 'acts resembling intercourse' between men. It included both homosexual acts between women and other sexual activity which involved a member of the same sex. A large body of contradictory and inconsistent case law on questions of detail had given rise to some confusion in the interpretation of the law. It also led to some confusion in the courtroom, where men arrested under the provisions of the act were at pains to establish the precise meaning of 'unnatural practices' and to ascertain in what way they had behaved immorally. There were effectively no limits to the application of the law since its interpretation was dependent on what the presiding judge considered 'unnatural' – only anal intercourse, or any physical contact with a deliberate or unconscious sexual motive. Even the Supreme Court was unable to apply the law consistently.

Sometimes there was only a case to answer if acts had taken place which resembled sexual intercourse or involved masturbation, in other words acts by which it was possible 'to achieve sexual satisfaction in the ways akin to natural sexual intercourse'. In other cases it was enough for acts to have taken place by which 'sexual *satisfaction was sought and gained* [my emphasis] from the body of a person of the same sex'. [12] Proof of the intention to masturbate was not necessary according to this interpretation. An earlier Supreme Court decision of 1902 had defined 'unnatural practices' as 'any activity which, *serving to arouse the sex drive* [sexual desire], *oversteps the boundaries of morality*' (my emphasis).

In so far as a 'homosexual' community existed in Vienna after the First World War, it came together primarily in bars, bookshops and more clandestine meeting places. To be sure, there were also more formal events, such as the public lectures given by Magnus Hirschfeld in the early 1920s. These drew large audiences, but also attracted unwelcome attention, and Hirschfeld's 1923 lecture was drawn to a premature close after young Nazis bombarded the hall with stink bombs.[13] Attempts were frequently made to establish associations. The German 'League of Human Rights' opened a branch in Vienna's eighth district.[14] Branches of the 'Scientific Humanitarian Committee' were also founded several times in Vienna, but the authorities repeatedly refused to recognise them as properly constituted associations. And when the *Wissenschaftlicher Geselligkeitsbund Eos* published its articles of association in 1921, it was not recognised by the authorities either. As a result, meetings took place elsewhere and on an informal basis. In 1925 a letter to the editor of the Viennese literary journal *Die Fackel* described the bookshop Lanyi in the Kärntnerstraße as the 'meeting point of the Viennese homosexual intelligentsia'. Indeed, contact was maintained through the literary periodical press. Coded poetry appeared in Josef Kitir's *Poetische Flugblätter*, for example, and the same journal carried advertisements for *Der Eigene* a homosexual magazine published in Germany.[15] None of these events have gone down in Austrian history. Nevertheless they provided the infrastructure within which homosexual men (and sometimes women as well) were able to develop and express their identities, to meet prospective partners, and to participate in the politics of the emancipation movement.

Beyond the meeting points provided by the emancipation movement, however, was a much bigger sphere: that of the bars. This is a milieu whose inhabitants kept no records, and which is documented only in police records and the sensationalistic exposures of the press – a community documented almost entirely through the perspective of the authorities.

There are exceptions, however. A 'gay guide' published in Germany in 1920 provides three addresses in Vienna for 'respectable inverts': the Hubertuskeller, Aiglas Landesmutterkeller, and the Reisner-Stuberl.[16] These were only a few of the bars used by Vienna's homosexual subculture in the 1920s. Among the others were: Café Buchheim (Rauhensteingasse); the first floor of the famous Café Herrenhof (Herrengasse); Gasthaus Kandler (Grundsteingasse); Café Atlantis, Café Greilinger, Gasthaus Bauer, Café Mischka, Café Motz, Gösser-Bräu and Café Löffler (Zufahrtstrasse). Café Löffler, like many others, was in the Prater, traditional home of Vienna sub-cultures. Probably the most important meeting point by 1938 was the Automatenrestaurant OK in the Kärntnerstrasse, which was near traditional cruising grounds around the Karlsplatz.

Altogether there seem to have been between ten and fifteen 'gay' or 'gay-friendly' bars in Vienna during the 1920s. These ranged from *variété* bars frequented by men with glamorous or effeminate nicknames, and by prostitutes of both sexes, to the traditional Vienna *Beisl*, and other public houses which put on special events and dances. In one such establishment, visited by two students in 1936, there were 'young men holding each other's penis' in the stairwell. Three detectives investigating the place saw 'men sitting close together at desks, fondling, kissing and embracing each other, exciting each other by rubbing each other's thighs, by touching, and by rubbing their penises between each other's thighs'. A song was sung 'with feminine intonation and gestures', and the policemen managed to catch snatches of words and phrases: 'gay bar', 'long cocks' and 'I'll let you ride in my saddle'.[17] It can be assumed that the sub-cultural codes used in such bars had an important part to play in the construction of homosexual identities.

Finally there remained the traditional infrastructure of public baths, parks and public conveniences, places frequented by men who rejected the milieu of the emancipation movement or the bar 'scene', or whose sexual identity was insufficiently stable to support more than fleeting anonymous encounters. There were many dangers associated with such 'traditional' meeting places. If people became aware of what was going on, they were affronted, and by-laws or regulations were passed to prevent such practices. This had happened in 1911, for example, when the local authorities had forbidden men from entering the public baths unless accompanied by a woman.[18] In addition, such places were well known to the police and constantly under surveillance. Certainly, most of the men arrested and convicted in 1938 were caught in such places, and this probably remained true until the decriminalisation of homosexuality in Austria in 1971. In addition, of course, men frequenting such places, particularly in the Prater, were easy prey for gangs of blackmailers who threatened to denounce their suitors to the police for often quite trivial sums of money.

Many defendants had no precise knowledge of the criminal status of homosexual 'offences'. One defendant in 1938 said that he was 'aware that such behaviour was subject to prosecution . . . from newspaper reports'.[19] There were many reasons for public ignorance of the law: the relative freedom enjoyed by judges passing sentence, the diverse nature of the behaviour which led to prosecution, and the lack of publicity accorded to such cases, for fear that greater knowledge might lead to the spread of homosexuality through imitation. In addition, many defendants attempted to explain their sexual preference or the origins of their sexuality at their trials. A tailor, Johann D., for example, acknowledged that he was 'a hundred per cent homosexual' but claimed that his 'nature' was a result of his father being drunk when he was conceived: 'I can't help the way I am. It's not my fault that my father was drunk then.'[20] In 1936 an unskilled worker, Karl S., presented the court with a hand-written autobiography as an explanation of his situation. He was a fatherless child with sixteen brothers and tuberculosis of the bone. He had spent time in a number of orphanages, had been beaten for bed-wetting, and had had to share beds with other boys: 'And we played with our members and got used to masturbating'.[21] The defendant in a Gestapo interrogation of 1938 admitted being homosexual when 'the word homosexuality was explained' to him.[22]

The limited reporting of court cases involving homosexuality was exacerbated by widespread ignorance about the nature of one's own sexuality. Many of the men charged with 'sodomy' were unable to locate themselves by using the discourse which Foucault and others have identified as markers of sexual identity. They had no access to the terminology used in scholarly discourse. The construction of a false stereotype of 'the homosexual' was not without consequences for men who were sexually attracted to other men, distorting as it did their interpretation of their own sexuality; but it was simply beyond the grasp of many people.[23]

The ignorance produced by the suppression of public discussion on the one hand, and an inability of most homosexual men to follow the technical language of the educated elites on the other, meant that during the 1930s men were unable to use long-accepted definitions of homosexuality in defence of their own behaviour. Although it had been argued for decades that homosexuality was hereditary, a medical condition and incurable, Vienna's court records from the late 1930s show that none of the defendants attempted to use such theories to excuse their behaviour – nor were able to do so.[24] Sexual identities were based on gossip derived from older prejudices which characterised such sexual behaviour as criminal or immoral, or from what could be gleaned from sensationalist newspaper reports of trials, or from works of literary fiction. These sources were supplemented by discussion with friends, family and neighbours, from experience or from the reported experience of others.

It is difficult to judge, in this context, what was the most typical or widespread construction of male homosexual identity in the Austrian capital. Austria's first 'gay rights movement' enjoyed only a marginal existence (compared with the more successful movement in Berlin). Nevertheless, it can perhaps at least be assumed that the use of certain terms which derived from the scholarly or medical discussion of homosexuality were also used in public discussion, indicating that some ideas from the theoretical discourse had filtered through, albeit in popularised form, and persisted in 1938.

Nor was there necessarily any clarity on the part of the Nazis. There had been no coherent anti-homosexual strategy during the period immediately following the Nazi 'seizure of power', and this was not least a consequence of the Nazis' own ambivalence on the subject. There was, of course, widespread homophobia in the Nazi Party, but there was also homosexuality within the party's own ranks. Up to June 1934 Hitler's defence of Ernst Röhm's homosexuality was reluctantly accepted, but it ill suited the image of a party sworn to cleaning up the 'moral degeneracy' of the 1920s, and presenting itself as a bulwark of bourgeois respectability. Indeed, as early as February 1933, the government of Prussia had published a series of measures in a 'campaign against public indecency', which included a ban on nudism, the closing down of night-shelters and homosexual bars, and the prohibition of the 'gay' press.[25]

The development of a more explicitly homophobic public discourse and the large-scale persecution of homosexuals as a matter of policy came in the wake of the 'Night of the Long Knives' in 1934. Hitler used the charge of 'homosexual excesses' to establish a retrospective moral legitimation for the murder of Ernst Röhm, the leader of the SA (Sturmabteilung) and a number of senior stormtroopers and other leading figures. In the wake of the affair, a central office, the Gestapo-Sonderdezernat II1S was established, under the leadership of Josef Meisinger, a veteran Nazi, for the purpose of gathering and filing information on homosexuals, and in particular homosexual party members and functionaries.[26] The next important step was the amendment of the penal code in June 1935. In contrast to Austria, German law required 'acts similar to intercourse' as a prerequisite for prosecution; this was now extended by replacing the old formula with a much more vaguely defined 'indecency' which could be interpreted arbitrarily in practice. Such was the contribution of the legal profession, 'the most significant beneficiaries' of the Gestapo's investigation and intensified persecution of homosexuals.[27] On 10 October 1936 there followed a secret decree from Himmler, announcing the establishment of the Reich Central Office for the Campaign against Homosexuality and Abortion (Reichszentrale zur Bekämpfung der Homosexualität und Abtreibung), an institution whose activities were directed against the two most important perceived obstacles to Nazi population policies. The office was not directly concerned with prosecution as such, which was left to the Gestapo or the Kriminalpolizei; its purpose was the compilation of data on convicted or suspected homosexuals. The number of homosexual prisoners in concentration camps increased as the police derived ever greater authority from a succession of nebulously formulated decrees. In 1936 and 1937 in particular, the Gestapo launched a concerted series of investigations into the Catholic clergy and members of religious communities, accompanied by a shrill, if largely unsuccessful, media campaign with the aim of discrediting the church, of ending the days when 'every *Volksgenosse* assumed the inner purity of the occupants from the external cleanliness of the monastery'.[28]

In June 1935 the exemption of homosexuals from the law enforcing the compulsory castration of sex offenders was ended by a reform in the Law for the Prevention of Hereditary Illness of 1933.[29] Originally intended for application on medical grounds alone, the law was now extended to men for the purpose of 'freeing them from degenerate sexual urges, which might continue to lead them astray'. The provisions of the law were also extended so as to include not only men convicted of homosexual offences, but those who volunteered for castration as well. And in addition to those homosexuals convicted under the 1935 law who submitted themselves to 'voluntary castration', the 'men with the pink triangle' imprisoned in concentration camps also volunteered in the hope of reducing their 'sentence'. The tightening up of the penal code was followed by a dramatic intensification in public campaigns against homosexuals, and by no means only those in the church. By the time of the Anschluß the image of the homosexual propagated by Nazi ideologues was a standardised stereotype, simultaneously a seducer of youths and a threat to the regime's population policies. In the same year a record number of men (8,562) were arrested in accordance with paragraphs 175 and 175a.[30]

In fact, homosexuality had been an important element in Austrian perceptions of Germany at least since the time of the trial of Prince Philip Eulenburg and Count Kuno Moltke in 1907; and the publicity given to the 'First German Homosexual Movement' promoted and strengthened such impressions. Austrian public opinion seems to have been very well informed about the discussion of homosexuality in Germany from the turn of the century onwards. On 30 June 1934, for example, the day after the murder of Ernst Röhm, the events in Germany were front-page news in all the Austrian papers. The moral and political arguments advanced in the official German press reports were largely accepted by the Austrian press, but were used as propaganda against the Nazis and their claims to be 'leading the German people to a new morality'.[31] The SA leader's 'unnatural preferences' were only to be expected. The *Neues Wiener Tageblatt* commented on the day after the shootings:

The sudden revelation in a Nazi declaration that Röhm and his unnatural inclinations have proved to be a heavy burden to the party cannot fail to prompt a knowing smile. It has been an open secret for years. The columns of the world's press have been crammed with innuendo about Röhm and his 'co-ordinated' brothers.[32]

On the other hand the intensified legal persecution of German homosexuals which followed the 1935 reforms to the penal code were virtually ignored by the Austrian press. Reports on the matter were generally restricted to a brief notice with no explanation of the context, so that the implications of the reforms were probably missed by most members of the general public, who had no knowledge of what the previous legal situation had been.

In May 1938 three Austrian workers who had taken up casual jobs in the *Altreich* took lodgings in a small German town. While rummaging through their luggage their landlady found a letter from Austria addressed to one of them, Rudolf R., a nineteen-year-old tailor's apprentice, in which his correspondent asked whether it was true that sodomy was 'not such a rarity in Germany'. According to his landlady, the young man explained that this was just 'gossip' in Austria.[33]

Following the 'Anschluß' of 11 March 1938 the jurisdiction of the Gestapo was immediately extended to the *Ostmark* in accordance with the decision to incorporate Austria directly into the Reich. On the day after the occupation of Austria, Himmler landed at Vienna's Aspern airfield before daybreak with a staff of SD and Gestapo officials. The state secretary for security, Michael Skubl was immediately dismissed, and Reinhard Heydrich requisitioned the Hotel Metropol on Vienna's Morinzplatz as headquarters for the SS and SD. The local police was purged, and those remaining swore oaths of allegiance to Hitler. There then followed the first large-scale wave of arrests in which the functionaries of the outgoing Austrofascist regime were targeted, along with Communists, Social Democrats and Jews.[34]

The Gestapo estimated that 2,059 men were necessary for it to extend its operations to Austria. Heydrich ordered the establishment of a Gestapo *Leitstelle* (local head office) in Vienna on 15 March. The most important positions were held by Reich German officers whose experience was felt to be essential for the overseeing of the extensive new operation. The same was true of Section II s, which was responsible for homosexuality and abortion. Häusserer left his desk in Berlin and started work with a small staff in Vienna; and Josef Meisinger also probably visited Vienna during this period of construction. Only clerical-grade officers were recruited locally from the Austrian police.[35] It is clear from the Gestapo's 'daily reports' that the work of Section II s involved the surveillance of bars and public toilets in co-operation with the criminal police. They also generally called in for questioning all homosexuals who were known to the police from records before 1938 and threatened them with further charges.[36]

The arrested men were generally questioned at Gestapo headquarters in the Morinzplatz, and the principal purpose of the interrogation was usually an attempt to discover the names of other men who might be convicted. After the construction of card-index files, however, there seems to have been no further consistent policy on the part of the Gestapo. Some men were sent directly to concentration camps while others were dealt with in a quasi-legal manner and brought before the public prosecutor at the Vienna local court. Others were sent first to concentration camps, then brought back to court for trial and imprisonment, generally only to be returned to concentration camps after this procedure on the strength of a Gestapo application. In one instance the case was dismissed by the local court because the defendant had already been sent to Dachau.[37] Karl F., who was also accused of 'unnatural practices' was sent to Buchenwald by the Gestapo on the day of his arrest, sent back to Vienna on the day he arrived, and released from detention two months later by the Vienna local court. A week before his trial, which took place three months later, the court received a letter from Buchenwald stating that he had been imprisoned there again. He was sentenced to five months' imprisonment by the court, but his six months in detention was taken into account and the court ruled that he had served his sentence.[38]

The criminal police (Kripo), which took over the persecution of 'homosexuals' after the beginning of the war, was hardly involved at all in 1938. After the Anschluß, however, the established procedures for dealing with homosexuality continued to be used. Men were caught *in flagrante* by the local constabulary, or were reported to the police by men approached on the false assumption that they were homosexual. This was followed by the 'traditional' procedure: arrest, statements from witnesses, and trial.

Austrian legislation remained in force despite the Anschluß, and a wide-ranging discussion began of ways in which the law could be made consistent. On the one hand female homosexuality was criminalised in Austria (this had never been the case in Germany); and on the other hand, the vague wording of the Austrian law made a more lenient judgement possible, since it allowed the possibility of punishing only those 'acts which resembled sexual intercourse'. For the Austrian authorities, to comply with the Nazi interpretation of the law meant bringing as many cases to court as possible, that is interpreting Paragraph 129 I b so that it had exactly the same force as the revised German Paragraph 175 of 1935. It also meant passing more severe sentences than had been the case before

1938. In some cases where a harsher sentence was passed, it was explained in terms of a deficit in relation to German law.[39]

Discussion of plans to standardise the law on homosexuality in Austria and the Reich became more heated in February 1940 with the publication of an article in the SS journal *Das Schwarze Korps* under the heading 'Das fehlte gerade' ('At last!').[40] The article praised the severity of German sentencing following the death sentence for a man convicted of indecent acts with two boys,[41] and criticised Austrian sentencing practice for its leniency. Five days after the publication of the article, State Secretary Freisler wrote to the *Oberreichsanwalt* (attorney-general), Brettle, informing him that Reichstagspräsident Bumke considered this criticism valid. They had resolved to bring the next appropriate Austrian case before the Supreme Court (*Grosser Senat*). Freisler acted promptly, ordering a memorandum to be circulated to all Public Prosecutors' offices in Austria instructing them to interpret the law according to the German practice. On 27 November Brettle wrote to Freisler, informing him that the Sixth Senate of the Reich Court (which dealt with Austria) was in agreement with the German interpretation of the law governing 'sodomy'.[42]

As far as can be established from Vienna's local court records, the city's homosexual sub-culture was by no means extinguished in 1938. Despite the intensification of Gestapo persecution, and the appearance of increasing numbers of men in court, more emphasis was placed on the severity of sentences than on the number of arrests. Indeed, the attempts of the police to investigate homosexual meeting places seem at times to have been almost sloppy. When, for example, the local court in Innsbruck passed on to the Vienna authorities information from local men who had had 'experiences with Viennese homosexuals', the latter learned of the reputation of the Hubertuskeller and summoned three of its former landlords for questioning. The first who, according to the Tyroleans, had personally 'seduced masses of young boys', testified that 'in fact it is doubtless true that there were homosexuals among the guests of the Hubertuskeller. But it certainly was not their local when I was there . . . In fact when I recognised one or two of that kind I even threw them out'. The two other landlords told similar stories. All three were immediately released and the charges against them were dropped. The landlord of the Hubertuskeller, who had run the bar since 1936, had also testified that there were homosexuals before he took over, but he had not tolerated them himself.[43]

The records of the Vienna local court present a heterogeneous picture of the persecution of homosexuals, but in the first months after the Anschluß individual judges seem to have been allowed enormous latitude in the interpretation of the law when passing sentence, and this produced surprising results. The records, along with those of the Gestapo or the Kripo are also virtually the only clues we have to the history of a 'gay community' in Austria at this time. And it is important to remember that this history was not documented by the men themselves, but in the files of police interrogators, medical practitioners, courts and so on. In other words, the history of Austria's gay community, such as it existed, was written only by the authorities, and we have only the perspective of authority, not that of the 'community' or the individuals of which it was made up. Moreover, many of these victims of Nazi persecution would not have characterised themselves as homosexual. Many, of course, were falsely charged with homosexual acts for political reasons; but even among those who did have sex with other men there was a diversity of identities beyond the Nazi stereotype of 'the homosexual'.

10   'The years of consent'? Popular attitudes and resistance to Fascism in Italy, 1925–1940

Philip Morgan

In the fourth volume of his encyclopaedic life-and-times biography of Mussolini, Renzo de Felice caused considerable controversy by arguing for the apparently unlikely proposition that the Italian Fascist regime enjoyed its broadest level of 'consent' in the period from 1929 to 1934. It was precisely during the years of the Great Depression, he asserts, that the regime was most popular and stable, attracting wide-ranging support even among the working classes of town and country. This was 'more extensive and . . . more totalitarian'[1] than the enthusiastic, yet shallower and ephemeral 'consent' of 1935–6, during and immediately after the invasion of Ethiopia, which is where historians have conventionally located the peak of fascism's popularity.

This interpretation is already a long way from the prevalently anti-Fascist historiography of the 1950s and 1960s, where the only relationship portrayed between the working classes and the regime was one of hostility and antagonism. De Felice was quite deliberately and provocatively challenging what he regarded as the 'establishment' left-wing view in his allegedly neutral and value-free history of Mussolini and fascism. He returned to the anatomy of 'consent' in the fifth volume of the biography, asserting that widespread discontent was emerging among all social classes and groups in the period between 1936 and 1940, but never at any point became active anti-Fascist opposition. The discontent among the working classes was far less dissensual and politically worrying for the regime than the 'psychological distancing'[2] from fascism of its natural middle-class constituencies in reaction to the increasingly autarkic, totalitarian and warmongering policies of the late 1930s.

De Felice's conclusions on the quantity and quality of 'consent' and 'dissent' under the Fascist regime of the 1930s are controversial. They highlight the problems of method and sources confronted by historians attempting to reconstruct and understand popular attitudes at any time, let alone during a 'totalitarian' dictatorship, but they do not clarify them.

163

More will be said about sources later. But the historian's resort to the terminology of social and political science in order to make sense of historical phenomena about which the sources are silent or partial, comes close to being the scholarly camouflage of ignorance. There is always the danger that concepts borrowed from other disciplines will provide a consoling but largely unverified and perhaps unverifiable framework, glossing over the gaps in our historical knowledge and understanding: in this case of the workings of the Fascist regime and popular responses and reactions to it. Concepts are valid as analytical tools, but their usefulness is in illuminating reality, not in replacing it.

De Felice's analysis, which seems to draw on a functional sociology, arrives at rather unstable conceptualisations of 'consent' and 'dissent'. According to De Felice, during the Depression years manifestations of discontent by workers, whether employed or unemployed, singly or in groups, only ever involved a small minority; and such displays were usually the inevitable and understandable signs of economic distress at a particularly unfavourable economic juncture. Such incidents generally lacked any political organisation, content, significance or outcome, and could not be taken as indications of even an incipient anti-Fascist opposition.

One of the reasons for this, of course, was the efficiency and effectiveness of police surveillance and repression. Thus De Felice's introduction of the repressive dimension of the regime means that working-class 'consent' is deduced from the absence of political dissent and oppositional activity among workers. He thereby creates a positive out of a negative. Wishing to have it all ways, De Felice also finds evidence of 'increasing consent'[3] among workers as a result of the regime's own pragmatic efforts to alleviate the worst effects of the Depression: job-creating public works schemes; the Fascist syndicates' more vigorous defence of their members' material interests; and especially state and party welfare initiatives. What De Felice identifies as 'consent' is characterised as 'more or less passive fascistisation', the 'consent' of the 'good citizen' who accepts the fact of government and its policies, and not 'active fascistisation',[4] which suggests a high degree of identification and integration with the regime's goals and organisations.

Some critics of De Felice's concept of 'consent' and the ways in which it is applied to the Fascist regime, deny that such low-level 'consent' can be seen as proper 'consent' at all, since it was neither active, nor positive nor voluntary, but 'extorted' by a combination of police repression and diversionary methods of social control. 'Real' consent, such critics would argue, can only exist and be measured in democratic, pluralist societies, since the tolerance of dissent alone allows the quantification of consent, and nothing of the kind is possible in the Fascist dictatorship. It all depends on what is meant by 'consent'. For obviously differing understandings of the idea of 'consent' will produce diametrically opposed analyses of the same evidence. To take a banal example: it is noted that few of the peasants and shepherds of rural Sardinia joined Fascist organisations. This non-involvement could be taken as the sign of the shepherds' ingrained indifference to or apartness from fascism, an attitude bordering on a rejection of fascism. Alternatively, it could be taken as an indication of passivity, implying a basic acceptance of Fascism, a qualitatively different judgement which transforms a potentially negative indicator into a relatively positive one.[5]

The jumbling of concepts and meanings does not end here. Confusingly, the same word in Italian, *consenso*, can stand for both 'consent' and 'consensus'. One wonders whether De Felice knew of or wanted to make any distinction between the two. Certainly, 'consensus' is often used as if it is synonymous with 'consent', an elision of meaning apparent in the sociology presumably borrowed by De Felice as well as in ordinary daily usage. An attempt at a definition of terms would probably be useful at this point, though whether the concepts themselves are helpful is still another matter.

'Consensus' has been employed by sociologists as an explanatory concept regarding the existence or absence of stability and cohesiveness in societies. The risk of conceptualisation leading to the cul-de-sac of reification and tautology is already evident: if a society is stable, then consensus exists; consensus is therefore the set of conditions producing stability. 'Consent' is usually applied in the political context or setting, and in particular refers to the relationship between government and society – the attitudes of the governed towards their government, both in respect of individual policies and of the overall legitimacy of governmental authority. 'Consent' is best treated on a continuum or a spectrum to take account of its often ephemeral and volatile nature. It varies in intensity and duration over time, from a grudging acquiescence to total identification with and commitment to the government's aims and policies. Conversely, the term 'dissent' can equally encompass a range of attitudes and actions, from reactive and defensive grumbling and opposition to a specific government policy, to organised resistance aimed at the overthrow of the regime.

'Consensus', on the other hand, appears to have a wider and more general application than the political sphere, and might be said to incorporate or overlap with 'consent'. 'Consensus' treats a whole range of social relationships and patterns of behaviour in order to explain how social stability or cohesion is achieved. Attitudes of the governed to the government may be one of these relationships. At the core of the definition of 'consensus' is the idea of broad or approximate 'horizontal' agreement within and between different social groups. The intensity of attachment each group feels may vary over time, but the agreement expresses and reinforces harmony and some sense of unity, or at least reduces the incidence and impact of conflict between social groups.

This idea of 'consensus' has some passing affinity with the concept of 'hegemony', which the Italian Communist, Antonio Gramsci, employed to describe and explain the resilience of modern capitalist societies through the transmission of the cultural values and norms of the dominant classes to the subordinate classes. But Marxist historians and social scientists distrust the use of the term 'consensus' because it assumes a static harmony or community, and takes these as the objects to be analysed and explained. They would regard the stability of a given social and political system as reflecting something other than 'consent' or 'consensus': rather, the use of power to balance conflicting interests or subordinate one interest to another.

The terms 'consent' and 'consensus' are generally applied to the experience of pluralist, democratic societies and political systems. They may not be germane to the experience of living in a 'totalitarian' system, which Fascism aspired to create, if only imperfectly realised. Nevertheless, it is essential for a nuanced understanding of what the available sources tell us about people's responses to the Fascist regime to grasp the unique way in which the regime tried both to repress dissent and mobilise or organise 'consent'.

While repression might not be the distinguishing feature of Italian Fascism, the regime nevertheless rested on a refined and efficient police apparatus which, under public security laws and decrees passed in the late 1920s and early 1930s, had pervasive powers both to prevent and repress dissent.[6] The judicial system had no competence in the handling of offences under these laws and decrees. Instead, the police exercised these powers independently and unaccountably as a matter of administrative fiat: in other words, the police dispensed their own justice. They could apply a range of sanctions from *confino di polizia* (internal exile), through the *ammonizione* (a renewable two-year sanction restricting the liberty, movement and occupation of individuals), to the *diffida* (a kind of formal public warning administered to suspects to deter them from wrongdoing). Cases for *confino* or *ammonizione* were decided by provincial commissions covened and presided over by the prefect. A local magistrate was on the panel, but cases were usually heard in camera in the absence of those charged and there was no appeal against the commission's decisions. Individuals acquitted by the Special Tribunal, a military-style court set up to try offences against the security of the state, or whose cases never reached the Tribunal after the investigation stage, could expect as a matter of course to be referred to the provincial commissions for the application of police measures.

Police action was not limited to the detection and repression of militant anti-fascism. The defence of 'public order' also involved the safeguarding of institutions and policies which embodied the social and economic objectives of the Fascist state. This considerably widened the areas in which the police could intervene and to which police measures could be applied. It gave considerable elasticity to definitions of what constituted unacceptable behaviour; police sanctions could be imposed on those who were simply suspected of the intention to engage in 'subversive' activity.

The effect of almost unrestrained police powers exercised over ever wider areas of jurisdiction was that increasing numbers of people were trawled and their actions or intentions 'criminalised'. The figures may seem small, but they are nevertheless a good enough indicator of how far Fascist Italy had become a police state. About 5,500 individuals were tried by the Special Tribunal, a figure which has been used in the past to argue for the relatively restrained repressiveness of the Fascist system. But far larger numbers were investigated for referral to the Tribunal, even if they were eventually handled elsewhere in the system. There were apparently about 17,000 people sent to *confino* between 1926 and 1943, and about 160,000 appeared in police files over the same period as having received the *ammonizione* or being under special police surveillance and control. (This latter figure included common criminal as well as 'political' offences.)[7] To all the above must be added the certainly more numerous though unquantifiable cases of those who received the police's warning as to their future conduct, the *diffida*.

The problems of interpreting such figures, and the impact of the police apparatus which produced them, are by now self-evident. Do these figures denote a 'dissenting' society and, if so, what is the quality of that 'dissent'? By criminalising so many activities or at least making them a matter for police surveillance and intervention, the regime created 'dissenters' and inflated 'dissent'. Police measures hit people who, in acting as they did, probably had no intention of seeking to 'subvert' the Fascist state.

The cliché that Fascist Italy was somehow less repressive than Nazi Germany or Stalinist Russia cannot really be justified in the face of the extent of policing and its efficiency. What can be said is that policing in the years after 1926 seemed to be more routine and predictable than the often highly personalised, vindictive and indiscriminate terror practised by the Fascist squads in the early and mid 1920s. The Fascist Party never managed to infiltrate the career police service with its own men and methods, while the police themselves applied their wide powers in a relatively discriminating and selective fashion. Their measures were geared to the perceived degree of importance or danger of the activity being investigated.

This 'normalisation' of repression might in itself have been a source of 'consent' for the regime, especially since it rested on the restraint or marginalisation of party violence. But this probably made little difference to how workers in industry and agriculture were likely to view the regime. The continuing force of the police's investigative and repressive efforts was directed at the industrial working classes in particular, and with good reason. They were recognised by the regime itself to be the social group most fundamentally unreconciled to Fascism – the most serious threat to the regime's stability at a time when they were bearing the brunt of the Depression and of the government's deflationary policies. The most active and persistent clandestine organisation working against the regime from within Italy was the PCI (Partito Comunista Italiano, the Italian Communist Party), which alone of the anti-Fascist movements and parties had initially decided to oppose fascism inside Italy as well as from exile abroad after 1926.

Clearly there were limits to what coercion alone could achieve regarding people's attitudes and behaviour in a society marked by deep social and economic divisions, and where fascism had literally smashed and then outlawed organisations which had represented workers' interests. In a 'totalitarian' reflex, the regime sought to manufacture consent, developing mass organisations of its own where the elements of compulsion were less evident and through which it could attempt to integrate workers into the national community. The mass organising of society started with a will in the late 1920s, received impetus from the Fascist Party's 'going to the people' campaign of the Depression years and culminated in the 'totalitarian' phase of the mid to late 1930s. Its start coincided with the putting into place of the apparatus of the police state, and its development was symbiotically connected to the highly efficient operation of that machinery of repression.

The repressive component of the Fascist regime facilitated the task of integration in the following way. The police were extremely effective in locating, infiltrating and destroying the clandestine networks of the Communist Party, breaking or interrupting the channels of communication and organisational links between the internal and external party centres, the local and regional cells, and the party activists and workers. Continual police successes against the party's underground organisation was itself a factor in depressing the morale and level of activity of party members. It seemed impossible to contemplate overturning a regime whose permanence was secured by a police apparatus which employed refined techniques of control and surveillance – and repression – where necessary. The police's widespread use of networks of agents and informers, dispersed among all sectors of the population and in all walks of life, helped to create an atmosphere of mutual diffidence and insecurity and to inhibit people in what they felt they could do or say. The climate of repression induced a form of daily self-censorship, experienced perhaps most extremely by those who were opposed to the regime. Communist Party directives to activists on how to operate clandestinely emphasised the need for secretiveness, caution and suspicion in relations between members, reflecting the obsessive fear of police infiltration and provocation. Internal party reports also testified to the debilitating effects of such a conspiratorial atmosphere. The fear of discovery inhibited activity; to survive was enough and all that was possible.[8]

The PCI had great hopes of exploiting what it saw as the workers' inevitable discontent at the impact of the Depression, even to the point of anticipating that it could develop into a popular insurrection against the government. But repression, or the climate of repression, isolated whatever individual acts of discontent occurred from any organisation or collective effort capable of pulling together the specific strands of hostility into a general rejection of fascism which would be a platform for wider political action.

Essentially, repression removed on a continuing basis any possibility of articulating alternatives to the Fascist way, allowing the regime's organisations and propaganda to monopolise the field. The pull or credibility of the regime's mass organisations depended to an extent on their members being deprived of any alternatives. Just as the pervasiveness of police action and powers in the Fascist state affects our understanding of the nature and dimensions of 'dissent', so it skews our conventional and commonsensical view of 'consent'. Repression was indispensable to the regime's attempts to manufacture consent through propaganda and popular organisations. These very 'totalitarian' mechanisms for acquiring and consolidating consent could only operate in the context of coercion. The impressively large growth in membership of the regime's capillary organisations was not achieved without a vast effort of *organising* being undertaken from the late 1920s. This in itself allows us to question the regime's own self-image of winning massive adherence from all sectors of the population.

All Fascism's mass organisations uneasily combined different functions. They were a way of keeping an eye on people; they were also meant to mobilise people, engage them actively, 'fascistise' them. The regime wanted to generate a participatory enthusiasm within the controlled orbit of its organisations; this was the 'totalitarian' dream. It was illusory precisely because of the unique and paradoxical combination of force and consent underpinning the Italian 'totalitarian' system. In a regime where there was an obligation to join or participate, not necessarily enforced by actual physical coercion but by the absence and exclusion of alternatives, then a willing 'consent' was impossible to guarantee and to measure.

Organised spontaneity was a long way from genuine enthusiasm. Who could say whether or not the acclaim of the crowds at Mussolini's set-piece rallies was genuine? Locating and gauging 'consent' in Fascist Italy is very problematic. What has to be taken into account is the kind of 'totalitarian' consent the regime wanted to generate, and the repressive, intolerant atmosphere darkening any expression of popular feeling. When open dissent was impossible, or at least very risky because it invited punishment, people were inhibited in what they said and did. In such a system, the lack of dissent could not be necessarily taken as a sign of consent. It was difficult to judge whether apparent approval or accept-ance of what the government was doing was due to enthusiasm, or simply due to repression, indifference and the desire for a quiet life.

This is a methodological problem in all popular history. The people themselves were silent, at least on paper, and their actions and lives were usually recorded by others. In the Fascist period, these others included activists and organisers of the clandestine PCI who tried to work politi-cally on and among them. But even these sources are mainly silent about popular attitudes. Memoirs of party militants are understandably retro-spective and judgemental pieces rather than recollection, and often tell us more about the organisation they worked for than the people they claimed to represent, which is also true of the few extant party archives. What remains useful in PCI documentation are the reports on the position in the country filed by agents and emissaries sent on clandestine expeditions to Italy by the party's external centre.

For apparent lack of alternatives, historians have used official sources – the voluminous archives of the police, prefects and Fascist Party – for some sense of what was actually happening in the country in the 1930s. Their use has been controversial, and has considerably muddied the waters of the debate over 'consent'. This is not least because De Felice relied on this kind of documentation for his analysis of the extent and nature of support for the regime, complementing it with reference to contemporary PCI perceptions, including Togliatti's *Lezioni sul fascismo*,[9] where this confirmed the message of the regime's own agencies. The problem of using these official records is that they convey a perspective on people and events peculiar to the role of the organisation reporting on them. People's lives and actions are regarded from the standpoint of the powerholders, or at least the executors of power, not of the people themselves as protagonists. It is difficult for historians to distance themselves from this top-down perspective of the deviant popular behaviour which the regime's state and party organs were meant to record, correct and repress.

In reporting to their superiors, police chiefs, prefects and Fascist Party leaders were reporting on their own activities and were bound to put as rosy a construction as possible on them. Most of the incidents of popular protest and discontent registered in police files during the Depression years and afterwards were described as being caused by economic difficulties and therefore of no political consequence, and certainly constituting no political threat to the regime. They were often reported to be isolated, sporadic, localised events, and so easily repressed or contained by the police. All of this might be true, of course, but the constant refrain that protest was passing and contingent on economic hardship was also a way of minimising popular discontent, playing down the level of conflict in their patch and demonstrating to their superiors that matters were under control.

Again, police and prefectural summary reports to the Ministry of the Interior often distinguished between 'public order' and 'anti-Fascist' incidents, and the distinguishing factor was the absence or presence of anti-Fascists and their organisations in inciting or exploiting the agitation. What mattered to prefects and police was maintaining order, and their concern was to prevent and repress disaffection which might threaten the system's stability. So, from their perspective, protest was only significant when politically motivated or directed, and it was only politically motivated when the hand of anti-Fascist propaganda and organisation was evident or suspected. The Special Tribunal operated on the same rule of thumb. It only dealt with the serious 'political' crimes – by definition those where there were signs of Communist and anti-Fascist subversion. Other cases classified as 'economic' and again, by definition, less dangerous to state security, were referred for police action further down the apparatus of repression. Interestingly, De Felice asserts that his view that the stimulus to popular agitation was primarily economic, precluding any real anti-fascism, is confirmed by the reading of police records. It is pretty clear that De Felice has reproduced the interpretation of the police themselves. The provenance may be different, but some of the older Marxist historiography of anti-Fascism shares the same reductive separation of the economic from the political in taking the view that workers could do and express nothing outside working-class organisations. Bereft of the guidance and direction of parties and unions, workers were only able to articulate economic demands and not engage in properly class-conscious political activity.

In other words, the ways in which the police saw their own role in the Fascist state, and how they reported on and interpreted incidents of popular protest, can in turn shape the historian's evaluation of the popular mood, unless allowance is made for the inherent bias of police accounts. The clues to reconstructing the authentic world of workers and peasants are often left inadvertently in police files, thanks to the manic recording of all possible detail of even quite trivial events. The police not only summarised and glossed what happened; they also sometimes reproduced verbatim the letters they intercepted, the anti-Fascist slogans appearing on walls and in public places, the subversive songs sung and insults passed by individual or groups of workers, the confiscated posters and leaflets. These at least convey the authentic voice of popular protest, and give some direct access to popular feeling. Making sense of them, however, is another matter, as we shall see.

The regime itself wanted to know and control what people thought and felt, while realising that a climate of repression made this difficult to achieve. This imperative was one of the reasons for the development of surveillance and information-gathering services by both the Fascist Party and the national Chief of Police, Arturo Bocchini, whose networks of secret agents and informers covered the country. Characteristically, the mysteriously named OVRA began as a special political police unit in the Interior Ministry for the monitoring and investigation of clandestine Communist Party activity, but its network of informers came to extend to all social classes and walks of life. Anonymous informers were expected to mix with people and register what they actually said, to gauge a public mood which had no open way of self-expression in a dictatorship and was potentially prey to optimistic misrepresentation in official reports.

These informers' reports, swelling the central party and ministry files, were often used as a check on the operations of their provincial and local organisations. Indeed they became the most important source of information for the regime's leadership on the fluctuations in popular attitudes (and later, of course, for historians). Nevertheless, as historical sources, these reports have self-evident limitations of which the historian should be aware. Opinions and conversations overheard in various public places were welded by informers into the generalisations of their reports. These could obviously be massaged to fit the reporter's own ideas and predilections. There was, and is, no such thing as objective reporting. In contrast to the vested interest of the prefect or police chief, which was to reassure his superiors, the informers tended to be more alarmist and exaggerated popular disaffection, because if they had nothing 'juicy' to report they were making themselves redundant.

Yet the evidence of the informers' reports is sometimes so cumulative as to be compelling. For example, it is difficult to doubt their accuracy when in the late 1930s practically all police and party informers throughout the country were in agreement about the widespread popular discontent at rising prices and shortages, and fears of an impending European war. But their use still requires the same critical handling which the historian brings to other official sources. Although Simona Colarizi's study of public opinion during the 1930s[10] is prefaced by a consideration of their credibility as source material, the book almost subliminally takes on the viewpoint of the informers' reports on which it is largely based. What is really a reconstruction of changing popular attitudes as refracted in the perceptions of the regime's agents and informers becomes the definitive portrayal of people's actual attitudes towards fascism and its policies: a perception is transformed into the reality.

The challenge of detecting the popular voice which was otherwise muffled in the climate of repression and self-censorship under the dictatorship, or filtered through the apparatus of control and repression, has led to the exploration of rather more unconventional sources and methods. Taking their cue from the work of British historians such as Edward Thompson and Eric Hobsbawm, working-class and popular attitudes during the Fascist era have been approached from the wider and more complicated perspective of social and cultural history. The forms and symbols of social protest against the institutions of authority and power, even as revealed in the records of the state's repressive agencies, have been seen as indicative of the values, codes of behaviour, and outlook on life of the otherwise historically silent masses. The analysis of popular protest lays bare an autonomous popular culture, and the indefatigable 'subversiveness' of the popular classes. This idea of a subterranean anarchic rebelliousness running through popular attitudes and behaviour is a fresh way of reclaiming the 'people' for anti-fascism. It can take on board the uncomfortable truth that organised party-political anti-fascism was largely ineffectual in mobilising working-class resistance to the regime. Moreover, it helps to explain the apparently unco-ordinated and spontaneous nature of popular protest in the 1930s, involving people who had never been organised by socialist movements at all. The persistence of a stubborn rebelliousness in popular culture showed that ordinary people were resisting fascism all along, albeit in different forms and through different channels from the political.[11]

An increasingly fashionable element of this cultural approach is the use of the oral testimony of old workers, who retrospectively become the protagonists of their own pasts. At least these men and women are speaking for and of themselves, and about the everyday experiences of their lives. But as oral historians are careful to point out, what their testimonies provide is not a factual or sequential account of their lives, rather their memory of them which will obviously be selective and coloured by the circumstances of the present. Where memory scores is in the revelation of the person's mentality, exposing the attitudes, perceptions and values which constitute his or her identity, or 'culture'. In Luisa Passerini's view,[12] oral testimony opens up whole new areas of people's conduct and feelings which go far beyond political attitudes. It thereby uncovers a wider span of potential dissidence under fascism which cannot be described or accounted for by political categories, or accommodated between the conventional poles of 'consent' and 'dissent'.

The analysis of 'culture' and what might be called 'cultural resistance' is difficult, because once again the historian's basic skills do not seem to be adequate to the task. Passerini's study of the 'culture' of working-class men and women in Turin draws heavily on the terminology and concepts of anthropology and psychology to provide the keys to interpreting nuances of mundane language and behaviour which otherwise would apparently be impenetrable. So a joke at the expense of a Fascist leader could be read 'politically' as a release, a diversion, a small surrogate protest in a repressive society. Read 'anthropologically', the joke may be indicative of a deep-seated cultural resistance to an invasive dominant culture; but a resistance which was nevertheless ambivalent, because it combined symbolic rebellion with a recognition of impotence in the face of that authority. There may be problems with this approach, but the idea of ambivalence is an extremely suggestive one. As a source uncovering the small-scale dramas of daily working-class life, oral testimony can be usefully set alongside the meticulous recording of minor conflicts and acts of protest in police documentation.

Any survey of the methodological and source problems of defining and analysing popular attitudes in the Fascist 'totalitarian' system might well conclude that the mission is a hopeless one. It is no easy matter to match evidence of very different kinds and provenance to conceptual frameworks lacking the precision they are meant to provide. With this in mind, it is possible to attempt some evaluation of De Felice's controversial view of the 'years of consent'.

When De Felice talks of 'consent', a term with positive connotations, he means the lack of dissent, or more precisely the lack of any political opposition to fascism. It can be broadly accepted that neither anti-Fascist movements, whether operating from exile or clandestinely in Italy, nor any of the overt signs of popular protest and dissent, organised or not, posed a real threat to the survival of the Fascist regime in the 1930s. Put in these absolute terms, those of the police and then of De Felice, the regime was stable, its overthrow from within unlikely, and this was the achievement of the regime's machinery of repression. The problem is that De Felice's own cataloguing of protest during the Depression years, which is dismissed as 'economic' and not 'political', contradicts the sense of social peace and harmony conveyed by his use of the term 'consent'. The evidence from police documentation indicates that the regime was in no danger, but not that it was a peaceful society. The real disagreements arising from De Felice's work concern the significance and meaning to be given to the myriad examples of protest and dissent minutely recorded in police files.

An obvious first point to make is that all forms of protest bore the imprint of the routine repressiveness of the Fascist state. Most, if not all, were micro-incidents, small in scope, short in duration, local in setting, reflecting not only the way these events were reported by the police but also the real impact of repression. On the capitalist farms of Emilia-Romagna, in the years before the First World War and during the 'Two Red Years' of 1919–20, the socialist-affiliated agricultural leagues of Federterra had organised zonally, calling out thousands of landless labourers and other peasant farmers in support of strikes for better contracts which had lasted weeks and months. During the Depression, the aims and targets of protest were the same, against cuts in agricultural wages by employers violating even the punitive labour contracts imposed under fascism, against the failure of public and private employers to allocate available work according to agreed quotas and against the use of machines rather than men at harvest time. These were all to do with the employment and conditions of employment of the *braccianti*. But speedy police intervention and divisive Fascist Party and syndicate action helped to fragment and isolate protest when it occurred. Stoppages at the place of work were soon dealt with, and did not usually spread either to other peasants or to neighbouring communes. The old collective solidarity of the *braccianti* was also undermined by the local Fascist Party and unions taking action to exclude migrant 'foreign' labourers (meaning men from the next commune or province) from working locally, a defence of employment which side-stepped the issue of there not being enough jobs to go round and set worker against worker.[13]

In the south and the islands, popular agitation showed a degree of craftiness and premeditation which belied the assumption that protest was unorganised and a kind of spontaneous combustion. Protests occur-

red on holidays or after Sunday mass, occasions when the coming together of groups of people was unlikely to provoke an exceptional police
presence. Women were prominent in collective public demonstrations,
not only to give them a popular flavour, but also to soften or deflect police
intervention when it came to making arrests or forcibly dispersing the
crowd. Marchers carried banners and shouted slogans which simultaneously declared 'Up with Mussolini' and 'Down with the *Podestà*' (the
Fascist mayor), a deliberately confusing combination of loyalty and protest again designed to avoid the march being broken up by the police.[14]

In these examples we are looking at protests with very specific targets
and motivation for discontent which were economic and conjunctural.
The incidence of protest, at a peak in the Depression period 1930–34,
dipped in the years following. The demand was for bread and work, above
all, though in some cases in the south and islands, there was clearly an
accumulation of popular grievances against falling wages and agricultural
prices coinciding with increased municipal taxation and duties on property, consumer goods and utilities. This spread the distress around. For
example, in Calabria in 1930–1, practically the whole population of some
rural communes was involved in protests. Again it was characteristic of
the south and islands that popular rage was directed against the *Podestà*
and the local administration, who were condemned for their negligence
or inability to service the community.

What did protesting for or over material needs actually mean in conditions of dictatorship? For De Felice, of course, nothing at all beyond the
economic sphere. For the New Left historians of the late 1970s and early
1980s, if protest was 'active', then it was 'political', against the regime.[15]
Workers in factories and farms striking for higher wages were waging a
political battle against Fascism. This linking of the economic and the
political is intelligible only because of the repressiveness of the regime:
since strikes were illegal, workers knew that stopping work would lead to
police intervention and possible police sanctions against strikers. Looking
again at those popular tumults in the south and islands, there was no
evident and stated political challenge to the Fascist government as such,
and nor could there be, because that would invite immediate and severe
repression. Professing loyalty to Mussolini while going for the *Podestà* was
the only way to stage a public protest at all in such circumstances. This
was the thinking behind the ways protest was camouflaged: the protesters
were pushing to the limits of what was permissible and possible in the
circumstances.

The focusing of popular resentment on the local centre of power was
typical of the traditional mode of protest adopted in southern communities, and the same kinds of tactics and devices had been employed to fox

the Bourbon as well as the Fascist police. Such continuity would suggest that much of southern protest in the 1930s was the recurrence of long-standing antagonism to any governmental authority, the Fascist included. This was the case since Fascism had 'conquered' the south after 1922 by coming to terms with the local notables and hence not challenging the traditional social and land tenure system, which was at the root of peasant grievances. What made the Fascist government unpopular at this particular juncture was the impact of its deflationary policies on agriculture from the late 1920s onwards. In this light, it seems casuistry to regard protest against the effects of government policy as 'non-political' when the protesters were forced by repression to dissemble their motives and simply because the Fascist state was not put in mortal danger.

Other forms of popular protest seemed to lack the specific and contingent targeting of matters related directly to material conditions of life and the daily struggle for existence. Police reports monitored a range of recurrent small-scale individual and group protests: anti-Fascist and pro-Communist slogans and symbols daubed on walls; scurrilous jokes and puns scrawled in public and factory toilets; *braccianti* singing the 'Internationale' as they walked to work at dawn; workers the worse for drink or pretending to be, bawling out subversive songs and making obscene gestures at figures of authority; factory and farm workers wearing red ties or scarves on what used to be May Day. These incidents were scarcely life-threatening for the regime. But they were indicative of undeniably anti-Fascist attitudes, especially when, whatever the mode of protest adopted, the anonymous protesters actually spelt out their attachment to the goal and ideal of proletarian revolution, using names (Lenin, Stalin) and symbols (hammer and sickle) evocative of the Bolshevik Revolution and the USSR first employed by the working-class movement during the 'Two Red Years' of 1919–20.

Communist activists were undoubtedly directly responsible for some of this explicitly anti-Fascist activity, but not all such behaviour indicated planning or incitement. It went on even when the party's internal cells were inactive. Again, protest of this kind was obviously 'political' in its content and made so by the police's response: an agricultural labourer was sentenced to three years' *confino* in 1930 for singing the 'Internationale' at work.[16] When the police were bound to monitor the funeral of a local 'subversive',[17] mourners attending with a red buttonhole knew the likely consequences of what would be taken as a provocation. By choosing to do so and almost inviting police intervention, they challenged authority, asserting in a tiny way their opposition to and rejection of fascism. Such dissent was also symbolic, a matter of gestures, once again reflecting the force of repression. In a repressive climate, gestures of defiance were all that were left and there could be no expectation that such acts would actually change anything.

Some parts of Emilia-Romagna and Tuscany, which were socialist bastions before and immediately after the First World War, were later strongholds of the anti-Fascist resistance in 1943–5 and the 'red belts' of the Italian Republic after 1945. Workers' allegiance and votes had shifted in many such cases from the Socialist to the Communist Party. Thus the political continuity from the pre-Fascist to the post-Fascist period suggests a recent tradition of popular subversiveness pushed on to the defensive by fascism but nevertheless persisting and surviving.[18]

There is still the danger of portraying these forms of popular protest in too polarised a way: as a negligible threat to the regime and therefore of no significance, or as a permanent and unyielding anti-Fascism. The value of the oral testimonies of workers who lived through Fascism is what they reveal of people's everyday conduct and attitudes in relation to a regime which through its organisations and personnel increasingly attempted to cross the boundaries between the political and the private, and 'politicise' the latter.

This was a regime difficult to keep at arm's length. It took notice of and action against people who shared a joke about Mussolini or who gossiped in the market place about high food prices and shortages. It offered material blandishments to workers and their families in various forms, such as welfare, recreation and sport. It wanted to put workers' children in the uniform of the youth organisations, themselves an opening to other material opportunities like holiday trips and summer camps. The Communist Party came to recognise that the regime was, if only for lack of alternatives, organising among workers, and that the way to regain contact with workers and their lives was to infiltrate rather than ostracise Fascist organisations.

The enforced absence of alternatives meant that fascism was the norm, the given for young workers whose age and formation during the regime distanced them from the violent anti-proletarian origins of fascism. Similar inferences about the potential openness to Fascist penetration could be made of newly urbanised immigrant labour,[19] and workers who had not previously been unionised. Even older workers, with good memories of the recent past, had to live in the present. It might well be distasteful to join the Fascist syndicate, but membership often provided some guarantee of employment, some access to low-level material aid, and redress in a situation where there was literally no other recourse, no other way of even marginally improving things.

The oral accounts, although they do not often touch on 'political' matters, provide several interesting examples of a sort of interaction with the regime, of small compromises with 'power', such as the worker who did not want his son to join the Fascist youth organisation but nevertheless gave way because it helped to prolong his schooling.[20] We are given here small signs of a pragmatic acceptance of what was on offer, a kind of selective susceptibility. Fascist Party membership might be ruled out, but joining the less overtly political Dopolavoro, the regime's umbrella organisation for 'after-work' leisure and recreation, or receiving party-organised welfare, was acceptable.

Rejection of and discontent with some areas of the regime's activity could co-exist with acceptance and enjoyment of others, an ambivalent mix of attitudes. The ambiguous character of 'cultural resistance' expressed in the joke, the gesture, symbolically and momentarily challenging authority while simultaneously acknowledging and accepting its existence, could perhaps usefully be extended, if only by analogy, to the whole range of workers' attitudes and actions during the period of the Fascist regime. This 'mix' does not appear positive enough to constitute what De Felice has called 'consent'. But given that the elements of rejection or disapproval of the regime did not lead to a general rejection of the system until the Second World War, and did not, in the PCI's phrase, break Fascist 'legality',[21] then the 'mix' might plausibly be understood as 'consensus'.

11 Saints and heroines: re-writing the history of Italian women in the Resistance

Perry R. Willson

Frida [Malan] . . . dressed as a country bride, with a handful of confetti (and a different groom each time) used to go round bars in working class areas pretending to celebrate her wedding, in reality contacting union groups.[1]

The story of the much married Frida is but one example of the great variety of roles played by Italian women in the Resistance movement during the Second World War. The stories of their involvement are tales of bravery, humanity, pathos and fear, include acts of courage or simple pity, and are often both moving and inspiring. It is no wonder that many of them have described this as either the most terrible or the most wonderful period of their lives. These were indeed terrifying and exciting times.

Although most of the copious historiography of this formative period of modern Italian history focuses on male activities, many highly courageous women were involved. Accurate statistics do not exist. Women have proved more modest than men in coming forward to claim the diplomas and medals later awarded to partisans, and formation commanders often proved unwilling to propose their names. Written records are scarce, and assumptions about the primacy of the armed aspects of Resistance activities have shaped official figures, making it appear that far fewer women than men played a significant role. If, however, a broader view is taken of what constitutes Resistance activity, this gender disparity disappears, and it has been estimated that the women may have numbered as many as two million.[2] Furthermore, unlike many of the men who got involved because they were faced with a choice between being called up to fight a war they no longer believed in and the life of a partisan, the women were mostly real volunteers, who could have chosen to do nothing. Women from all age groups, social classes and geographical areas of occupied Italy took part and were present in the work of every political grouping within the Resistance.

But roles were highly gendered. Women who were fighting members of armed formations were exceptional. Some took direct action such as opening sealed trains to release prisoners on their way to concentration camps, transporting bombs, or even personally killing Germans or Fascists; but most were involved in other ways, only some of which were connected to armed activities. Large numbers worked as couriers, carrying messages and anti-fascist literature concealed in bicycle tyres, shopping baskets or handbags. Some typed news-sheets, sheltered deserters or Jews, and collected money, clothes and food for the fighting groups. They led protests for food and participated in the huge strikes in northern factories, at times taking the lead. They nursed the sick or wounded, prepared and buried the dead (often secretly and against German orders), did the painful task of informing and assisting the relatives of those fallen in combat, and performed innumerable acts of symbolic defiance such as laying flowers on the tombs of those killed in action. Much of the extremely dangerous work of spying was done by women, work for which they were particularly well suited due to the relative lack of suspicion they aroused. They frequently escorted deserters or escaped prisoners across road blocks. From November 1943 some of these activities, particularly the collection of food and money and the making of clothing, were carried out in special groups – the *gruppi di difesa della donna e per l'assistenza ai combattenti della libertà*,[3] comprising women of various political persuasions.

Despite the apparent traditionalism of female Resistance roles which saw women knitting socks and nursing the sick while men carried out armed raids, laid bombs and camped out in the mountains, this period did see a 'widening of the female sphere'. For many women this was a time when the urgency of the situation enabled them to transgress the boundaries of 'respectable' feminine behaviour. The job of courier, for example, often involved travelling alone in unknown areas, meeting members of the opposite sex and going out after nightfall.

The large numbers of oral and written testimonies collected from women involved in this movement record the fear, the tragedy, the grief and the moments of hunger and despair. But they also record moments of great euphoria, the joy of getting a message through against all odds, the satisfaction of a job well done, relief at a lucky escape, the feeling of solidarity and unity against a common enemy. Such testimonies make moving reading. Even those involved in the most seemingly humble ways – such as providing food or refuge for those on the run – risked their own lives. Some of the accounts are characterised by great modesty. Some women do not even give their own names, or spend their interview time recording the exploits of others. Others recount with pride what they did and for most this was a formative moment in their life histories.

The collection of testimonies has been prompted by the great interest in the history of the Resistance during the post-war period. In volume alone, writings about women and the Resistance still far outnumber studies of women's experience in the much longer Fascist period: a disproportionate interest which reflects the huge symbolic importance of the Resistance in the history of the Italian Republic, and the claims that have been made of it. Although varying in its finer points according to the politics of the commentator and the period in which he or she wrote, the Resistance has frequently been presented as a purge of Fascism, showing that there was another, alternative Italy capable of wiping the slate clean after Mussolini's regime.

There has been much debate on the place of the Resistance in Italian history. At various moments, and with various meanings, it has been called such diverse things as a war of liberation, a patriotic war, a class war, a civil war or the second Risorgimento.[4] It has been crucial to the collective process of burying the past and dealing with questions of national guilt. Such questions have undoubtedly been far less traumatic in Italy than in Germany,[5] but the Resistance mythology, more than any other single factor, has contributed to this national ability to avoid certain questions. Despite the fact that the real core of the Resistance – the communists – never got into power, and despite repeated right-wing attempts to discredit the partisan movement, on the whole a Resistance background has been of benefit to the image of public figures, political parties and movements. A whole chain of institutes exist throughout Italy dedicated to celebrating and analysing the history of the Resistance through research, publications and exhibitions.[6]

The writing and re-writing of Resistance history has often reflected present politics and many have used it as a means of legitimising or discrediting political viewpoints. The intense politicisation of this subject has meant that there has been little pretence of objectivity.[7] In some ways this has made the debate on the Resistance rather sterile and repetitive. Positions have been so entrenched due to attacks on the Resistance legacy. During the Cold War, for example, some ex-partisans were prosecuted for their Resistance activities. Such attacks on the very acceptability of the Resistance rendered it something of a 'sacred cow' which could not be discussed, only celebrated. Even today some politicians make great use of it as a symbol, declaring themselves as 'for' or 'against' the Resistance as the underlying national symbol which legitimises the Italian political system.[8] Only now, with the changes wrought by the end of the Cold War in Italy, does the debate appear to be freeing up.

If the Resistance could bestow political legitimacy on an entire nation, it is hardly surprising that women wished to share in the citizenship this conferred. The way in which women's role in the Resistance has been

remembered has similarly been shaped by political trends. Women, however, have responded to this national mythology in a gender-specific way.
In particular, the Resistance has often been presented as not just demar-
cating fascism from democracy, but as ushering in a new era of greater
emancipation which the female partisans had earned for post-war
women.

Early days: saints and heroines

Even before the liberation of Italy was complete, the heroines of the
Resistance began to be celebrated and commemorated in a style which
was to set the tone for years to come. During a speech addressed to the
delegates of the First National Conference of Communist Women, the
party leader Palmiro Togliatti argued that the Resistance marked the first
real entry of Italian women on to the stage of history. He said of women
who had died in the Resistance that:

their heroic sacrifice must be made known . . . it is your duty to make them so
popular that every Italian woman knows their names. If I might make a sugges-
tion, I'd like to see millions of colour pictures of these women made so that they
can be given out to ordinary women to keep together with their pictures of saints.
These women died for you, for your emancipation. They made the victory of
women's cause certain, because they have proved to the entire nation that Italian
women . . . are capable of contributing, in a front-line position, to the new history
of Italy . . . Carried forward by the guiding example of these martyrs, Italian
women will know how to emancipate themselves from all backwardness and all
slavery. They will know how to be at the forefront of the construction of a new
democratic regime. [9]

Such bold and optimistic words were typical of the dramatic period at the
end of the war, but Togliatti's speech does exemplify some of the huge
claims that were being made at the time about the impact of women's
Resistance role on post-war politics. These heroines were to be the new
female saints. In the new Italy, where Communists and Catholics would
stand together against the Fascist menace, the martyred saint would be
flanked by the martyred Resistance heroine. The 'canonisation' of such
women, which continued in a spate of celebratory publications after the
war, formed a weighty and problematic legacy for the post-war generation
of women which remained substantially unchallenged until the 1970s.
Saints, by definition, are somewhat unreal figures, hard to emulate, who
can only with great difficulty be criticised.

  The business of 'saint-creation' began rapidly, and indeed was already
under way by the time of Togliatti's speech.[10] Women's 'contribution'
and 'sacrifice' began to be celebrated in newspapers and magazines and in

other publications, mostly hagiographic pamphlets like the aptly named *Eroine del secondo Risorgimento*, published in 1944.[11] Written in a dramatically heroic style, this was dedicated to commemorating women who had died. For a number of years after hostilities ended the themes and style of language of this pamphlet were emulated in innumerable other texts. Thus the heroic personal characteristics of the 'martyrs', their bravery, their essential femininity, and their contribution to the nation were presented. Such writings often used the category 'woman' loosely in a way that suggested that all women had been involved in the Resistance. They also frequently referred to women in terms of their relationship to men, as mothers, sisters and wives rather than as simple individuals.[12] But despite such limitations, these texts did emphasise women's bravery, patriotism and dignity, and quickly began to talk of equal rights.

Meanwhile, many early Resistance commemorations not explicitly dedicated to women tended to ignore, minimise or even denigrate their role. In this early period the emphasis was very much on recording the role of the perceived leaders, particularly Communists, few of whom were female. But it was also due to the backlash against the emancipatory vision of the Resistance which set in almost immediately with many, including some male ex-partisans, placing a renewed emphasis on women's domestic role.[13] Central to this backlash were numerous accusations about the sexual immorality of women who had been active in armed formations. Such attitudes also permeated much of the avalanche of literary works inspired by the Resistance, many of which appeared in the first ten years after the war. In Italo Calvino's famous fictional depiction of the life of a partisan band, *Il sentiero dei nidi di ragno*, first published in 1947, for example, there are only two sketchily described female 'characters'. One is a prostitute who sleeps with Germans. The other, who lives with the partisans, causes endless trouble, including the burning down of their hideout because the leader of the band is sexually distracted by her presence. In this account the Resistance was a man's world where survival was apparently possible without so much as a courier to supply them, and where women figure largely as the subjects of the men's conversations and dreams, or as intruders – a hindrance to the 'real' Resistance.[14]

Such depictions of women in one of the bestsellers of Resistance literature is some indication of the problems they faced in trying to assert the importance of their role. Much of the literature echoes such themes, portraying the Resistance as an all-male culture where women appear only as objects of male sexuality, both 'other' and a threat to the Resistance. The equation of women with sex discouraged many from coming forward to tell their stories.

Such considerations must have weighed on Renata Viganò in her choice of heroine for her compelling novel *L'Agnese va a morire* first published in 1949.[15] Viganò sidesteps this issue neatly by casting as her main protagonist a middle-aged barely literate village washerwoman, and making constant references to her lack of physical beauty, her aged appearance and her heaviness, thereby unequivocally avoiding any sexual potential in her encounters with male partisans.[16] The novel is an evocative account of how a woman with very narrow horizons could react to the invasion of her country and be drawn into the Resistance by a chain of events. In the course of the novel she grows in stature, taking on an increasingly responsible role in the provisioning and maintenance of her partisan band. Far and away one of the most positive literary representations of this topic, Agnese is a heroic, powerful and dignified figure, who knows right from wrong, and who is always brave and modest.

Apart from its literary merits, *Agnese* should also be seen as an example of didactic celebration at its very best. It was far more likely to succeed in conveying a positive vision of the Resistance to future generations than many of the more tedious conference proceedings (*Agnese* sold well, won a literary prize, and was translated into fourteen languages). Indeed it would be a mistake to set fictional narratives in a totally separate category from other writing, since the borders between 'fictional' and 'historical writing' are fragile in Resistance historiography. Viganò herself wrote much later that Agnese was a 'real' person, in the sense of a composite, emblematic figure representing the actual experience of thousands of women.[17] Similarly, as Penelope Morris has noted, supposedly 'true' autobiographical accounts – in themselves another important genre for remembering women's role in the Resistance – are actually no more than a reconstruction of the past. Much of Giovanna Zangrandi's 'diary' of the Resistance, for example, which she claimed to have written at the time, dated from after the war.[18]

The Resistance generated a veritable spate of such autobiographical writing as many women felt legitimised by the exceptional nature of the period to write and eventually publish their diaries and autobiographies. The majority of these were published in the 1950s when remembering the Resistance moved on from mainly commemorating the dead to include also those who survived. Many of these accounts interweave intensely personal and subjective considerations with what they see as 'historical facts and events'. And although they ostensibly wrote to record the latter, Marina Zancan has convincingly argued that the real motivation for much of this writing was a consciousness of the writer's own value, and the feeling that this was a moment when things were opening up for women.[19]

Equally emotionally charged but often far less exciting and readable are the other types of writings devoted to women's role in the Resistance which appeared in the first two decades after the war. This period, when Italy lay in the frozen shadow of the Cold War, was one of political deadlock with the Christian Democrats maintaining a stranglehold on Italian politics, whilst the Communists remained in the political wilderness despite considerable electoral support. Meanwhile, the Resistance was solemnly celebrated on each anniversary of the Liberation.[20] Such rememberings usually recalled the cross-party Resistance against fascism. The driving force behind many of these occasions was the Communist Party, forced to reiterate the importance of anti-fascism and its own central role in it as the foundation stone of the Republic. This was a defensive counter-argument against those who now presented communism not fascism as the real danger. A substantial proportion of the publications on women in the Resistance stem from such conferences. Some are products of research projects inspired by, or commissioned by, celebratory committees. Many of the writers were either protagonists themselves or representatives of political parties. Many were both.

Such celebratory volumes all followed more or less the same pattern. Generally taking a fairly narrow view of what constituted Resistance activity, they tended to remember female partisans through such things as scraps of oral testimony, statistics, pictures, 'exemplary lives', letters and documents.[21] Written in a direct, emotive, and often heroic style, to commemorate rather than discuss, these books avoid any uncomfortable or contradictory aspects. Women are normally presented as making a 'contribution' to the 'real' (i.e. male and armed) Resistance. This is reinforced by the fact that women are usually remembered in separate books and figure little in the 'general' histories of the Resistance.

Re-reading many of these speeches and articles today, it is striking how almost formal they seem in their heroic conventions. Their lack of intimate detail or contradictions renders the protagonists more symbolic than real, and makes them dull reading compared with some literary works or the full-length autobiographies such as Ada Gobetti's *Diario partigiano*.[22] Their rather empty and rhetorical tone is at least in part due to their explicit didactic intent. That the young must learn the moral values of the Resistance was repeated again and again, and frequently ex-partisans gave this as their reason for coming forward to testify about their own role.[23] However, exactly what these values were is more debatable. Speeches often referred to the values of the Resistance with great vagueness. Many stressed liberty as a core value, but the actual definition of this depended on the political viewpoint of the speaker.

Despite the persistence of the commemorative approach, discussion became a little more sophisticated in the 1960s. Although the simple narration of heroic acts and deeds continued, there was also more recognition of the different types of women involved and the range of their roles. The best example of this new approach is *Mille Volte No!*, published in 1965. In commemorative vein, and largely heroic in style, it contained a vast number of short extracts from the testimonies of women partisans, with each chapter introduced by a famous male partisan. As such it followed a well-trodden path, but it was a broader book than its predecessors because it was not limited to one geographical area or type of woman, and showed some of the variety of female Resistance roles from gun-toting in a partisan brigade to laying out the dead.

Despite the homogeneously commemorative tone of this material, some of the better examples of the genre during the 1960s did try to be more analytical and address new issues: why women got involved; why their contributions were so hidden; how innovative a phenomenon this was; on what terms the Resistance itself tried to mobilise women;[24] and what women actually did. By this time even the protagonists themselves were beginning publicly to reflect more on what the values were. Yet such new attempts to rethink the past were not backed up by any serious research, and there was still far too much uncritical quotation from testimonies, reproduction of documents, and the description of 'facts' and 'events', rather than analysis. And there was still a reluctance to criticise the male members of the Resistance.

A legacy of emancipation?

One common theme in much of this commemorative literature is the idea that there was a clear relationship between the Resistance and women's emancipation. The most obvious evidence of this was, of course, the vote, granted to women 'in recognition of their Resistance contribution'. The news-sheets and leaflets produced by Resistance women themselves included calls for women's suffrage and for equal pay which shows that, among the female leaders at least, there was a commitment to working for greater emancipation. The Resistance was the first time large numbers of women were involved in an important political movement, and, as we have seen, it took many women outside their traditional sphere. This was a break with the past. In the 1950s and 1960s many repeatedly emphasised the compatibility of the aims of the Resistance as a whole with women's emancipation and presented this as but one of the general aims of Resistance activists of both sexes.[25] Some even went so far as to argue complacently that it was enough to be a member of the Resistance to be more or less automatically a supporter of women's emancipation.[26]

Such optimism about the emancipatory potential of the Resistance, it must be admitted, was more often found in male commentators. Some women, even as early as the mid 1940s, struck a note of greater realism, recognising that even men 'on their side' could in this respect be less than perfect. Communist women, for example, did not take long to begin to admonish their comrades for a lack of interest in women's issues.[27] By the 1960s even many women at celebratory conferences were bitterly stressing the limits of emancipation in the Republic.[28]

Early publications are rather vague about the exact nature of the link between Resistance and emancipation. But gradually, especially in the 1960s, there was more attempt to define it. The emancipatory thrust of the Resistance was seen as a matter for all classes and generations of women, and for those of all political and religious beliefs. It was portrayed as a benefit for all of society,[29] an essential element of democracy and liberty, and not in conflict with male privilege. Women, after all, had stood up to be counted by helping the men, whilst maintaining their feminine specificity. Implicit in all of this was the idea that women had won the right to equality and freedom by contributing to an essentially male activity, namely, armed warfare. The Resistance version of emancipation was claimed to be a more advanced notion than turn-of-the-century feminism which was condemned as too intellectual, class-bound and overly concerned with a few narrow issues. The Resistance definition of emancipation now appears somewhat naive and optimistic. Too much emphasis was placed on simply winning formal equal rights while male roles went unchallenged, but at the time few voices were putting forward more advanced ideas. The official position of the Communist Party, for example, included a vigorous defence of the institution of the family and a belief that women needed only equal legal rights and access to employment to be free.

Moreover, cross-party unity meant celebrating the Resistance with Catholics. Although female suffrage is welcomed, particularly as many of the new electorate voted Christian Democrat, the term 'emancipation' is markedly absent in Catholic Resistance commemorations. Instead women's sacrifice, humility and suffering are praised and their activities presented more as acts of Christian charity than political actions.[30]

In practice, of course, the Resistance failed in many respects to open up a new period of great emancipation for women. With Christian Democracy firmly in power, many Fascist laws, such as the ban on abortion, remained on the statute books, and the post-war period was marked in many aspects of women's lives by continuity rather than change. Many elements of even formal legal equality had to wait for the 1970s.

But in one respect at least, the language of commemoration differed little between Catholics and the left. Much of this writing, whether written by female resisters or other commentators, constantly emphasised that at heart these women acted as mothers. This imagery was so pervasive as to render difficult the choice of an illustrative quotation. It surfaced in all the genres from literary representations (perhaps most memorably in Viganò's 'mamma Agnese'[31]) through celebratory speeches to oral testimony. Women were presented, and presented themselves, as acting as mothers, whether they were sheltering an escaped Allied prisoner in their homes or camping out with an armed brigade in the mountains.[32]

The wind of change: feminism in the 1970s

In the following decade, however, much of this tradition was challenged. Some pure commemoration continued, which saw women as a largely undifferentiated category about which generalisations could be made.[33] Other work concentrated on gathering more 'facts' about women's role without really adding any fresh insights.[34] Many such books tended to be amateurish and the 'analytical' or 'general' sections were often closely based on previously published texts.[35] Others were yet more of the 'personal testimony' genre.[36] Commemorative conferences continued with programmes dominated by speakers from political parties.

But from the mid-1970s there was an identifiable wind of change, following the emergence of one of the strongest feminist movements in western Europe. This led to a far more critical, and at times even denunciatory, analysis, amounting less to a rethink than a total rejection of Resistance values. Whereas in the previous period most of those who wrote about women in the Resistance were men, now the field was invaded by a new generation of female historians, passionately dedicated to addressing the issues in new ways. Some asserted that women historians writing as women could shed new, gender-specific, light on the past. Most previous publications were dismissed as either the product of male prejudice or empty celebration. The new history stressed how women had been an intrinsic part of the movement, rather than 'contributors' to the 'real' Resistance'. Without them, it was now pointed out, partisans could not have survived in the mountains, nor operated in cities and lowland areas. Gradually this led to the emergence of a new vision, directly centred on women, now seen as important in their own right. The focus shifted perceptibly, eventually making anti-fascism a topic for women's history, rather than women just a sub-section of Resistance historiography. Although some of these new works were fairly amateurish in their approach, others began to show an interest in questions of methodology. Oral history still predominated and some of the best of the new writing, such as *Compagne*, included discussions of how interviewees were selected and the problems of the reliability of memory.[37]

A hallmark of this period is the great attention paid to the emancipatory legacy of the Resistance. There is a world of difference between a book like *La questione femminile nella politica del PCI 1921–1963*,[38] a party-political account published by communist women in 1972, which takes the emancipatory potential of the Resistance for granted, and publications of only a few years later. The feminists did not abandon the idea of the Resistance as a watershed, a moment when horizons broadened and women's issues were put on the political agenda, but they began to stress the limitations of its challenge to traditional gender roles.[39] With the iconoclasm characteristic of the 'great cultural revolution' of the 1970s, the new generation jettisoned the notion that the Resistance underpinned their right to liberation. This new critical stance on the sexual politics of the Resistance opened up debate and eventually marked the end of complacent statements about how much the Resistance had done for women. The new feminists broke with their 'foremothers' on the question of men, and the attitudes of male partisan leaders were subjected to scrutiny, often unfavourable.

Perhaps the best-known example of this new feminist writing is *La Resistenza taciuta*.[40] This fascinating book is justly regarded as a milestone in Italian women's history. Admittedly, as a local study using oral testimony which mobilised the past in the service of present politics, there was some continuity with its predecessors. But its long in-depth testimonies were far richer and more complex than the brief, heroic fragments used in many earlier volumes. They considered the morality and even the humour of the period, and presented women's fears and contradictions as well as their bravery. Rejecting the 'male-female unity' approach, this book argued that women had been doubly betrayed, both by the reconstruction and by male partisans. It stressed how many men wanted women back in the home after the war, and there is much emphasis on how little commitment male partisans of all parties had to female emancipation.

Many men were affronted by such arguments. In an article on women and the Resistance in Liguria published in 1979, for example, Giuseppe Benelli accused the feminists of reducing the history of the Resistance to purely a part of the history of feminism, and argued against separating the role of women in the Resistance from the history of the movement as a whole.[41] Men such as Benelli (and some women) were made distinctly uncomfortable by feminist criticisms of male partisans. Attacks on the Resistance by neo-fascists were somehow easier to deal with than 'disloyal' condemnations from troublesome young feminists.

But opposition to the feminist position also came from some female partisans themselves, who, without denying that the Republic had given women far less than emancipation, were at pains to defend a more unified vision of the Resistance. Gisella Floreanini, for example, in 1979, argued strongly that the relationship between men and women had become more equal during the armed struggle.[42] She and other ex-partisans stressed the strength of the unitary nature of the Resistance, in contrast to the new largely separatist feminist politics. The Resistance, they asserted, was what made the Italian feminist tradition different from feminism in other countries, for Italian women had won the vote by their participation in solidarity and co-operation with men in a movement which transcended party and class.[43]

But others saw things differently, as is clear from *L'altra metà della Resistenza*[44] – the proceedings of a conference held in 1978 – where ex-partisan women met with younger feminists. Some of the ex-partisans' speeches cover familiar ground, little different from innumerable speeches of past decades.[45] Some expressed distress at feminist attacks on Resistance men. Others, however, infused with a renewed desire to investigate the past and really show in what numbers and strength 'women were there too', praised the new politics and re-evaluated their own experiences, casting a more critical eye over the role of their male comrades-in-struggle. This new approach was neatly summed up by Isotta Gaeta who, after praising the valiant role of many women in the Resistance side by side with men, asserted that: 'today this is no longer enough', and argued that the attitudes of some male partisans had limited the ability of the Resistance to achieve its great potential as a vehicle of social and political change.[46]

Overall, despite the reticence in some quarters, feminism irreversibly reset the agenda for discussions of women and the Resistance, and indeed of the Resistance as a whole. It paved the way for a deeper understanding of individual Resistance activism by placing it in the context of life stories, helped redefine the definition of what constituted Resistance activities, and challenged the overly heroic vision of many Resistance men. All these trends were ultimately potentially enriching for the historiography of the Resistance in general.

In terms of women themselves, one aspect of the new approach was a re-thinking of the question of motivations. Motherly feelings were not, as might be imagined, simply jettisoned, but there was some attempt to re-interpret the meaning of this.[47] Others focused on how problematic this emphasis was, noting how the stress on women's maternal role had contributed to their exclusion from post-war public life.[48] Many preferred to put this aside and look instead at the range of factors which could mobilise women. With the aim of disproving the oft-repeated idea that women were mobilised because they were following their fathers, brothers or lovers into the struggle, they tried to uncover women's autonomous reasons for activism. These might arise from personal experiences of the war, pacifism, class politics, humanitarian views or a desire to stake a place in a man's world.[49] Others explored how motivations related to the specific socio-economic characteristics of particular regions.[50] Some of these analyses were perhaps a little infused by the romanticism of the years of 'sisterhood', which assumed a whole string of supposedly female virtues such as 'spontaneity, a rejection of self-interested calculation, a sense of justice, a passionate capacity to love and suffer'.[51]

The late 1970s and early 1980s formed a turning point in debates on women and the Resistance with a host of new challenging issues raised and debated. But, with a few exceptions,[52] the discussion was still very much in the vein of 'let the protagonists speak for themselves'; and most of the research continued to be done, with varying levels of skill, by amateur historians such as students, ex-partisans themselves and even schoolchildren.

'Women's history' in the 1980s

The next few years, however, saw an increased professionalisation and the emergence of 'women's history' as a small but assertive section of historical study in Italy. Rejecting the idea of simply adding women on to the major events of 'male history' it has striven to set its own, separate agenda. This agenda did not, at first, include the Resistance. Although some work continued to be published, including a modest stream of purely commemorative texts even in the late 1980s,[53] the flood of publications on women and the Resistance abated to the point of an almost pathological avoidance of this subject by the new generation of feminist historians. *Memoria*, for example, the Italian journal of women's history, published by a feminist collective from 1981 to 1993, paid it little attention.[54]

The reasons for such neglect were complex, and part of a general decline in interest in the Resistance shared by many historians, both male and female. Clearly one element was boredom with the subject for a generation which grew up with tedious, pompous celebrations. Many feminists now preferred to leave the saints and their canonisers to their

own devices. If women's history had hitherto been devoted almost exclusively to this topic, then they wished to consider new questions, even
though it was clear that in many ways the Resistance had still only been
poorly studied. As Laura Mariani commented in 1989: 'everything seems
already said and everything still seems to be said'.[55]

New directions: subjectivity and the war

The 1990s, however, have seen a radical change in this picture with a
veritable renaissance of Resistance research by feminist historians, much
of it both serious and innovative. The main reason for a revival of interest
in what only a few years ago had become a truly unfashionable subject is
the political situation. One aspect of the enormous political changes,
largely produced by the end of the Cold War, has been the inclusion of
'neo-fascists' in government for the first time since the war, a fundamental and impossible challenge to a political system supposedly legitimised
by the events of 1943–5. Such changes made many rush, once again, to
the defence of the Resistance legacy.

That this had implications for women was underscored when Catholic
fundamentalist Irene Pivetti, shortly after becoming Speaker of the
Chamber of Deputies early in 1994, asserted in a press interview that
Mussolini had done some good things for Italian women. Such crude
historical revisionism and the fact that 1995 was the fiftieth anniversary of
the Liberation, have stimulated a dramatic revival of interest. Although
some of the new debate simply attempts to use or discredit the Resistance
legacy for new political ends, it has also produced some excellent new
work. The debate now seems unprecedentedly open, in part due to the
fragmentation of political certainties since the fall of the Berlin Wall.[56]

Over the last few years, numerous new research projects, supported by
their local Resistance institutes, have mushroomed around Italy and their
initial findings have been aired in a series of conferences and in a 'travelling seminar'. Some of this work is clearly focused on the Resistance,[57]
but most concentrates on subjective attitudes to the war. Many of these
projects draw on literary techniques, with historians studying diaries,
letters, memoirs, and fictional representations as 'texts' rather than
'documents'. Given the relative lack of enthusiasm in Italy for pure
textual analysis, however, those studying these forms of female autobiography have largely grounded their analysis in a firm belief in a link
between text and 'reality'.[58]

Oral history, however, remains the main source, but now it is used less
to simply record 'what happened' than to address issues of subjectivity
and memory.[59] Some historians are treating oral testimonies as 'narra-

tives' and using tools borrowed from other disciplines, mainly literary study, anthropology and psychology to analyse the symbolic meanings of acts, emotions and feelings, and how these are remembered and recounted. Such studies look, for example, at how interviewees remember fear and courage, and their use of modesty and pride, jokes, understatement, or the recourse to dialect forms or metaphor as ways of telling difficult or painful tales.

This revival of interest is not unproblematic. It could be argued that a disproportionate amount has been written on this period already, and the historiography of women's Resistance is still impoverished by a lack of understanding of the historical context. It seems limiting to be going into one single aspect – subjectivity – of one very brief period in such depth when little is known about so much else. Even the new studies of the war tend to concentrate mostly on the occupation period, with much less interest on the early years of hostilities – perhaps yet another example of a desire to avoid questions of national guilt. The use of literary tools of analysis has brought many new insights. As Luisa Passerini rightly notes, sometimes as much can be told about how someone experienced something by their silences and their use of language as by what they actually say.[60] Yet some of this work does seem to reveal more about narrative technique than the Resistance itself.[61]

On the whole, however, much of this research is extremely interesting and the use of such innovative and interdisciplinary approaches has shed new light on this period. Undoubtedly the most influential of the new work is that of Anna Bravo, who set much of the agenda for the new studies by demonstrating that it was possible to look at a tired old topic in fresh and innovative ways. Her research on written and oral memories of the war by women in Turin[62] suggests some useful avenues of enquiry for Resistance historians. Bravo highlights the widespread use of what she calls the 'maternal register' in how women recollect and give meaning to their memories of the war. Interviewees, whether actual mothers or not, repeatedly used maternity as a way of making sense of what they had lived through and done. Such 'mothering' extended beyond the biological family to become what Bravo calls 'mass *maternage*', where many female Resistance activities were explained in terms of assistance to symbolic sons.

Bravo's findings on the pervasiveness of the maternal register lead her to be pessimistic about the impact of wars on gender roles.[63] She challenges the idea, prevalent in some writings about countries such as Britain, that wars lead to greater female emancipation. Constant reference to the maternal image does suggest that the war did little to liberate women, and can help explain why women demanded so little after the war, as maternity is a difficult terrain for demanding rewards. 'Mothers' are supposed to give selflessly. However, Bravo's interpretation of maternal symbolism goes beyond this. Taking a complex approach she sees the maternal image as full of contradictory meanings such as devotion and possession, sacrifice and power, a mobiliser of men for war, or a symbol of peace. Of course this choice of symbol partly reflects Catholic maternalist ideology and the marian tradition which legitimises the prolonged power of the mother over the son, but Bravo argues that, more importantly, women stressed motherhood because it was the strongest female image on which they could draw, and the only socially acceptable one in which women could be stronger than men. This image was also appealing as it was comfortably asexual.

According to Bravo, the use of the image of symbolic mothers helping symbolic sons in the shape of deserters is also a way of recounting the war which avoids problems of national guilt. The childlike image of the deserter was one of innocence, of victims betrayed by bad leadership and saved by women, despite the fact that, in reality, many of these young, vulnerable 'sons' had shed blood as soldiers. Once they became partisans, however, they could be remembered with admiration rather than pity. Thus on one level the Resistance could be seen as a kind of recuperation of Italian masculinity.

Although Bravo's work is densely argued and is considerably less accessible than much of the work discussed so far, its importance is undeniable. It suggests some ways in which historians might rethink the pervasive emphasis on maternity, an emphasis which suggested that women were just doing something natural to them.

Other new research tends broadly to concur with at least some of Bravo's hypotheses. Margie Fraser's fascinating research on family and politicisation among left women active in the Resistance in the Veneto[64] confirms the importance of the maternal register in female narratives. She also agrees that in the testimonies she collected this appears as a symbol of strength not weakness. Fraser's own interviewees also recounted similar tales of weak and vulnerable 'symbolic sons' in hiding and active women supplying and rescuing them. However, she also looks at how some women, particularly those who were quite young at the time, recount their experience of the Resistance less as 'mothers' than as 'sisters', an important reminder that Bravo's 'maternal register' explains much, but not everything.

As well as focusing on women's perceptions of their experience and how they recount it now, there is also much interest in shedding new light on the question of motivations: the complex, varied, and sometimes contradictory paths which could lead women to Resistance activism.[65]

Perhaps the most important new aspect, however, is the fact that some historians are beginning to challenge the traditional 'hierarchies of importance' of Resistance activities.

Both Gianni Sciola and Margie Fraser argue that some female Resistance activities dismissed as secondary because they were primarily motivated by 'humanitarian' reasons, should be reassessed. Fraser argues, and illustrates with a careful and subtle reading of her oral testimonies, that the distinction between 'humanitarian' and 'political' is a false one, since many 'merely humanitarian' acts were deeply political in this context. Sciola's work on the Brescian peasantry shows how the traditionally female activity of cleansing and burying the dead could become imbued with new meaning during the war. Its significance lay in the fact that, as Luisa Passerini has argued: 'It becomes essential – and not of secondary or subordinate importance – in a war which aims to refound a civilisation – to perform certain ritual activities which restore a sense of humanity where it has been denied'.[66] These peasant women were defending a moral code which included the absolute need to honour the dead even where this meant defying German and Fascist orders.[67] Such arguments help reposition female roles in the Resistance, showing that these had value not, as earlier work argued, in quantitative terms – the level of support to the implicitly more important fighters – but in qualitative terms of women performing their own, equally important, but different, tasks.

Unlike Fraser's and Sciola's research, however, most of the new work focuses not on Resistance women, nor on those who chose to actively support fascism in its dying moments,[68] but on those who made no clear-cut choice. Their attitudes ranged from passive resistance or active collaboration, to simply waiting the war out, or even helping both sides at different moments. This group, largely ignored by historians up to now in their preoccupation with the Resistance, probably constituted the majority of the population. A consideration of the experiences of such 'ordinary women' is essential to understanding the contradictions and complexities of this period.

This new work looks at a whole host of hitherto ignored themes. Evacuation, for example, was a truly traumatic experience for some who experienced it, evoked in memoirs as a moment of hunger, fear, loss of everything known and leading to total disorientation. It was a time when people were forced to eat wild roots and live in caves, and was referred to in one of the memoirs used in Francesca Koch's work as a 'silent tragedy': silent because history had forgotten it.[69] Many other 'silences' are explored in this new wave of research, such as the experience of those who had witnessed huge massacres.[70] Another important aspect is the theme of confusion about who was the enemy,[71] a problem which illustrates just how much more complex the legacy of the war is than implied in the romanticised celebrations that formerly passed for historical writing. This new work is not looking for victims or heroines, although many personal stories contain elements of both, as women had to cope in a situation which amounted to the virtual disintegration of their world. It was a situation where food was scarce, and where it was far from clear whose side they were on, where the partisans could appear as dangerous as the Germans if they provoked reprisals against the civilian population.

Although this research marks an attempt to get away from a narrow view of the Resistance, its attempts to challenge notions of what constituted resistance itself are equally important. Anna Bravo, for example, draws on the concept of 'civilian resistance', employed by French historians, which broadens out the notion of resistance to include autonomous actions of civilians orientated towards explicitly civilian goals.[72] This type of resistance encompasses actions which entailed neither being in an armed band nor assisting one, but aimed rather at keeping together the fabric of civilised society, defending basic freedoms, and not submitting to the enemy, either physically or mentally, in the situation of occupation.

This concept is extremely useful in understanding the role of women in the opposition to Nazism and Fascism. It underscores the value of numerous female roles not directly aimed at servicing armed fighters, such as the distribution of the clandestine press and the sheltering of Jews and deserters. Nonetheless, the use of the concept of civilian resistance is not without its dangers as it can lead to historians finding resistance where there was none. The term 'resistance' can be stretched so far as to lose its meaning, so that it appears to include even people who were simply waiting for the end of the war.[73] Laura Capobianco, for example, has argued that the concept of civilian resistance has enabled the South to be, at last, included in the history of women and the Resistance,[74] even though her research focuses on women who simply organised their own individual survival and that of their families – activities which seem unrelated to any form of resistance, armed or otherwise. The inclusion of the South is essential to getting a broader picture of women's experience in this period, but it seems telling that historians feel more legitimised to explore this subject if the label 'resistance' can somehow be attached to it.

The work of Angela Scali, too, betrays a similar fascination with this term. She goes so far as to call the strength and endurance, which women drew upon to piece together their lives after a horrendous massacre by the Germans, a form of resistance, albeit an internal, private and individual form of resistance,[75] even though these same women had been peacefully co-existing and co-operating with the occupying troops previously.

Scali's recourse to such terminology illustrates just what an enduringly powerful and emotive term 'resistance' still is, and how difficult it is for historians to get away from the notion that ultimately the history of the war is primarily the history of the Resistance.

Conclusion

Despite the problems that historians have in disentangling themselves from the attractiveness of the Resistance as a concept, and their difficulties in viewing this period through any other lens, much of the new work is very important. It shows what a long path writing about women's role in this period has travelled since Togliatti's speech cited at the beginning of this chapter. Recent research has built on the work begun in the 1970s to explode the myth that the 'real' resisters were largely men who forsook home and family for the armed struggle. Such brave men had a role to play, but it is now clear that they were but one part of a complex story. The new work poses a challenge to the idea that the violent aspects of the Resistance were in fact the most important ones, by placing a new emphasis on the unarmed role of, mainly female, 'civilians'; and by showing the horrors of war divested of the romantic sheen that often clung even to many of the most horrific tales of partisan violence. It recovers the experience of millions of ordinary women. Undoubtedly, in some respects, the preoccupations of the new researchers are no less shaped by current political trends than the previous historiography, but the new approach does feel like the end of rhetoric, and a real sign, perhaps for the first time since the end of the war, that historians are ready to look more dispassionately at this complex and contradictory period. Far from depoliticising the history of this period, however, this research gives a new meaning to the need to remember, for, as the women interviewed by Maria Grazia Camilletti argued,[76] the horrors of war need to be remembered so that they will not be repeated.

Notes

INTRODUCTION

1 The term is from Charles S. Maier, *The Unmasterable Past. History, Holocaust and German National Identity* (Cambridge, Mass. and London), ch. 5; see also Geoff Eley, 'Nazism, Politics and the Image of the Past: Thoughts on the West German *Historikerstreit* 1986–1987', *Past and Present* 121 (1988), pp. 171–208; and Richard J. Evans, *In Hitler's Shadow* (London, 1989).

2 See Detlev J. Peukert, 'Der Deutsche Arbeiterwiderstand 1933–1945', *Aus Politik und Zeitgeschichte: Beilage zur Wochen-Zeitung das Parlament*, B 28-29/79, 14 July 1979, and Peukert, *Inside Nazi Germany. Conformity and Opposition in Everyday Life* (London, 1989), originally published in 1982.

3 Charles S. Maier, *Recasting Bourgeois Europe: Stabilisation in France, Germany and Italy in the Decade after World War I* (Englewood Cliffs, N.J., 1975). See Neil Barrett's contribution in chapter 3.

4 F. L. Carsten, *The Rise of Fascism*, second edition (London, 1982); Stein Ugelvik Larsen, Bernt Hagtvet and Jan Peter Mykelbust (eds.), *Who were the Fascists? Social Roots of European Fascism* (Bergen and New York, 1980); Stanley G. Payne, *A History of Fascism 1914–45* (London, 1997); Peter Sugar, *Native Fascism in the Successor States, 1918–1945* (Santa Barbara, Ca., 1971).

5 Sir Percival Phillips, *The 'Red' Dragon and the Black Shirts. How Italy Found Her Soul. The True Story of the Fascisti Movement* (London, 1922); Richard Griffiths, *Fellow Travellers of the Right: British Enthusiasts for Nazi Germany 1933–39* (London, 1980).

6 A. J. P. Taylor, *The Course of German History: A Survey of the Development of Germany since 1815* (London, 1951, originally published 1945); Daniel Goldhagen, *Hitler's Willing Executioners: Ordinary Germans and the Holocaust* (New York, 1996).

7 *Rot-Weiß-Rot-Buch. Darstellungen, Dokumente und Nachweise zur Geschichte und Vorgeschichte der Okkupation sterrreichs (nach amtlichen Quellen)* (Vienna, 1946); Paul Ginsborg, *A History of Contemporary Italy. Society and Politics 1943–1988* (London, 1990); Hans Rothfels, *Die Deutsche Opposition gegen Hitler. Eine Würdigung* (Krefeld, 1949); see especially, Rothfels, 'Das politische Vermächtnis des deutschen Widerstands', *Vierteljahreshefte für Zeitgeschichte* 2(4) (Oct. 1954), pp. 329–45, here p. 338, where conservative conspirators were not only 'good Germans' but also 'good Europeans'; Peter Hoffmann, *Stauffenberg. A Family History* (Cambridge, 1995). For a critical collection on the theme of 1944, see Gerd R Ueberschär (ed.), *Der 20. Juli*

1944. Bewertung und Rezeption des deutschen Widerstandes gegen das NS-Regime (Cologne, 1994).

8 See David Reynolds, 'The Origins of the Cold War. The European Dimension, 1945–51', *Historical Journal* 28 (1985), pp. 497–515.

9 Karl Dietrich Bracher, *The Age of Ideologies: A History of Political Thought in the Twentieth Century* (New York, 1984); Elizabeth Wiskemann, *Europe of the Dictators, 1918–1945* (London, 1966; reprinted 1985); Stephen J. Lee, *The European Dictatorships 1918–1945* (London, 1988); Roger Griffin, *The Nature of Fascism* (London, 1991).

10 Robert Morrison MacIver, *Community: A Sociological Study. Being an Attempt to Set Out the Nature and Fundamental Laws of Social Life* (London, 1928); Susan Keller, *The Urban Neighbourhood* (New York, 1967); Robert Roberts, *The Classic Slum* (Harmondsworth, 1900); Anthony P. Cohen, *The Symbolic Construction of Community* (London, 1989); Albert J. Reiss, 'The Sociological Study of Communities', *Rural Sociology* 24 (June 1959), pp. 118–30; Benedict Anderson, *Imagined Communities. Reflections on the Origin and Spread of Nationalism*, revised edition (London, 1991).

11 MacIver, *Community*, p. 144; Cohen, *The Symbolic Construction*, pp. 20, 108.

12 See Max Weber, *Economy and Society. An Outline of Interpretative Sociology*, ed. Günther Roth and Claus Wittich (2 vols., Berkeley and London, 1978): vol. II, *Political Communities*, pp. 901–3.

13 Lewis A. Coser, *Continuities in the Study of Social Conflict* (Glencoe, 1962), pp. 103–4, 107. Cf. Richard Sennett, *Authority*, second edition (London and Boston, 1993).

14 Adrian Lyttelton, *The Seizure of Power: Fascism in Italy, 1919–1929* (London, 1973), p. 63; Frank Snowden, *The Fascist Revolution in Tuscany 1919–1922* (Cambridge, 1989); Alice A. Kelikian, *Town and Country under Fascism: The Transformation of Brescia, 1915–1926* (Oxford, 1986); Jeremy Noakes, 'The Nazi Party and the Third Reich: The Myth and Reality of the One-Party State', in Jeremy Noakes (ed.), *Government, Party and People in Nazi Germany* (Exeter, 1980), pp. 11–15, see also the editor's introduction; Detlef Mühlberger, 'Central Control versus Regional Autonomy: A Case Study of Nazi Propaganda in Westphalia 1925–1932', in Thomas Childers (ed.), *The Formation of the Nazi Constituency 1919–1933* (London 1986), pp. 64–103; Erik Hansen, 'Fascism and Nazism in the Netherlands 1929–39', *European History Quarterly* 11(3) (July 1981), pp. 355–85, here pp. 372–4.

15 Werner Rings, *Kollaboration und Widerstand. Europa im Krieg 1939–1945* (Zurich, 1979).

16 Michael Geyer, 'Resistance as Ongoing Project: Visions of Order, Obligations to Strangers, Struggles for Civil Society', *Journal of Modern History* 64, supplement (December 1992), pp. 217–41, here p. 224.

17 Jacques Semelin, *Unarmed Against Hitler. Civilian Resistance in Europe, 1939–1943* (Westport, Conn. and London, 1993), pp. 27, 30, 163; see also: Rings, *Kollaboration und Widerstand*.

18 Semelin, *Unarmed*, pp. 65, 73, 77, 80. Cf. Eve Rosenhaft, *Beating the Fascists? The German Communists and Political Violence 1929–1933* (Cambridge, 1983), esp. chapter 6.

19 Semelin, *Unarmed*, pp. 25, 168–9, for a useful typology.

20 Anthony McElligott, *Contested City. Municipal Politics and the Rise of Nazism in Altona, 1917–1937* (Ann Arbor, Mich., 1998), introduction.
21 Anderson, *Imagined Communities*, p. 22.
22 Griffin, *The Nature of Fascism*.
23 For a critical review of this research, see Ulrich Herbert, 'Arbeiterschaft im 'Dritten Reich'. Zwischenbilanz und offene Fragen', *Geschichte und Gesellschaft* 15 (1989), pp. 320–60.
24 For the background to post-war historiographical development, see Paola Di Cori, 'Women's History in Italy', in Karen Offen, Ruth Roach Pierson and Jane Rendall (eds.), *Writing Women's History. International Perspectives* (London, 1991).

1 THE GERMAN REVOLUTION DEFEATED AND FASCISM DEFERRED: THE SERVICEMEN'S REVOLT AND SOCIAL DEMOCRACY AT THE END OF THE FIRST WORLD WAR, 1918–1920

1 Two recent studies of the disintegration of the military are to be found in Richard Bessel, *Germany After the First World War* (Oxford, 1993) and Wolfram Wette, 'Demobilisation in Germany 1918–19: The Gradual Erosion of the Powers of the Soldiers' Councils', in Chris Wrigley (ed.), *The Challenge of Labour in Europe* (London, 1993), pp. 176–95.
2 The facts were kept hidden from the British and French publics as well. Had the scale of German desertions been published earlier, charges by the Allies of war guilt against the German nation would have carried less weight. Erich Volkmann, who worked on the Reichstag Commission of Enquiry into the German collapse of 1918, estimated that there were up to one million deserters in the last months of the war and documented them in a paper, 'Social Grievances in the Army during the World War', *Wissen und Wehr* 10 (1929), p. 157. Dr Arthur Rosenberg, who worked on the same enquiry as Volkmann, reported only three million soldiers on 1 October: two and a half million in the western army, half a million in the east. Dr Arthur Rosenberg, *The Birth of the German Republic, 1871–1918* (New York, 1962), pp. 219, 236. This amounts to the loss from desertion of all kinds in the last two years of the war of approximately half the German army and is documented in my article 'Shirkers in Revolt – Mass Desertion, Defeat and Revolution in the German Army: 1917–1920', in Colin Barker and Paul Kennedy (eds.), *To Make Another World – Studies in Protest and Collective Action* (Aldershot, 1996), pp. 113–38.
3 Report from Crown Prince Rupprecht, Commander in Chief, VI Army, to Prince Max von Baden. *Erinnerungen und Dokumente* (Stuttgart, 1968), p. 440.
4 David Engel, 'Patriotism as a Shield – The Liberal Jewish Defence Against Antisemitism in Germany during the First World War', *Leo Baeck Institute Year Book* 31 (1986), p. 150.
5 Erich Otto Volkmann, *Der Marxismus und das deutsche Heer im Weltkriege* (Berlin, 1925), cited in Bessel, *Germany*, pp. 46–7.
6 Bernard Huldermann, *Albert Ballin* (Berlin, 1922), p. 373. Cited in Joachim

Petzold (ed.), *Deutschland im Ersten Weltkrieg* (Berlin, 1970), vol III, p. 418.

7 Bessel, *Germany*, p. 1.

8 General Ludendorff, *The General Staff and its Problems* (London, n.d.), vol. I, p. 145.

9 Harold J. Gordon Jr., *The Reichswehr and the German Republic* (London, 1957), p. 3. Details of locations and death penalty order in 'Histories of the 251 Divisions of the German Army which Participated in the War (1914–1918)'. From the intelligence records of the American Expeditionary Force, Chaumont, 1919. Published as US War Department Document 905 (Washington, 1920; reprinted London, 1989), p. 450. There are several cases throughout 1917 and 1918 of mutiny and desertion cited in these abbreviated reports.

10 General Ludendorff, *My War Memories, 1914–1918* (London, n.d., probably 1924) vol. II, pp. 680–3.

11 *Preliminary History of the Armistice*, compiled by the Carnegie Endowment for International Peace (New York, 1924), p. 83. Translated from the 1919 German government's own records and minutes of proceedings leading to the signing of the Armistice to counter nationalist propaganda that it had 'stabbed the army in the back'.

12 *Ibid.*, p. 45.

13 Von Baden, *Erinnerungen*, pp. 439–40.

14 *Preliminary History*, pp. 45, 84–5.

15 Ludendorff, *War Memories*, p. 762.

16 Gordon, *Reichswehr*, pp. 3–4.

17 Walter Goerlitz, *History of the German General Staff, 1657–1945* (New York, 1953), p. 206.

18 Quote from the wartime memoirs of Heinrich Brüning, later German Chancellor, in H. W. Koch, 'The Collapse of Germany', *Purnell's History of the First World War* (London, 1971), vol. VII, p. 3026.

19 Alternative reports of these events are quoted in F. L. Carsten, *Revolution in Central Europe* (London, 1972), pp. 56–7.

20 Oskar Hippe, *And Red is the Colour of Our Flag* (London, 1991), pp. 29–30.

21 Ludwig von Maercker, *Vom Kaiserheer zur Reichswehr* (Leipzig, 1921), pp. 19–20.

22 Philip Scheidemann, *Memoirs of a Social Democrat* (2 vols., London, 1929), vol. II, p. 460.

23 Press reports dated 11, 13 and 18 November from The Hague, Cologne, the Press Office of the Cologne Soldiers' and Workers' Council, and from Berlin in the *Pester Lloyd* newspaper, 14–15 November; *Kölnische Zeitung*, 14 November, translated from paraphrased reports in Eberhard Buchner, *Revolutionsdokumente* (Berlin, 1921) vol. I, pp. 202–4. British diplomatic report from the Hague, PRO, FO 371/3165, fn. 189861, 16 November 1918.

24 Pierre Broué, *Révolution en Allemagne, 1917–23* (Paris, 1971), p. 162.

25 N. P. Howard, 'The Social and Political Consequences of the Allied Food Blockade of Germany, 1918–19', *German History* 11(2) (1993), p. 185.

26 Sir James Edmonds, *The Occupation of the Rhineland, 1918–1929* (London, 1987), p. 30.

27 Berliner Tageblatt, 18 November 1918, quoted in Buchner, *Revolution-*

sdokumente, vol. I, p. 204.

28 Edmonds, *Occupation*, p. 29.

29 Buchner, *Revolutionsdokumente*, vol. I, pp. 118–29.

30 Holger H. Herwig, *The German Naval Officer Corps: A Social and Political History, 1890–1918* (Oxford, 1973), p. 262.

31 *Berliner Lokal-Anzeiger*, *Der Reichsbote*, 14 November 1918, from Buchner, *Revolutionsdokumente*, vol. I, pp. 204–5. Herwig reports gaps in the naval archives over this period.

32 Paul Fröhlich, *Illustrierte Geschichte der Deutschen Revolution* (Berlin, 1929), p. 518.

33 Richard Bessel, 'The Great War in German Memory', *German History* 6(1) (1988), p. 24.

34 Scheidemann, *Memoirs*, vol. II, p. 480.

35 William Hoegner, *Die verratene Republik – Deutsche Geschichte 1919–1933* (Munich, 1979). 'Asiatic' etc., from Scheidemann, *Memoirs*, vol. II, p. 533.

36 Wilhelm Groener, *Lebenserinnerungen* (Göttingen, 1957), p. 452.

37 Von Baden, *Erinnerungen*, p. 591, fn 1.

38 *Ibid.*, p. 587.

39 Groener, *Lebenserinnerungen*, p. 456.

40 *Ibid.*, pp. 455–6.

41 Dieter Groh, 'The Kiel Mutiny', *Purnell's History of the First World War* (London, 1968), vol. VII, p. 3115.

42 Groener, *Lebenserinnerungen*, pp. 452–3.

43 Buchner, *Revolutionsdokumente*, p. 195.

44 Wolfram Wette, 'Demobilisation in Germany, 1918–19', in Wrigley (ed.), *The Challenge of Labour*, pp. 180–1.

45 Groener, *Lebenserinnerungen*, p. 470.

46 Jens Flemming, *Landwirtschaftliche Interessen und Demokratie* (Bonn, 1978), p. 87.

47 'Die Geborene und Gestorbenen nach Monaten in den Jahren 1918–19', *Statistisches Jahrbuch für das Deutsche Reich* (Berlin, 1922), vol. XLII, p. 42, table 8.

48 *Ursachen und Folgen vom Deutschen Zusammenbruch, 1918–1945* (Berlin, n.d.), vol. II. p. 372.

49 Buchner, *Revolutionsdokumente*, vol. I, p. 228.

50 Bessel, *Germany*, pp. 81, 242.

51 Fröhlich, *Illustrierte Geschichte*, p. 518. *Volkswille* (Hanover), 14–15 November 1918, Buchner, *Revolutionsdokumente*, vol. I, p. 218.

52 *Berliner Tageblatt*, 14 November 1918; *Hannoverscher Kurier*, 14–15 November 1918, from Buchner, *ibid.*, pp. 216–18. F. L. Carsten, *Revolution in Central Europe* (London, 1972), p. 69.

53 Reinhard Rürup, 'Problems of the German Revolution 1918–19', *Journal of Contemporary History* 3 (1968), pp. 109–35, 124–31.

54 *Ibid.*, pp. 119, 124. See Evelyn Anderson, *Hammer or Anvil* (London, 1945), 44–5.

55 *Kieler Zeitung*, 15 November 1918; *Leipziger Volkszeitung*, 15 November 1918; *Hamburger Nachrichten*, 18 November 1918; *Freie Presse* (Strasburg), 20 November 1918; from Buchner, *Revolutionsdokumente*, pp. 223–6.

56 Nick Howard, 'Der Wilde Necker – An Essay in Oral History, Wilhelm Necker Recalls the Weimar Years', *Labour History Review* 58(3) (winter, 1993), pp. 38–50, here p. 42. Carsten, *Revolution*, pp. 62–3.
57 Hans-Joachim Bieber, *Burgertum in der Revolution* (Hamburg, 1992), p. 54.
58 Wireless message. PRO, FO 371/3776, p. 152, 16 November 1918.
59 French Intelligence to British Foreign Office. PRO, FO 371/3776, p. 135, 13 January 1919. *Berliner Lokal-Anzeiger*, 16 November 1918, Buchner, *Revolutionsdokumente*, vol. I, pp. 231, 257.
60 *Kölnische Zeitung*, 17 January 1919.
61 John Riddell, *The German Revolution and the Debate on Soviet Power* (New York, 1986), p. 159.
62 Wette, 'Demobilisation', p. 182.
63 John Keegan, 'Demobilisation', *Purnell's History of the First World War* (London, 1971), vol VIII, p. 3146.
64 Gerhard A. Ritter and Susanne Miller (eds.), *Die deutsche Revolution, 1918–19* (Frankfurt, 1983), p. 139.
65 The MSPD won 11.5 million votes, or 38 per cent of the vote; Eberhard Kolb, *The Weimar Republic* (London, 1988), p. 193.
66 Heinrich Ströbel, *The German Revolution and After* (London, 1923), p. 143. Gordon, *Reichswehr*, p. 33. The quote is from Maercker, *Vom Kaiserheer*, p. 64.
67 M. Philips Price, *Germany in Transition* (London, 1923), p. 35.
68 Fröhlich, *Illustrierte Geschichte*, pp. 518–21.
69 Howard, 'Der Wilde Necker', p. 43.
70 Charles B. Burdick and Ralph H. Lutz, *The Political Institutions of the German Revolution, 1918–1919* (Stanford, Ca., 1966), p. 74.
71 Wette, 'Demobilisation', p. 188.
72 Chris Harman, *The Lost Revolution, Germany 1918 to 1923*, revised edition (London, 1997), pp. 102–4.
73 Wette, 'Demobilisation', p. 181.
74 Susanne Miller and Heinrich Potthof, *A History of German Social Democracy* (New York, 1986), pp. 78–81, 93–4.

2 DANGEROUS COMMUNITIES AND CONSERVATIVE AUTHORITY: THE JUDICIARY, NAZIS AND ROUGH PEOPLE, 1932–1933

1 This chapter draws partly on a previously published article: Anthony McElligott, 'Authority, Control and Class Justice: The Role of the *Sondergerichte* in the Transition from Weimar to the Third Reich', in *Criminal Justice History* 15 (1995), pp. 209–33.
2 For an idiosyncratic account of 'Bloody Sunday': Léon Schirmann, *Altonaer Blutsonntag 17. Juli 1932: Dichtungen und Wahrheit* (Hamburg, 1994). For the Reichstag fire and the *lex van der Lubbe*, see Martin Broszat, 'Zum Streit um den Reichstagsbrand', *Vierteljahreshefte für Zeitgeschichte* 8 (1960), pp. 275–9. Lothar Gruchmann, *Justiz im Dritten Reich* (Munich, 1990), pp. 826f.
3 Gerhard Kramer, 'The Courts of the Third Reich', *The Third Reich* (London, 1955), p. 626; Hermann Weinkauff, *Die Deutsche Justiz und der National-*

sozialismus. Ein Überblick. Die deutsche Justiz und der Nationalsozialismus, Part 1 (Stuttgart, 1968); Eberhard Kolb, 'Die Machinerie des Terrors. Zum Funktionieren des Unterdrückungs- und Verfolgungsapparates im NS-System', in Karl Dietrich Bracher, Manfred Funke and Hans-Adolf Jacobsen (eds.), *Nationalsozialistische Diktatur 1933–1945. Eine Bilanz* (Bonn and Düsseldorf, 1983), pp. 270–84, here p. 280.

4 Hinrich Rüping, 'Strafrechtspflege und politische Justiz im Umbruch vom Liberalen Rechtsstaat zum NS-Regime', in Josef Becker (ed.), *1933. Fünfzig Jahre danach. Die nationalsozialistische Machtergreifung in historischer Perspektive* (Munich, 1983), pp. 159, 163; Dieter Simon, 'Waren die NS-Richter "unabhängige Richter"' im Sinne des §1 GVG?', in Bernhard Diestelkamp and Michael Stolleis (eds.), *Justizalltag im Dritten Reich* (Frankfurt am Main, 1988); Klaus Bästlein, 'Als Recht zu Unrecht wurde: Zur Entwicklung der Strafjustiz im Nationalsozialismus', *Aus Politik und Zeitgeschichte. Beilage zur Wochenzeitung Das Parlament* B13-14/89 (24 March 1989); Ingo Müller, *Hitler's Justice. The Courts of the Third Reich* (Cambridge, Mass., 1991).

5 *Deutschlandberichte des Sozialdemokratischen Partei Deutschlands (Sopade)* (Salzhausen and Frankfurt am Main, 1980), vol. II, p. 251; Martin Broszat, 'Zur Perversion der Strafjustiz im Dritten Reich', *Vierteljahreshefte für Zeitgeschichte* 6 (1958), pp. 390, 397, 403; Werner Johe, *Die gleichgeschaltete Justiz. Organisation des Rechtswesens und Politisierung der Rechtsprechung 1933–1945, dargestellt am Beispiel des Oberlandesgerichtsbezirks Hamburg* (Frankfurt am Main, 1967), p. 93. Gruchmann, *Justiz*, pp. 1143–4.

6 Franz Neumann, *Behemoth. The Structure and Practice of National Socialism 1933–1944* (New York 1983; originally published 1942), pp. 20–3. Klaus Marxen, 'Strafjustiz im Nationalsozialismus Vorschläge für eine Erweiterung der historischen Perspektive', in Diestelkamp and Stolleis (eds.), *Justizalltag im Dritten Reich*, p. 102.

7 Weinkauff estimates that before 1933 only about thirty of the 7,000 judges in Prussia belonged to the NSDAP and that these were most likely to be younger members of the profession: Weinkauff, *Deutsche Justiz*, p. 108.

8 Gruchmann, *Justiz*, pp. 150ff, 221–40, 1117. Müller, *Hitler's Justice*, p. 61, gives 1,500 as the number affected by the measures. Both authors make the distinction between lawyers admitted to practice in general and legal personnel (prosecutors, judges, etc.) employed by the state. Cf. H. Schorn, *Der Richter im Dritten Reich. Geschichte und Dokumente* (Frankfurt am Main, 1959), p. 730.

9 Gruchmann, *Justiz*, pp. 226, 228. For the court in Altona, STAH 421-5, Regierung Schleswig, Akten der Dienststrafkammer (Reichsdisziplinärkammer Schleswig), DK1-46.

10 Weinkauff, *Deutsche Justiz*, portrays a beleaguered, angry, but impotent judiciary during the 'two years of Nazi lawlessness' (i.e. 1933 and 1934), pp. 113, 151, 160; Kramer, 'Courts', p. 626; Johe, *Die gleichschaltete Justiz*, p. 107; Rüping, 'Strafrechtspflege', pp. 161, 168; K.-D. Bracher, *The German Dictatorship. The Origins, Structure and Consequences of National Socialism* (Harmondsworth, 1970), pp. 269–71; E. R. Huber, *Verfassungsrecht des Grossdeutschen Reiches* (Hamburg, 1937), p. 280; Müller, *Hitler's Justice*, pp. 45, 52–3.

11 Gotthard Jasper, 'Zur Innerpolitischen Lage in Deutschland im Herbst 1929', *Vierteljahreshefte für Zeitgeschichte* 8 (1960). pp. 280–9, here pp. 285–9.

12 Franz Osterroth and Dieter Schuster (eds.), *Chronik der deutschen Sozialdemokratie* (2 vols., Berlin, Bonn-Bad Godesberg, 1975), vol. II: *Vom Beginn der Weimarer republik bis zum Ende des Zweiten Weltkrieges*, p. 253.

13 'Sitzung des Preußischen Staatsministerium vom 4. August 1932', printed as Document 96, *Akten der Reichskanzlei Weimarer Republik: Das Kabinett von Papen 1. Juni bis 3. Dezember 1932*, vol. I: Juni bis September 1932, bearb. von Karl-Heinz Minuth (Boppard am Rhein, 1989), pp. 349–57, especially p. 353. Thilo Vogelsang, *Reichswehr, Staat und NSDAP* (Berlin 1962), pp. 475ff.

14 IML/ZPA St 3/622 Bl. 31–2: Der Polizeipräsident Landeskriminalpolizeistelle I 41-06- (Flensburg) Betr. KPD Geheim!, 4 November 1930; IML/ZPA St 18/8 Bl. 2–34: 'Anklageschrift Der Oberreichsanwalt 15J24/32/25 Leipzig, 20 May 1932', p. 15 and 'An das preußische Min.d.I., 9 Aug. 1932'. See *Ursachen und Folgen. Vom deutschen Zusammenbruch 1918 und 1945 bis zur staatlichen Neuordnung Deutschlands in der Gegenwart* (Berlin, n.d.), vol. VIII, Document 1774, pp. 347–8.

15 See *Akten der Reichskanzlei: Kabinett von Papen*, p. 249, fn. 1. Arnold Brecht, *Preussen contra Reich vor dem Staatsgerichtshof: Stenogrammbericht der Verhandlungen vor dem Staatsgerichtshof in Leipzig vom 10. bis 14. und vom 17. Oktober 1932* (Berlin, 1933), pp. 14–17.

16 Harry Graf Kessler, *Tagebücher 1918–1937. Politik, Kunst und Gesellschaft der zwanziger Jahre* (Frankfurt am Main, 1961), entries for 12 July and 18 July, pp. 676, 678; Richard Bessel, *Political Violence and the Rise of Nazism. The Storm Troopers in Eastern Germany 1925–1934* (New Haven and London, 1984); Eve Rosenhaft, *Beating the Fascists? The German Communists and Political Violence 1929–1933* (Cambridge, 1983); Thomas Childers and Eugene Weiss, 'Voters and Violence: Political Violence and the Limits of National Socialist Mass Mobilization', *German Studies Review* 13(3) (1990), pp. 481–98, here p. 483.

17 Landesarchiv Schleswig 309/22721, 'Übersicht über politische Ausschreitungen im Polizeibezirk Altona-Wandsbek (für die Zeit vom . . .)', Rg.Vfg.v. 16 September 1932, -IPP 1239/6. Stadtarchiv Kiel, Akten des Ausschusses zur Feststellung der Entschädigungen für Aufruhrschäden für Kiel und Umgebung, Tumult-Schäden, file series 28640–51; Anthony McElligott, *Contested City. Municipal Politics and the Rise of Nazism in Altona, 1917–1937* (Ann Arbor, 1998).

18 IML/ZPA St 18/217 Bl. 51–2: Der Minister des Innern II (Diels) 1272 OP Schleswig-Holstein/65, Berlin 17 August 1932, 'Entwurf', p. 4; McElligott, *Contested City*, ch. 2.

19 Landesarchiv Schleswig Rep. 352 *Sondergerichtsakten* (hereafter LAS followed by serial number), 352/1241, Der Oberstaatsanwalt als Leiter der Anklagebehörde. Altona. 11 Son. J. 3/32. Namenverzeichnis zur Strafsache gegen Meyer u. Gen. wegen Aufruhrs: Getötete und verletzte Personen. Cf. *The Times* (London), 2 August 1933; details in McElligott, *Contested City*, ch. 6.

20 A copy of the official report dated 19 July is in LAS 301/4709. Published as 'Bericht des Regierungspräsidenten in Schleswig Abegg an den Preußischen

Innenminister Severing', printed as Document 67, *Akten der Reichskanzlei*: *Kabinett von Papen*, pp. 248–56; IML, ZPA, IV 3/2/1078, St. 18/217, Bl. 87–100: Der Pr.Min. des Inn. II 1272 O.P. Schleho, Berlin 18 November 1932 (final report). In this final report from the Prussian Interior Ministry, the authorities claimed that at least ten armed five-man groups had fired upon the police. This version of events has carried over into the literature: E. R. Huber, *Deutsche Verfassungsgeschichte seit 1789*, second edition (Stuttgart, Berlin, Cologne, Main, 1991), vol. VII: *Ausbau, Schutz und Untergang der Weimarer Republik*, pp. 1052–3; Ursula Büttner, Werner Jochmann, *Hamburg auf dem Weg ins Dritte Reich. Entwicklungsjahre 1931–1933* (Hamburg, 1983), pp. 30–1; Wolfgang Kopitzsch, 'Der 'Altonaer Blutsonntag''', in Arno Herzig, Dieter Langewiesche and Arnold Sywottek (eds.), *Arbeiter in Hamburg. Unterschichten, Arbeiter und Arbeiterbewegung seit dem ausgehenden 18. Jahrhundert* (Hamburg, 1983), pp. 509–16, and has been challenged by Schirmann, *Altonaer Blutsonntag*, who uses the original court sources: LAS 352/1242 sub-file 102: Report of Pol.Lt. Schieritz; LAS 352/1244 sub-files 249 and 252: reports of Pol.Maj. Wendt.

21 'Minister Besprechung vom 11. Juli 1932, 16.30 Uhr', printed as Document 57: *Akten der Reichskanzlei: Kabinett von Papen*, pp. 204–8.

22 IML, ZPA, IV 3/2/1078, St. 18/217 Bl. pp. 63ff: Der Pol.präs. A/W IA 3557/32, 17 September 1932: Betr. 'Politische Ausschreitungen und Straßenunruhen v. 17.7.1932'. Some idea of the sort of 'stern and consequential measures' Diefenbach had in mind can be gauged from the order of the Reich minister of the interior, von Gayl, to the police to make free use of their firearms and with impunity, LAS 309/22804, Polizeifunkdienst, Berlin 25 July 1932. This order antedates Goering's notorious 'Schießbefehl' of 17 February 1933.

23 Elke Fröhlich (ed.), *Die Tagebücher von Joseph Goebbels. Sämtliche Fragmente. Teil I Aufzeichnungen 1924–1941*, vol. II: *1.1.31–31.12.36* (Munich, New York, London, Paris, 1987), pp. 204, 206, diary entries: 13 July 1932 and 17 July 1932.

24 Arnold Brecht, *Preußen contra Reich vor dem Staatsgerichtshof. Stenogrammbericht der Verhandlungen vor dem Staatsgerichtshof in Leipzig vom 10. bis 14. und vom 17. Oktober 1932* (Berlin, 1933), pp. 18–86. Rudolf Morsey, 'Zur Geschichte des ''Preußenschlags''' am 20. Juli 1932', in *Vierteljahreshefte für Zeitgeschichte* 9 (1961), pp. 430–9; Hagen Schulze, *Otto Braun oder Preußens demokratische Sendung. Eine Biographie* (Frankfurt am Main, Berlin, Vienna, 1981). For the general background to the conflict between Prussia and the Reich, Dietrich Orlow, *Weimar Prussia 1925–1933: The Illusion of Strength* (Pittsburgh, Pa., 1991).

25 Fröhlich, *Tagebücher*, diary entry 19 July 1932, p. 207; *Schleswig-Holsteinische Tageszeitung*, 20 July 1932.

26 Huber, *Verfassungsrecht*, p. 40.

27 *Reichsgesetzblatt* (hereafter RGBl) I (1932), pp. 404–7: 'Verordnung der Reichsregierung über die Bildung von Sondergerichten. Vom 9. August 1932'.

28 Müller, *Hitler's Justice*, ch. 18. Müller argues that the eventual purpose of the *Sondergerichte* was to strengthen the 'inner front' during World War II.

29 By stating that 'punishable political acts had to be brought to expeditious trial under the law'. *International Military Tribunal, Nuremberg Trials Major War Criminals* (42 vols., London, 1947), vol. XVI, p. 281. See also the evidence of Schlegelberger, *ibid.*, vol. XX, p. 233. Cf. Huber, *Verfassungsgeschichte*, vol. VII, p. 1054. On nationalist fears, see *Akten der Reichskanzlei: Kabinett von Papen*, pp. 190–1, 246–7: Documents 53 and 66.

30 Neumann, *Behemoth*, p. 20.

31 'Ministerialbesprechung vom 21 März 1933, 16. Uhr', *Akten der Reichskanzlei Weimarer Republik: Die Regierung Hitler* (2 vols., Boppard am Rhein, 1983), vol. I: *1933/34, bearb. von Karl-Heinz Minuth*, Document 70, p. 244. RGBl I (1933), pp. 136–8: 'Verordnung der Reichsregierung über die Bildung von Sondergerichten. Vom 21. März 1933'.

32 Dr Crohne, 'Bedeutung und Aufgabe der Sondergerichte', *Deutsche Justiz* (1933), pp. 384–5.

33 See McElligott, 'Authority, Control and Class Justice', pp. 215–17.

34 *Statistisches Jahrbuch für das Deutsche Reich 1935* (Berlin, 1935), p. 529. Cf. Martin Broszat, *Der Staat Hitlers. Grundlegung und Entwicklung seiner inneren Verfassung* (Munich, 1969), pp. 407–9.

35 Supreme Court Judge Otto Schwarz, cited in Müller, *Hitler's Justice*, pp. 153–4.

36 *Justiz-Ministerial-Blatt für die preußische Gesetzgebung und Rechtspflege*, vol. XCIV, no. 31, 10 August 1932, Sondernummer Ausgabe A, pp. 195–96: 'Bildung von Sondergerichten. AB. d. IM. v. 9. 8. 1932 (I 4197)'; Huber, *Verfassungeschichte*, vol. VII, p. 1054. For details of the operational procedures of the *Sondergerichte*, see Gruchmann, *Justiz*, pp. 949–50, and Johe, *Die gleigeschaltete Justiz*, pp. 81–116.

37 Gruchmann, *Justiz*, p. 947.

38 Between 1919 and 1922, 354 political murders were committed by the right, for which the perpetrators received a total of ninety years imprisonment; the left was responsible for twenty-two political killings over the same period, for which ten death penalties were passed and 248 years of prison meted out: Emil Gümbel, *Vier Jahre Politische Mord* (Berlin, 1922, 1924; reprinted Heidelberg, 1980), pp. 73–81.

39 Preußischer Staatsrat 24. Sitzung am 9. September 1932, 'Allgemeine Verfügung vom 9. August 1932, betr. Bildung von Sondergerichten', cols. 540–4.

40 Preußischer Landtag, 4. Wahlperiode, I. Tagung 1932, Nr. 854 Urantrag (Winzer, Gehrmann, Küttner, SPD); Nr. 1157 Urantrag (21. Oktober 1932), (Kube, Lohse, Haake, Hinkler, Dr. Freisler, NSDAP). For the Potempa murder, see Preußischer Staatsrat, col. 541. Paul Kluke, 'Der Fall Potempa', in *Vierteljahreshefte für Zeitgeschichte* 5 (1957), pp. 279–99: Richard Bessel, 'The Potempa Murder', *Central European History* 10 (1977), pp. 241–54.

41 The motion was carried with a sizeable majority but the result had no immediate effect, Preußischer Staatsrat, col. 550.

42 LAS 352/1240, Der Oberstaatsanwaltschaft als Leiter der Anklagebehörde beim Sondergericht 11.Son.J. 3/33, 1 April 1933: 'Sondergerichtsanklage'.

43 Der Oberstaatsanwalt als Leiter der Anklagebehörde bei dem Sondergericht 11.Son. J. 401/34, 17 October 1934 (1935), Sondergerichtsanklage. Copy kindly made available to me by the Verein der Verfolgten des Naziregimes

Hamburg (VVN, Association of the Persecuted under the Nazi Regime in Hamburg).

44 LAS 352/1244/278, Alex Kuhlmann, interrogation 17 November 1932; LAS 309/22813, Polizeipräsident (Altona) Abt. IA, 29 July 1932; Regierungspräsident Schleswig IPP 961 II/6, 10 August 1932 to Min.d.I. 'Betr. Vorbereitungen der KPD zu einem bewaffneten Aufstand'. Heinz Karl Kücklich and Erika Kücklich, *Die Antifaschistische Aktion. Dokumentation und Chronik Mai 1932 bis Januar 1933* (East Berlin, 1965), p. 260.

45 Martin Broszat, 'A Social and Historical Typology of the German Opposition to Hitler', in David Clay Large (ed.), *Contending With Hitler. Varieties of Resistance in the Third Reich* (Cambridge, 1991), p. 27; P. Berger, *Gegen ein braunes Braunschweig. Skizzen zum Widerstnd 1925–1945* (Hannover, 1980), pp. 79, 132.

46 Rudolf Olden, 'Sondergerichte', *Die Weltbuhne* 28(33) (16 August 1932), p. 224. Cf. Robert Gellately, 'The Gestapo and German Society: Political Denunciation in the Gestapo Case Files', *Journal of Modern History* 60 (1988), pp. 654–94.

47 Geheimes Staatsarchiv preußischer Kulturbesitz (GStA) Rep. 84a/24143 Landgericht Altona, Bd. IX (1931–34), Bl. 108: Der Landgerichtspräs. III A 6/10292, to O/G.präs. Kiel, 8 August 1932; Bl. 119: Der OP VA 117/4795I, 14 September 1932; Bl. 140: Der OP VA 117/6643, 14 November 1932. *Ibid.*, 84a/797 Bl. 79: Abschrift: Der Oberstaatsanwalt und Leiter der Anklagebehörde VII 96, Altona 12. August 1932, Bildung von Sondergerichten A.V. 9/8.32.

48 Stanislaus Switalla was believed to have escaped to the Soviet Union after Bloody Sunday. LAS 352/1240, Staatsanwaltschaft bei dem Landgericht Hamburg-Altona, Not-Akte Switalla u. And., 11 Son.J.3/33 Sdg.7/33, 'Im Namen des Volkes!'. *Altonaer Nachrichten*, p. 127, 2 June 1933, 1 Beilage.

49 LAS 352/1246, Sb.E Strafsache Reese u. Gen. (Meyer u. Gen), Wegen Beihilfe zum versuchten Mord, Bl. 13: Vermerk (Gerichtsassessor de la Motte), for reservations; LAS 352/1242, files 90, 102, 122, 147, 148; 352/1244, files 278, 280, 281; 352/1245, file 304; and those in 352/1246. Cf. IML ZPA St.3/129, Bl.16–30ff: for the 5,000 marks reward money and its disbursement.

50 Claims by the defence counsel recapitulated in *Hamburger Anzeiger*, 30 May 1933, *Schleswig-Holsteinische Tageszeitung*, 1 and 2 June 1933, have been subsequently confirmed by my own findings, originally presented to the Hamburg Justice Ministry in 1985, 'Zum Altonaer Blutsonntag und der Rolle des Sondergerichts in Deutschland, 1933' (Rede vor der Hamburg Justizbehorde, Landgericht Max-Brauer-Allee), and more fully in McElligott, 'Authority', and supported by the recent study carried out independently by Léon Schirmann, *Altonaer Blutsonntag*.

51 G. Dahm and F. Schaffstein, *Liberales oder autoritäres Straffrecht?* (Hamburg, 1933), pp. 3ff, cited in Martin Hirsch, Diemut Majer and Jürgen Meinck (eds.), *Recht, Verwaltung und Justiz im Nationalsozialismus. Ausgewählte Schriften, Gesetze und Gerichtsentscheidungen von 1933 bis 1945* (Cologne, 1984), p. 447. See Huber, *Verfassungsrecht*, p. 200.

52 Peter Hüttenberger, 'Heimtückefälle vor dem Sondergericht München', in

Martin Broszat, Elke Fröhlich and Anton Grossmann (eds.), *Bayern in der NS-Zeit* (Munich and Vienna, 1981), vol. IV, pp. 435–526, here p. 448.

53 GStA Rep. 84a 797, Bl. 398–9: 'Übersicht über der Tätigkeit der Sondergerichte (Preußen) o.D' (December, 1932). The other two were at Kiel and Flensburg. Klaus Bästlein, 'Die Akten des ehemaligen Sondergerichts Kiel als zeitgeschichtliche Quelle', *Zeitschrift der Gesellschaft für Schleswig-Holsteinische Geschichte* 113 (1988), pp. 157–211.

54 For instance, the *Sondergericht* in Altona passed a total of 209 years and 4 months in 167 cases, whereas the *Sondergericht* in Königsberg, another judicial blackspot, passed sentences totalling 190 years in 271 cases, while the Bochum *Sondergericht* handed down a total of 77 years and 7 months in 158 cases, 'bersicht über der Tätigkeit der Sondergerichte'.

55 O. Rietzsch, 'Die Abwehr des Gewohnheitsverbrechertums. Deutsche Gesetze und Gesetzentwürfe bis zur Machtübernahme', *Deutsche Justiz* (1938), pp. 134ff. Gruchmann, *Justiz*, pp. 719–45. Reinhard Mann, *Protest und Kontrolle im Dritten Reich. Nationalsozialistische Herrschaft im Alltag einer rheinischen Großstadt* (Frankfurt and New York 1987), pp. 157–8. *Altonaer Nachrichten*, p. 127, 2 June 1933, 1 Beilage, 'Der Blutsonntag und seine Sühne'. Cf. McElligott, *Contested City*, ch. 3; Michael Schwartz, '"Proletarier"' und "Lumpen"' Sozialistische Ursprünge eugenischen Denkens', *Vierteljahreshefte für Zeitgeschichte* 42(4) (1994), pp. 537–70.

56 LAS 352/1252, 'Gnadensachen Wolff, Tesch, Lütgens, Möller': Der Oberstaatsanwalt als Leiter der Anklagebehörde bei dem Sondergericht, 6 July 1933: Strafsache gegen Switalla und Genossen wegen Landfriedensbruch. Betrifft Gnadenverfahren hinsichtlich der zum Tode verurteilten Lütgens, Möller, Wolff und Tesch, pp. 1–4.

57 *Ibid.*, Rechtsanwalt Harry Soll, 24 June 1933, In der Strafsache gegen Switalla und Genossen an den Herrn Ministerpräsidenten in Berlin: Gnadengesuch, p. 3.

58 *Ibid.*, Der Oberstaatsanwalt, Gnadenverfahren.

59 See the 'Anklageschrift' in 352/1240: 'Not-Akte Switalla'.

60 Lothar Danner, *Ordnungspolizei Hamburg. Betrachtungen zu ihrer Geschichte 1918–1933* (Hamburg, 1958), p. 264.

61 See *Notarbeit 51 der Notgemeinschaft der Deutschen Wissenschaft Gemeinschädigende Regionen des Niederelbischen Stadtgebietes 1934/35* (Hamburg, 1935; reprinted 1984); Rosenhaft, *Beating the Fascists*, p. 5; Rosenhaft, 'The Unemployed in the Neighbourhood: Social Dislocation and Political Mobilisation in Germany 1929–33', in Richard Evans and Dick Geary (eds.), *The German Unemployed. Experiences and Consequences of Mass Unemployment from the Weimar Republic to the Third Reich* (London, 1987), p. 194.

62 Broszat, 'Social and Historical Typology'; Klaus Tenfelde, 'Soziale Grundlagen von Resistenz und Widerstand', in Jürgen Schmädecke and Peter Steinbach (eds.), *Der Widerstand gegen den Nationalsozialismus. Die deutsche Gesellschaft und der Widerstand gegen Hitler* (Munich 1994), p. 806; McElligott, *Contested City*, ch. 6.

63 Hartmut Mehringer, 'Die KPD in Bayern 1919–1945. Vorgeschichte, Verfolgung und Widerstand', in Martin Broszat and Hartmut Mehringer (eds.), *Bayern in der NS-Zeit*, vol. V (Munich, 1983), p. 144.

64 Sauer had been at the centre of the notorious Marburg student case in 1922, when as the prosecuting counsel he pleaded with the judge to acquit the student members of a Free Corps detachment on trial for cold-bloodedly gunning down fifteen unarmed and innocent workmen from Bad Thal, Thuringia. Gümbel, *Vier Jahre*, p. 57–8. Gruchmann, *Justiz*, p. 128.

65 Freisler, in Hirsch *et al.*, *Recht*, pp. 432–4.

66 'Gnadensachen', Der Generalstaatsanwalt, E.R. 403/32, 13 July 1933, Ausserung in der Strafsache geen Switalla und Genossen, pp. 3–4.

67 'Gnadensuchen', Der Oberstaatsanwalt, Gnadenverfahren, p. 3.

68 Broszat, 'Social', p. 28. See, Mehringer, 'Die KPD', pp. 51ff.

69 IML/ZPA St.3/622, Bl. 119–20: Abteilung 1A.d. Altona, Geheim! Betr. Situationsbericht über die KPD im Bereich der B.L. Wasserkante (v. Rauch), 21 April 1933; *ibid.*, Bl. 185: Der Polizei-Präsident Altona-Wandsbeck, Betr. illegales KPD-Büro in Altona, 6 July 1933; *ibid.*, Bl. 253: Staatspolizeistelle Altona 590/33 an das Geheime Staatspolizeiamt in Berlin: Betr. Stand der kommunistischen Bewegung, 4 Sept. 1933; *ibid.*, Bl. 328ff: Staatspolizeistelle in Altona 1970/33: Geheim! Betr. Stand der kommunistischen Bewegung, 2 December 1933. See also 'Mitteilungen des Preußischen Ministers des Innern an die Regierungspräsidenten über die Richtlinien des Zentralkomitees der KPD für einen neuen Informationsapparat, 10 April 1933'; 'Bericht der Staatspolizeistelle Kassel an das Geheime Staatspolizeiamt in Berlin, 28 July 1933'; and 'Nachrichten des Geheimen Staatspolizeiamtes an die Staatspolizeistelle Hannover, 9 August 1933', printed as Documents 2040a, d and e, in *Ursachen und Folgen. Vom deutschen Zusammenbruch 1918 und 1945 bis zur staatlichen Neuordnung Deutschlands in der Gegenwart* (Berlin, n.d.), vol. IX, pp. 171–2, 174–7; Hermann Weber, 'Die Ambivalenz der kommunistischen Widerstandsstrategie bis zur "Brusseler"' Parteikonferenz', in Schmädecke and Steinbach, *Der Widerstand*, pp. 76–81.

70 Otto Chr. Kühbacher, 'Wie stehts am Wedding?', in *Die Tat* 25(8) (November 1933), p. 651.

71 See IML/ZPA St.3/622, Bl. 255, for reports on the impact of police surveillance and harassment of local communities for the Communist Party's underground work; Mehringer, 'Die KPD', pp. 113, 162–3, 179, 181, 185; Lothar Bembenek and Axel Ulrich, *Widerstand und Verfolgung in Wiesbaden 1933–1945. Eine Dokumentation* (Gießen, 1990), pp. 73–4, 78, 82–4.

3 THE ANTI-FASCIST MOVEMENT IN SOUTH-EAST LANCASHIRE, 1933–1940: THE DIVERGENT EXPERIENCES OF MANCHESTER AND NELSON

My thanks to Professor David Howell for his comments on an earlier draft of this essay.

1 From the end of 1935 the BUF aligned itself more closely with the German National Socialists, and changed its official name to the British Union of Fascists and National Socialists. This seems to have been a fairly short-lived change, as by the middle of 1937 the terms 'fascist' and 'National Socialist' disappeared from BUF literature and the movement referred to itself from that time as simply the 'British Union'. On the proliferation of fascist move-

ments in Britain, see R. Thurlow, *Fascism in Britain. A History 1918–1985* (Oxford, 1987).

2 See R. Thurlow, 'The Failure of British Fascism 1932–1940', in A. Thorpe (ed.), *The Failure of Political Extremism in Inter-War Britain* (Exeter, 1989), pp. 67–84.

3 This analysis is developed at some length in P. Williamson, *National Crisis and the National Government. British Politics, the Economy and Empire 1926–1932* (Cambridge, 1992).

4 For further details of the experiences of a number of anti-fascist activists in Spain, see D. Corkhill and S. Rawnsley (eds.), *Anti-fascists at War 1936–9* (Dunfermline, 1981).

5 See S. Rawnsley, 'Fascism and Fascists in Britain in the 1930s – A Case Study of Fascism in the North of England in a Period of Political and Economic Change' (Ph.D. thesis, University of Bradford, 1983), p. 124.

6 See *Blackshirt*, 10 January 1936, p. 5.

7 G. Webber, 'Patterns of Membership and Support for the British Union of Fascists', *Journal of Contemporary History* 19 (1984), pp. 575–606. While Webber's figures rely heavily on those of the Home Office, notably the 144 Series, the trends they suggest are readily discernible, and probably more reliable than any other assessment of bare membership numbers. The agencies compiling such data were possibly too ready to take at face value estimates of BUF strength which came either from the movement itself, which had a clear motive for overestimating, or from local organs of the state, which may also have had an interest in such overestimation by promoting the threat of the BUF in order to attract more resources.

8 For more on the growth of Nelson, see A. and L. Fowler, *The History of the Nelson Weavers' Association* (Manchester, 1984).

9 *Ibid.*, p. 13.

10 Taped interview with Iveson available for study in the Working Class Movement Library. See also J. Liddington, *The Life and Times of a Respectable Rebel. Selina Cooper, 1864–1946* (London, 1984). pp. 37–8.

11 My thanks to Max Druck for this information. Druck was a secretary of the Challenge Club in the 1930s. Born in Cheetham in 1917, he was the son of immigrants. His father came from Lithuania and his mother from Romania. Interview in possession of the author.

12 *Manchester Guardian*, 12 March 1933, p. 9.

13 Indeed, the famous Olympia debacle of 7 June 1934, which was witnessed by a number of prominent politicians at first hand, coincided almost exactly with the Roehm purge in Germany. This was a connection, no matter how tenuous, that anti-fascist activists made great play of, much to the detriment of the BUF. In relation to this meeting, Mosley's son, Nicholas, has concluded that 'the Communist propaganda victory was due to the fact that the image of fascists as thugs was being imprinted in people's minds'. N. Mosley, *Beyond the Pale* (London, 1983), p. 63. However, he probably overestimates the importance of the fact that there was much about the BUF which ran counter to British culture.

14 *Manchester Guardian*, 26 November 1934, p. 11.

15 The incident was reported with satisfaction by the BUF weekly newspaper,

Blackshirt, 25 January 1935, p. 2. Evelyn Taylor, born in Knutsford, Cheshire, in 1913, later married George Brown, the political organiser of the CPGB in Manchester, who was killed fighting on the Madrid front in Spain in 1937. On his return from Spain, Jack Jones, the future leader of the Transport and General Workers' Union, met and later married Evelyn Brown. Interview in possession of the author.

16 *The Times*, 29 June 1936, p. 9.
17 The quotation is from Driver's unpublished autobiography, 'From the Shadow of Exile', pp. 36–8. It is lodged in Nelson Public Library.
18 *Manchester Guardian*, 29 June 1936, p. 9.
19 Interviews in possession of the author. Bernard (Benny) Rothman was born in Cheetham in 1911. His parents came from Romania in the early years of the century. He is best known for leading the Kinder Mass Trespass in 1932, for which he was jailed for six months. Lily Wilde was born in 1917, also in Cheetham; her father came to Britain from Russia in 1905, her mother from Poland around the same time.
20 *Manchester Guardian*, 1 October 1934.
21 On two occasions, in the first six months of 1936, the BUF held meetings at Cheetham Town Hall – a clear challenge, particularly to Jewish anti-fascist activists. The opposition to these meetings will be dealt with later.
22 Bill Williams, 'The Anti-Semitism of Tolerance: Middle Class Manchester and the Jews, 1870–1900', in A. J. Kidd and K. W. Roberts (eds.), *City, Class and Culture. Studies of Cultural Production in Victorian Manchester* (Manchester, 1985), pp. 74–103.
23 Neville Laski, *Jewish Rights and Jewish Wrongs* (London, 1939), p. 105.
24 Minutes of the Co-ordinating Committee of the BoD, 12 November 1936. BoD Archive, London.
25 Minutes of the Executive Council of the CMSJ, 21 September 1938. CMSJ Archive, Manchester.
26 PRO, Home Office Report 144/21379/502735/232, 30 November 1936.
27 *Manchester Guardian*, 18 September 1934, p. 6.
28 Minute Book of the Manchester First Branch of the AEU, 21 September 1934, Working Class Movement Library. Anti-fascists such as Rothman clearly had a number of channels for their activism, itself a function of the interconnected nature of the labour movement in the city and their integration within it.
29 *Manchester Guardian*, 20 September 1934, p. 11.
30 Manchester Watch Committee Report Book number 186, 29 August 1934, Manchester Police Museum. Levine was born in Cheetham in 1907. His parents came to Britain from Lithuania in the mid 1890s. He was a prominent figure in the local CPGB, and has written of his experiences in the 1930s, most notably in Spain, in a short book entitled *Cheetham to Cordova. A Manchester Man of the Thirties* (Manchester, 1984). Interview in possession of the author.
31 *Manchester Guardian*, 22 September 1934.
32 Quoted in Millie Toole, *Our Old Man. A Biographical Portrait of Joseph Toole* (London, 1948), p. 116.
33 *Manchester Guardian*, 27 September 1934, p. 11.
34 Sir Stafford Cripps, *National Fascism in Britain* (n.d.).

35 PRO, Home Office File 144/20142/674216/199. After the event a note from the Chief Constable to the under-secretary of state at the Home Office reported that opposition to the BUF in Belle Vue consisted 'very largely of Jews [who] . . . persistently attempted to break up the Fascist meeting by yelling slogans, etc.'. Home Office File 144/20142/674217/200B.

36 *New Leader*, 5 October 1934, p. 5.

37 *Daily Worker*, 1 October 1934, p. 5.

38 *Manchester Guardian*, 17 June 1936, p. 13.

39 Manchester Watch Committee Report Book number 206, 4 February 1937. The jibe at the other representative bodies may well have been a reference to the apparent inactivity of the CMSJ.

40 *Manchester Guardian*, 22 October 1936.

41 *Ibid.*, 22 October 1934.

42 See Liddington, *Life and Times*, chs. 22 and 23.

43 *The Times*, 23 July 1934, p. 14.

44 *Cotton Factory Times*, 28 December 1934, p. 6.

45 M. McCarthy, *Generation in Revolt* (London, 1953), p. 239. This, however, may tell us more about the nature of the political affiliation of the activists outside the mainstream in troubled times than the rival attractions of the BUF and CPGB.

46 The left replied with numerous pamphlets, such as William Rust's *Mosley and Lancashire*, a reprint of a *Labour Monthly* article.

47 Fowler and Fowler, *Nelson Weavers' Association*, p. 70. In Blackburn, by contrast, unemployment topped 39 per cent in 1936. *Cotton Factory Times*, 22 May 1936, p. 3. The figures for Blackburn also included nearby Rishton, Clitheroe and Great Harwood.

48 A. Raven Thomson, 'Cotton and the Left', *Fascist Quarterly* 1 (1935) p. 276.

49 Len Dole was born in Colne in 1918. He was expelled from the Labour Party in the late 1930s, along with a number of other local activists, for his support for the Unity Movement. He briefly joined the YCL, but quickly rejoined the Labour Party. He was the agent for the radical Nelson MP, Sidney Silverman, from 1953 until Silverman's retirement in 1966.

50 Interview in possession of the author. Sutherst was born in Shaw, near Oldham, in 1919 and joined the BUF in 1936.

51 PRO, Home Office Report 144/21281/807060/34.

52 Driver, 'From the Shadow', p. 45.

53 Bill Whittaker was born in Colne in 1908. He too left the Labour Party over the Unity issue and joined the Communist Party. He attended a number of BUF meetings across the country, and saw at first hand what he describes as Blackshirt brutality.

54 *Nelson Leader*, 21 October 1938, p. 8.

55 *Nelson Gazette*, 15 November 1938, p. 2. The paper was the organ of the local Labour and Co-operative Party. Silverman had been elected in 1935 and was clearly on the left, which made him attractive to the Nelson Labour Party and, indeed, to the wider left in the town. His radicalism can be clearly seen in a letter to the *Nelson Leader* before his election, in which he condemned the national Labour Party leadership for failing to countenance a United Front, and concluded: 'What big things could be done in Nelson if we had the united

efforts in question, for instance, for increased children's allowance, against wage cuts, against Part Two of the Unemployment Act and against Fascism and War.' *Nelson Leader*, 14 June 1935, p. 11.
56 *Nelson Gazette*, 7 March 1939, p. 4.
57 Liddington, *Life and Times*, p. 429. PRO, Home Office Report 144/20164-692242/239. The key word would seem to be 'active'.
58 Interview of Nellie Driver by Brenda Crosby, in Nelson Public Library.
59 Nelson Labour Party Minutes, 12 May 1933.
60 Liddington, *Life and Times*, p. 429.
61 *Ibid.*
62 Nelson Labour Party Executive Minutes, 16 March 1937.
63 Gilbert Kinder was born in Nelson in 1906 and joined the ILP in 1925. He remembers that in the 1930s the ILP, CPGB and Labour Party invariably shared each other's platforms in the town, despite the fact that each was critical of the others over certain issues. Interview in possession of the author.
64 Albert Shaw was born in Nelson in 1915 and joined the YCL in 1929. He was secretary of the Nelson Weavers' Association from 1957 to 1974, when it merged with the Amalgamated Textile Workers' Union. Interview in possession of the author.
65 Fowler and Fowler, *Nelson Weavers' Association*, p. 120.

4 SPAIN 1936. RESISTANCE AND REVOLUTION: THE FLAWS IN THE FRONT

1 Leon Trotsky, 'The class, the party and the leadership' (unfinished), 20 August 1940.
2 The Popular Front's signatories were as follows: the left, centrist and Catalan republican groups (respectively Manuel Azaña's Izquierda Republicana, Diego Martínez Barrio's Unión Republicana and the Esquerra) and Spain's Socialist Party (PSOE) which signed on behalf of itself and the following groups: socialist-led trade union (UGT); Spanish Communist Party (PCE); left communist (anti-Stalinist) POUM and former CNT leader Angel Pestaña's Syndicalist Party (Partido Sindicalista).
3 Helen Graham, *Socialism and War. The Spanish Socialist Party in Power and Crisis, 1936–1939* (Cambridge, 1991), pp. 26–7.
4 Adrian Shubert, 'A Reinterpretation of the Spanish Popular Front: The Case of Asturias', in Martin S. Alexander and Helen Graham (eds.), *The French and Spanish Popular Fronts: Comparative Perspectives* (Cambridge, 1989), pp. 213–25.
5 Industrial collectivisation occurred predominantly in Barcelona province. The city itself was the capital of both industrial and commercial collectivisation. Agrarian collectivisation occurred most notably in Aragón, in parts of the Levante and in the Republican south (e.g. UGT-CNT agrarian collectives of Jaen). There is an enormous bibliography on collectivisation: see especially Walther L. Bernecker, *Colectividades y revolución social. El anarquismo en la guerra civil española 1936–1939* (Barcelona, 1982); German original, *Anarchismus und Bürgerkrieg. Zur Geschichte der Sozialen Revolution in Spanien 1936–1939* (Hamburg, 1978); Julián Casanova, 'Anarchism and Revolution in the

Spanish Civil War: The Case of Aragon', *European History Quarterly* 17 (1987), pp. 423–45; Casanova, *Anarquismo y revolución en la sociedad rural aragonesa 1936–1938* (Madrid, 1985); and Casanova (ed.), *El sueño igualitario. Campesinado y colectivizaciones en la España republicana* (Zaragoza, 1989); Luis Garrido González, *Colectividades agrarias en Andalucia: Jaen (1931–1939)* (Madrid, 1979); Aurora Bosch Sánchez, *Ugetistas y libertarios. Guerra civil y revolución en el país valenciano 1936–1939* (Valencia, 1983); Graham Kelsey, *Anarchosyndicalism, Libertarian Communism and the State: The CNT in Zaragoza and Aragon* (Amsterdam, 1991); Pierre Broué and Emile Témime, *The Revolution and the Civil War in Spain* (London, 1972); see also oral testimonies in Ronald Fraser, *Blood of Spain* (London, 1979). In addition, there is a substantial amount of material in individual memoirs both by Spaniards and non-Spaniards. This is of variable quality, but with the proviso that such material always offers a 'worm's eye view' it also provides invaluable insights into the passionate commitment and hope – also a condition of history – which fuelled collectivisation as a cultural as well as a social and economic endeavour. For a brief, useful summary of the current state of the historiographical debate, see Julián Casanova, 'Anarchism, Revolution and Civil War in Spain: The Challenge of Social History', in *International Review of Social History* 37 (1992), pp. 398–404.

6 Graham, *Socialism and War, passim* and Helen Graham, 'The Eclipse of the Socialist Left: 1934–1937', in F. Lannon and P. Preston (eds.), *Elites and Power in Twentieth-Century Spain. Essays in Honour of Sir Raymond Carr* (Oxford, 1990), pp. 127–51.

7 For a general historical perspective on this process see Adrian Shubert, *A Social History of Modern Spain* (London, 1990); also Manuel Suárez Cortina, 'La quiebra del republicanismo histórico, 1898–1931', in Nigel Townson (ed.), *El republicanismo en España (1830–1977)* (Madrid, 1994), pp. 139–63.

8 On the collapse of the centre and republican fragmentation there is little currently in English: see Nigel Townson, 'The Collapse of the Centre. The Radical Republican Party during the Second Spanish Republic' (unpublished PhD thesis, University of London, 1991); Stephen Lynam, '"Moderate" Conservatism and the Second Republic: The Case of Valencia', in Martin Blinkhorn (ed.), *Spain in Conflict 1931–1939* (London, 1986), pp. 133–59. On the political contradictions and strategy failures of republicanism, see Pamela Beth Radcliff, *From Mobilization to Civil War. The Politics of Polarization in the Spanish City of Gijón 1900–1937* (Cambridge, 1996) and Helen Graham, 'Community, Nation and State in Republican Spain 1931–1938', in C. Mar-Molinero and A. Smith (eds.), *Nationalism and the Nation in the Iberian Peninsula* (Oxford, 1996), pp. 133–47. See also S. Juliá, 'La experiencia del poder: la izquierda republicana, 1931–1933', and N. Townson, '"Una República para todos los españoles": el Partido radical en el poder 1933–1935', both in Townson (ed.), *El republicanismo en España*, pp. 165–92 and pp. 193–222. On the (still-debated) nature of the mass catholic party CEDA (christian democratic or quasi-fascist), see Richard A. H. Robinson, *The Origins of Franco's Spain* (Newton Abbot, 1970) for the former view, and both José Ramón Montero, *La CEDA: el catolicismo social y político en la II República* (Madrid, 1977) and Paul Preston, *The Coming of the Spanish Civil War.*

Reform, Reaction and Revolution in the Second Republic, revised edition (London, 1994) for the latter view. On the responses and strategies of capital, employers' associations, etc., see also Mercedes Cabrera, *La patronal ante la II República. Organizaciones y estrategia 1931–1936* (Madrid, 1983).

9 Cf. 'In every respect, economic, religious, political and in everyday relations, the workers wanted to demonstrate the power and support which the electoral victory had given them . . . *The attitude, the new tone, was even more important than the actual number of violent conflicts*. Of course the period following the Popular Front elections saw conflict but in quantitative terms not much more than had occurred in 1933 for example', in Manuel Pérez Yruela, *La conflictividad campesina en la provincia de Córdoba 1931–1936* (Madrid, 1979), p. 206 (my italics).

10 The bibliography on the popular revolution is enormous. See sources in note 5 above and note 16 below (Lorenzo and Peirats).

11 Although they were not always so. Moreover, the militia's attitude to militarisation was much more varied and complex than the often rather abstract terms of the 'revolution versus war' debate usually convey – see Casanova, *Anarquismo y revolución*, pp. 111–14.

12 It might be objected that the well-known case of Catalan republican leader Lluís Companys persuading the CNT to disband the anti-fascist militia committee and join a reconstituted Catalan government (*Generalitat*) in September 1936 constitutes an exception here. But what this incident reveals is an experienced politician operating at the level of instinct in conditions of republican disarray. At the same time, as I discuss below, his interlocutors had no political strategy of their own. Companys' 'solution' imposed itself by dint of a lack of competing options.

13 See Graham, 'Community, Nation and State in Republican Spain'.

14 For a classic exposition of this, see Vernon Richards, *Lessons of the Spanish Revolution* (London, 1953, 1972, 1983).

15 This division of opinion was already present before the 1920s, and in the Primo years some in the CNT were prepared to consider the pragmatic acceptance of the terms of legality offered by the dictator. The hostility of purist anarchists to this tendency led to the formation of the FAI in 1927. So the FAI's emergence itself symbolised the growth of internal differences in the CNT as much as it did radicalisation *per se*.

16 Eulàlia Vega, *El trentisme a Catalunya. Divergències ideològiques en la CNT* (Barcelona, 1980) and *Anarquistas y sindicalistas 1931–1936. La CNT y los Sindicatos de Oposición en el País Valenciano* (Valencia, 1987), pp. 222–6; César M. Lorenzo, *Los anarquistas españoles y el poder* (Paris, 1972); José Peirats, *La CNT en la revolución española* (Madrid, 1978).

17 Cf. Chris Ealham's thought provoking article, 'Crime and Punishment in 1930s Barcelona', *History Today* (October 1993), pp. 31–7.

18 The CNT's major regional federations – Catalonia, the Levante and Andalusia/Extremadura – all experienced a significant decline across the period 1931–6, losses which were bound up in a variety of ways with the dispute over the movement's future strategy. By spring 1936 the Catalan CNT claimed less than half of its 1931 membership of just over 300,000. See CNT Congress report for June 1931 cited in Susana Tavera and Eulàlia Vega, 'La

afiliació sindical a la CRT de Catalunya: entre l'eufòria revolucionària i l'ensulsiada confederal 1931–36', in *Revolució i socialisme* (Barcelona, 1990), pp. 343–63. For the south, see José Manuel Macarro Vera, *La utopía revolucionaria. Sevilla en la Segunda República* (Seville, 1985), p. 62.

19 Santos Juliá, 'La experiencia del poder: la izquierda republicana, 1931–1933', in Townson (ed.), *El republicanismo en España*, pp. 181, 185.

20 For the agricultural sector, see Manuel Pérez Yruela, *La conflictividad campesina en la provincia de Córdoba 1931–1936*, pp. 111, 119ff, 228–9; for the construction strike, Santos Juliá, *Madrid 1931–34. De la fiesta popular a la lucha de clases* (Madrid,1984), pp. 229–58, and summary in S. Juliá, 'Economic Crisis, Social Conflict and the Popular Front: Madrid 1931–6', in Paul Preston (ed.), *Revolution and War in Spain 1931–1939* (London, 1984), pp. 137–58; Stanley Payne, *Spain's First Democracy. The Second Republic, 1931–1936* (Wisconsin, 1993), p. 144.

21 And in Spain, too, such inroads as the very small Spanish Communist Party could make prior to 1935 were also in those areas where social fascism/'class against class' appealed precisely because it fitted pre-existing tensions and conflicts between working-class constituencies which were generated or exacerbated by economic depression. For example, in Seville, where 'the conclusion of Primo's extravagant works programmes had left a mass of unemployed construction workers': Preston, *The Coming of the Spanish Civil War* (revised edition), p. 29; see also José Manuel Macarro Vera, *La utopía revolucionaria. Sevilla en la Segunda República*.

22 See note 15 above.

23 Its national executive could neither advise nor adequately gather information. John Brademas, *Anarcosindicalismo y revolución en España 1930–1937* (Barcelona, 1974), p. 73.

24 Cf. Santos Juliá, 'De la división orgánica al gobierno de unidad nacional', in Fundación Pablo Iglesias (various authors), *Socialismo y guerra civil (Anales de Historia*, vol. II, Madrid, 1987), p. 237.

25 On the eve of the war the POUM had an estimated 6,000 members, though by December 1936 it claimed 30,000. B. Bolloten, *The Spanish Civil War. Revolution and Counterrevolution* (London and New York, 1991), p. 405. Again, a major factor in the political ghettoisation of these groups was Spain's very uneven industrial development.

26 See Graham, 'The Eclipse of the Socialist Left: 1934–1937', esp. pp. 131–2, for analysis and a bibliographical resumé of material on the socialist left.

27 Graham, *Socialism and War*, p. 185.

28 On the Catalan origins of the Workers' Alliance and (Madrid) socialist attitudes to it, Payne, *Spain's First Democracy*, pp.195–6.

29 See José Manuel Macarro Vera's suggestive discussion of the Andalusian case, in Santos Juliá (ed.), *El socialismo en las nacionalidades y regiones* (Fundación Pablo Iglesias, Madrid, 1988), pp. 105, 118.

30 See Santos Juliá, *Madrid 1931–34*.

31 The *Jurados Mixtos* in Madrid had broken down under grass-roots pressure in 1933, see *ibid.*

32 Some details in Payne, *Spain's First Democracy*, pp. 339–40, and for an analysis of UGT leadership mentality, Preston, *The Coming of the Spanish*

Civil War (revised edition), p. 29.

33 Santos Juliá, *La izquierda del PSOE (1935–1936)* (Madrid, 1977), p. 260.

34 Gabriel Jackson, *The Spanish Republic and the Civil War 1931–1939* (Princeton, 1965), p. 285; Chris Ealham, 'Anarchism and Illegality in Barcelona 1931–37', *Contemporary European History* (July 1995); UGT executive committee minutes, Dec. 1936/Jan. 1937, see Graham, *Socialism and War*, p. 271, n. 51.

35 For examples of this ongoing conflict, Graham, *Socialism and War*, p. 64, n. 45, p. 8, n. 51.

36 See Graham, 'The Eclipse of the Socialist Left: 1934–1937', for details.

37 By 1936, in the context of the aspirations of a radicalised rural base and its post-Popular Front expectations, there was some collaboration between the CNT and sectors of the UGT's landworkers' federation, the FNTT, in the rural south. See the reference in Payne, *Spain's First Democracy*, pp. 301–3.

38 The wartime Popular Front and the PCE's role therein are explored in my forthcoming book on the Republican state at war, and also in a preliminary article, 'Community, Nation and State in Republican Spain 1931–1938' (see note 8 above).

5 THE BLUESHIRTS IN THE IRISH FREE STATE, 1932–1935: THE NATURE OF SOCIALIST REPUBLICAN AND GOVERNMENTAL OPPOSITION

1 The popular usage and understanding of the term 'Blueshirt' is demonstrated by the journalist John Waters, *Jiving at the Crossroads* (Belfast, 1991), while the labelling of the Blueshirts by historians as fascist-inspired is best illustrated in Paul Bew, Ellen Hazelkorn and Henry Patterson, *The Dynamics of Irish Politics* (London, 1985).

2 *Irish Independent*, 10 February 1932, p. 6.

3 Frank Munger, *The Legitimacy of Opposition: The Change in Government in Ireland, 1932* (Beverly Hills, 1975), p. 7.

4 National Archive of Ireland, H.306/23 Justice Department file, *The National Guard*, 6 October 1932.

5 Details from conversation with Tom O'Higgins (Dr O'Higgins' son), 25 March 1993 in Monkstown, Co. Dublin.

6 *Irish Independent*, 12 August 1932, p. 6.

7 *Irish Press*, 16 August 1932, p. 4.

8 *An Phoblacht*, 20 August 1932, p. 1.

9 National Archive of Ireland, H.306/23, Justice Department file, *The National Guard*, 6 October 1932.

10 These included Michael Tierney, James Hogan, John Marcus O'Sullivan and Alfred O'Rahilly.

11 See Eoin O'Duffy, *An Outline of the Political, Social and Economic Policy of Fine Gael (United Ireland)* (Dublin, 1934).

12 The threat of communism hung heavy on the politics of the early 1930s, despite the small number of communists in the country. For details of the atmosphere see Dermot Keogh, 'De Valera, the Catholic Church and the Red Scare, 1931–2', in J. P. O'Carroll and J. A. Murphy (eds.), *De Valera and his*

Times (Cork, 1983).

13 University College Dublin Archives, P/24/671[a], Ernest Blythe Papers, monthly membership returns (March 1934).

14 *The Times*, 12 August 1933, p. 10.

15 Interview with James MacCarthy Morrogh, Innisbeg, Co. Cork, May 1991.

16 *An Phoblacht*, 19 August 1933, p. 1.

17 *Irish Worker's Voice* 17 February 1934, p. 5.

18 For more details on the major groups, see Richard English, *Radicals and the Republic: Socialist Republicanism in the Irish Free State, 1925–37* (Oxford, 1994); Richard English, 'Socialism and Republican Schism in Ireland: The Emergence of the Republican Congress in 1934.' *Irish Historical Studies* 27(105) (May 1990), pp. 48–65; and Richard English 'Paying No Heed to Public Clamour': Irish Republican Solipsism in the 1930s. *'Irish Historical Studies* 28(112) (1990), pp. 426–40.

19 *An Phoblacht*, 14 August 1933, p. 4.

20 National Archive of Ireland, Department of Justice 1993 Release D/JUS.D28/34 (1 June 1935), pp. 1–6.

21 *Ibid.*, Superintendent's report, D/JUS.E24/2/34 (10 October 1934).

22 A major force behind the Congress, George Gilmour, gives much space in his memoirs of the organisation to their opposition to the Blueshirts. George Gilmore, *The 1934 Republican Congress* (Dublin, 1965).

23 *Irish Worker's Voice*, 5 August 1933, p. 2.

24 *The Irish Republican Congress* (New York, 1935), p. 10.

25 *Ibid.*, p. 15.

26 *Republican Congress*, 12 May 1934, p. 5.

27 National Archive of Ireland, H.306/23, Justice Department file, *The National Guard*, 6 October 1933.

28 See Maurice Manning, *The Blueshirts* (Dublin, 1987), p. 79.

29 *An Phoblacht*, 12 August 1933, p. 1.

30 Tim Pat Coogan, *The IRA* (London, 1970), p. 104.

31 *Irish Worker's Voice*, 23 December, 1933, p. 1.

32 *Dail Debates* (Dublin, 1934), vol L, cols. 2213–23, 24 February 1934.

33 *Ibid.*, cols. 2237–9, 25 February 1934.

34 For fuller details, see Joseph Lee, *Ireland 1912-85. Politics and Society* (Cambridge, 1989) and Roy Foster, *Modern Ireland 1600–1972* (London, 1988).

35 See Tim Pat Coogan, *De Valera. Long Fellow, Long Shadow* (London, 1983), pp. 408–520.

36 See Roger Griffin, *The Nature of Fascism* (London, 1991).

37 For example, Roger Griffin's sub-definition 'abortive fascist movements in Inter-War Europe', or Stanley Payne's sub-group the 'radical right'. See Griffin, *Nature of Fascism*, p. 121; Payne, *Fascism. Comparison and Definition* (New York, 1980), p. 182.

38 For details see J. J. Lee, 'Aspects of Corporatist Thought in Ireland: The Commission on Vocational Organization, 1939–43', in Art Cosgrave and Donal McCartney (eds.), *Studies in Irish History presented to R. Dudley Edwards* (Dublin, 1979).

39 See Paul Canning, 'The Impact of Eammon de Valera: Domestic Causes of the Anglo-Irish Economic War', *Albion* 15 (1983), pp. 179–205.

40 Letter from Frank MacDermot to General O'Duffy, MacDermot Papers 1065/3/1 (Four Courts, Dublin) (9 July 1934), p. 1.

6 TOWN COUNCILS OF THE NORD AND PAS-DE-CALAIS REGION: LOCAL POWER, FRENCH POWER, GERMAN POWER

1 Originally published as 'Les municipalités du Nord/Pas-de-Calais: pouvoir local, pouvoir français, pouvoir allemand', in: *Revue du Nord 2*, spécial hors-série (1987), pp. 219–68. The editors wish to thank the author for permission to publish this much-shortened and edited translation of the original. Archives Nationales, Paris (henceforth AN), FIA/3630.

2 On the conditions of the 1914–18 occupation in the Nord and the Pas-de-Calais, see R. Vandenbussche *Histoire du Nord/Pas de Calais, de 1900 à nos jours* (Privat, 1982), pp. 193–225.

3 See Maner, 'Les municipalités', appendix 2 for the mayors' date of entry into the town councils.

4 *Ibid.*, p. 266, appendix 1 for the age profile of mayors.

5 *Ibid.*, appendix 4 for the mayors' professions. On the origins of the notables, see Y. Le Maner, 'Les Maires de l'arrondissement de Béthune, 1871–1914', in M. Agulhon, L. Girard, J. L. Robert and W. Serman (eds.), *Les Maires en France du Consulat à nos jours* (Paris, 1986), pp. 235–78.

6 On this point, see Y. Le Maner, 'Le PCF dans le Nord/Pas-de-Calais à la veille de la guerre', in transactions of the conference 'Le PCF 1938–1941', October 1984.

7 Cf. E. Dejonghe's paper given at the conference on 'Le PCF 1938–1941'.

8 For example at Calonne-Ricouart and Douvrin.

9 Such was the claim made by the mayor of Labourse (Pas-de-Calais) on his return in September 1940 after having 'evacuated' to the Loir-et-Cher, and by the mayor of Sauchy-Lestrée, who claimed to have evacuated to Perigueux 'on the order to withdraw'.

10 Archives Départementales du Pas-de-Calais, Dainville (Arras) (henceforth AD Pas-de-Calais), M4969, report of 2 May 1941.

11 For example at Leforest (Pas-de-Calais) on 21 May 1940.

12 At Tourcoing the mayor had fled 'with the town's cash box and the fire engines'.

13 For example, in the *arrondissement* of Arras, at Berles-Monchel, Gaudiempré, Ivergny, etc.

14 There were at least forty such cases in the Pas-de-Calais: Oisy-le-Verger, Halloy, Sus-Saint-Léger, Tilloy-les-Mofflaines, Riencourt-les-Bapaume, Haucourt, etc.

15 AN, FIA/3999 and Archives Départementale du Nord, Lille (henceforth AD Nord), M2841: an identical initiative had come to grief at Halluin.

16 AN, FlV/C18. These included the town councils of Anzin in Finistère, of Lille at Rennes, of Roubaix at La Guerche and of Armentières at Granville.

17 At Croix (in the Nord) and Cagnicourt, Béthune and Bienvillers-au Bois (in the Pas-de-Calais), etc.

18 AN, F1V/C1.

19 Such was the case of A. Gerschel, a deputy who had been acting mayor of Calais since September 1939; he was dismissed and incarcerated on 7 June 1940 (AN, FlA 3999).

20 AD Pas-de-Calais, M4969, letter from the *Standortkommandatur* of Loos to the *Kommandantur* of Lens, 13 September 1940.

21 *Ibid.*, report of 24 October 1940.

22 AD Pas-de-Calais, M4968.

23 *Ibid.*, M4782.

24 AN, FlV/C18.

25 Thus, in December 1940, the prefect of the Pas-de-Calais tried to prevent the resignation of the president of the War Committee of Carvin 'so as not to destabilise the situation and create a dangerous precedent'.

26 AN, FIA/3641.

27 On this incident, see AD Pas-de-Calais, M4970, prefect's report to the OFK, 11 September 1940.

28 See, E. Dejonghe, 'Aspects du régime d'occupation dans le Nord et le Pas-de-Calais durant la Seconde Guerre Mondiale', *Revue du Nord* 209 (April–June 1971), pp. 253–68.

29 E. Dejonghe, 'Etre occupant dans le Nord', *Revue du Nord* 259 (October–December 1983), pp. 707–45.

30 AN, OFK 670 report, 20 March to 20 April 1941.

31 *Ibid.*, FlC/108 bis.

32 *Ibid.*, AJ40/44.

33 *Ibid.*, Flll B/5.

34 This danger had been perceived by the director of 'les Mines' of Carvin, Verrier, who immediately resigned from his post as president of the War Committee of Carvin in order to show his hostility to a decision which called into question the mayor's authority over his staff (December 1940). The effect was immediate: from then on the *Kommandanturen* refrained from carrying out operations on that scale.

35 The law was published in the *Journal Officiel* of 12 December 1940.

36 AN, AJ40/44, monthly report of the OFK 670, 21 March 1941.

37 *Ibid.*, report of 20 April 1941.

38 AD Pas-de-Calais, M4963.

39 AN, AJ40/44.

40 Report of the prefect of the Nord to the Home Secretary, 14 February 1941, AN, FIA/3637.

41 AN, AJ40/44, report of 20 May 1941.

42 Maner, 'Les municipalités', pp. 235–6.

43 Notable members of the management committee included the socialists Couteaux (Saint-Amand), Dehove (Lille) and Maës (Lens), radicals such as Dufour (Armentières) or Pouget (Le Touquet), members of the URD like De Diesbach, and staunch Pétainists like Tillie (Saint-Omer). At the time of the creation of the Association, twenty-three communes in the Nord and eighteen in the Pas-du-Calais were represented, and these were on the whole the largest ones.

44 Mayors were appointed by the minister in communes of over 10,000 inhabitants, and by the prefect in communes of between 2,000 and 10,000 inhabit-

ants (Art. 4).
45 Maner, 'Les municipalitiés, pp. 238–9.
46 See *ibid.*, p. 266, appendix 5.
47 AD Pas-de-Calais, M4966.
48 AN, AJ41/425: 'You will order your employees not to carry out instructions from the authorities of occupation if they consider them to be incompatible with the treaties currently in force, without prior reference to their ministerial department or even to the government, with regard to municipal finances, appointments etc.'
49 *Ibid.*, FIA/3640
50 *Ibid.*, FIA/3637.
51 On Roubaix, see the article by Jean-Pierre Florin, 'Pouvoir municipal et occupation à Roubaix', *Revue du Nord* 2, spécial hors-série (1987), and AN, FIA/3640.
52 Visit to the communes of October 1943, AN, FIA/3999.
53 AD Nord, 15 W 36.640.
54 *Ibid.*
55 Notably in the mining communes where the German authorities sometimes went against the decisions taken in the town council : thus in January 1942 the mayor of Henin-Liétard resigned 'believing that the decisions of the *Ortskommandantur* removed from him the authority necessary to adminstrate the town'.
56 AN, FIA/3641. On the matter of Boulogne, see the prefect's report of 19 September 1942, AD Pas-de-Calais, M4971.
57 On this episode, see AD Pas-de-Calais, M4782 and 4968; also AN, FlV/C28, note from Dr Schmidt to the regional prefect, 24 November 1942.
58 Maner, 'Les municipalités', p. 248.
59 AN, FIA/3634: for instance, as in the case of the mayors of Haillicourt (Pas-de-Calais) and Oignies (Pas-de-Calais).
60 AD Pas-de-Calais, M746.
61 *Ibid.*, M4963, report of 12 November 1940.
62 For example, the mayor of Widehem (Pas-de-Calais) was sentenced in July 1941 to two months in prison following the cutting of a telephone wire.
63 See the example of Tourcoing, AN, FIA/3999.0.
64 AD Pas-de-Calais, M4965, letter to the prefect dated 11 September 1941.
65 *Ibid.*, M721, letter of March 1941.
66 *Ibid.*, letter of July 1941.
67 *Ibid.*, M722, letter to the prefect of 25 June 1941.
68 *Ibid.*, M4966.
69 *Ibid.*, M4968, report of the special commissioner of Lens, 2 February 1941; another stormy protest had taken place at Lens on 31 January: 350 housewives had forced the mayor to receive them.
70 For example, in September 1943, the mayor of Chocques received a letter containing his own effigy with a blood-drenched rope around the neck.
71 These included denunciations by the clergy of mayors considered anti-clerical or against Pétain; and interventions by employers eager to regain control over working-class councils. At the beginning of 1941, the socialist mayor of Auchel was 'attacked not only by the reactionary pontiffs of the Compagnie

des Mines de Marles but also by the communists, both of which groups desired him to leave': report of the sub-prefect of Béthune, AD Pas-de-Calais, M4967.

72 *Ibid.*, M4963.

73 *Ibid.*, M4950. Similar words were uttered by the mayor of Bonnières ('I feel that I have always defended my fellow citizens against the demands of the occupying authorities up until the very limit').

74 Nine cases leading to dismissal were counted in four years in the Pas-de-Calais: traffic in ration cards (Bailleul-sur-Berthoult, Couin), clandestine slaughter (Fresnes-les-Montauban, Saint-Rémy-au-Bois and, on a large scale, Coulomby), 'watering-down of milk' (Neuville-Vitasse, Fortel-en-Artois), and false declarations over livestock (Bellebrune, Nort-Leulinghem).

75 AD Pas-de-Calais, M4973: same analysis for the mayor of Quercamps (canton of Lumbres), in March 1942.

7 STRUCTURES OF AUTHORITY IN THE GREEK RESISTANCE, 1941–1944

1 C. M. Woodhouse, *Apple of Discord: A Survey of Recent Greek Politics in their International Setting* (London 1948), p. 56.

2 G. Margaritis, 'Stemma kai svastika' (review of H. Fleischer, *Stemma kai Svastika: i Ellada tis katochis kai tis antistasis, 1941–1944*), *Ta Istorika* 11 (Dec. 1989), pp. 444–9.

3 M. Mazower, *Inside Hitler's Greece: The Experience of Occupation, 1941–1944* (New Haven and London, 1993); G. Margaritis, *Apo tin itta stin exegersi: Ellada, anoixi 1941–fthinoporo 1942* (Athens, 1993).

4 War Office, Public Record Office (hereafter WO) 204/8890, 'General administrative questions', 8 August 1943.

5 WO 204/8312, 23rd Armoured Brigade, 'Operations in Greece: 15 October 1944–January 7 1945'; see also Le Suire cited in my *Inside Hitler's Greece*, p. 265.

6 Foreign Office files, Public Record Office (hereafter FO) 371/43680 R 3208/9, 'Report by Lt. Col. R. P. McMullen on Present Conditions in the Peloponnese'.

7 A. Sevastaki, *To andartiko ippiko tis Thessalias* (Athens, 1978), p. 36.

8 *Ibid.*, pp. 183–4; WO 204/8869, 'Greek Resistance Organisations'.

9 Sevastaki, *To andartiko ippiko*, pp. 65–6.

10 G. Zaroyiannis, *Anamniseis apo tin Ethniki Antistasi: ELAS, 1940–1944* (Athens, n.d.), pp. 101–4; Sevastaki, *To andartiko ippiko*, pp. 62–4, 140–1; G. Papakonstantinou, *Enthymimata potismena me aima kai dakrya* (Athens, n.d.), pp. 384–5.

11 Koumbas case materials in OSS files, US National Archives, Washington, RG 226/154, box 40/260, Wines-West (Cairo), 31 May 1944.

12 See also, *ibid.*, box 39/571, 'Hughling Report', and box 39/576, 'Kimball Report'.

13 E. Barker, *British Policy in South-East Europe in the Second World War* (London, 1976), pp. 188–92.

14 P. Roussos, *I megali pentaetia, 1940–1945* (Athens, 1978), vol. I, pp. 355–59.

15 *Ibid.*, pp. 356–7.
16 Th. Tsouparopoulos, *Oi laokratikoi thesmoi tis ethnikis antistasis* (Athens, 1989), p. 260.
17 G. Kotzioulas, *Theatro sta vouna* (Athens, 1980), p. 178.
18 Tsouparopoulos, *Laokratikoi thesmoi*, pp. 235–51.
19 RG 226/190, box 2/26, 'Ap'ti drasi tis EPON Stereas Elladas'; RG 226/190, box 3/40, 'Voice of Youth', Serres, 23 December 1943.
20 J. Hart, 'Women in the Greek Resistance: National Crisis and Political Transformation', *International Labor and Working-Class History*, 38 (fall, 1990), pp. 46–62.
21 S. Veopoulos, *To Sfalma* (Athens, 1961), p. 181.

8 NAZI AUSTRIA: THE LIMITS OF DISSENT

1 Österreichisches Staatsarchiv: Archiv der Republik (AdR), Reichskommissar für die Wiedervereinigung Österreichs mit dem deutschen Reich (Rk) 192, Stimmungsberichte von Partei- und SS-Stellen: Der SD-Führer des Oberabschnittes Donau an den Reichskommissar und Gauleiter Josef Bürckel, Wien 16 February 1939.
2 Adam Wandruszka, 'Historische Einführung', in *Protokolle des Ministerrates der Ersten Republik. Abteilung VIII 20. Mai 1932 bis 25. Juli 1934*, vol. I: *Kabinett Dr. Engelbert Dollfuß 20. Mai 1932 bis 18. Oktober 1932* (Vienna, 1980), p. xvi. See also Gerhard Botz, 'Der "4. März 1933"' als Konsequenz ständischer Strukturen, ökonomischer Krisen und autoritärer Tendenzen' in Botz (ed.), *Krisenzonen einer Demokratie. Gewalt. Streik und Konfliktunterdrückung in Österreich seit 1918* (Frankfurt and New York, 1987) pp. 155–80.
3 See Everhard Holtmann, *Zwischen Unterdrückung und Befriedung. Sozialistische Arbeiterbewegung und autoritäres Regime in Österreich 1933–1938* (Munich, 1978), pp. 95ff.
4 See Jill Lewis, *Fascism and the Working Class in Austria* (New York and Oxford, 1991), pp. 152ff.
5 See Melanie Sully, *Continuity and Change in Austrian Socialism. The Eternal Quest for the Third Way* (Boulder, 1982), p. 44; Maren Seliger and Karl Ucakar, *Wien. Politische Geschichte 1770–1934. Entwicklung und Bestimmungskräfte großstädtischer Politik Teil 2: 1896–1934* (Vienna, 1985), pp. 1171–3.
6 See Willibald I. Holzer, *Im Schatten des Faschismus. Der österreichische Widerstand gegen Hitler 1938–1945* (Vienna, 1981).
7 Holtmann, *Zwischen Unterdrückung und Befriedung*, p. 280.
8 For a contemporary account, see G. E. R Gedye, *Fallen Bastions. The Central European Tragedy* (London, 1939) pp. 265ff.
9 See Robert Schwarz, *'Sozialismus' der Propaganda. Das Werben des völkischen Beobachters um die österreichische Arbeiterschaft 1938–9* (Vienna, 1975).
10 In the words of Karl Renner, the Social Democrat leader. Cited in Gerhard Botz, *Wien vom Anschluß zum Krieg. Nationalsozialistische Machtübernahme und politisch-soziale Umgestaltung am Beispiel der Stadt Wien* (Vienna and Munich, 1978). p. 135.
11 See SD reports on the impact of such new unemployment: United States National Archives, Washington, Captured German Records Microfilmed at

Alexandria (USNA), T-84 Roll 14.

12 Dokumentationsarchiv des österreichischen Widerstands, Vienna (DÖW), 5120. See also *Deutschlandberichte der Sozialdemokratischen Partei Deutschlands (Sopade)* (8 vols., Salzhausen and Frankfurt, 1980), vol. V, pp. 997–9.

13 See Evan Bukey, *Hitler's Hometown. Linz, Austria 1908–1945* (Bloomington and Indianapolis, 1986), pp. 183–207; Albert Speer, *Inside the Third Reich* (London, 1970), p. 154.

14 Copies of such reports are held at the DÖW, and are also among the documents microfilmed by the Americans.

15 On Communist resistance up to the invasion of the Soviet Union, see Helmut Konrad, *Widerstand und Verfolgung an Donau und Moldau. KPÖ und KSČ zur Zeit des Hitler–Stalin Paktes* (Vienna, 1978).

16 Radomir V. Luža, *The Resistance in Austria 1938–1945* (Minneapolis, 1984), p. 293. The estimate is based on a 'purposive' rather than a random sample of 2,795 activists involved in activities defined as resistance by the author.

17 German Federal Archives (Bundesarchiv, BA), R58 1081, Lagebericht über Österreich; R22 3668, Der Generalstaatsanwalt beim Oberlandesgericht Innsbruck; R22 3365, Der Generalstaatsanwaltschaft beim Oberlandesgericht Graz; R22 3377, Generalstaatsanwaltschaft beim Oberlandesgericht Linz.

18 See Konrad, *Widerstand und Verfolgung an Donau und Moldau*, pp. 97–140.

19 See Willibald Ingo Holzer, 'Die österreichische Bataillone im Verband der NOV I POJ. Die Kampfgruppe Avantgarde/Steiermark. Die Partisanengruppe Leoben–Donawitz. Die Kommunistische Partei Österreichs im militanten politischen Widerstand' (Phil. Diss., Vienna, 1971); Holzer, 'Am Beispiel der Kampfgruppe Avantgarde/Steiermark (1944–45). Zu Genese und Gestalt leninistisch-maoistischer Guerilladoktrin und ihrer Realisierungschance in Österreich', in Gerhard Botz et al. (eds.), *Bewegung und Klasse. Studien zur österreichischen Arbeitergeschichte* (Vienna, 1978), pp. 419–24. See also Luža, *Resistance*, pp. 193–209.

20 See Tim Kirk, 'The Limits of Germandom. The Resistance to the Nazi Annexation of Slovenia', *Slavonic and East European Review* 69 (1991), pp. 646–67.

21 Cf. Günter Morsch, *Arbeit und Brot. Studien zur Lage, Stimmung, Einstellung und Verhalten der deutschen Arbeiterschaft 1933–1936/7* (Frankfurt, 1993), pp. 384ff. Regular commentaries on responses to the *Winterhilfswerk* were to be found in the SD's situation reports: Heinz Boberach (ed.), *Meldungen aus dem Reich. Die geheimen Lageberichte des Sicherheitsdienstes der SS* (17 vols., Herrsching, 1984).

22 See Tim Kirk, *Nazism and the Working Class in Austria. Industrial Unrest in the 'National Community'* (Cambridge, 1996), p. 53.

23 BA, R58 723, Chef der Sicherheitspolizei, Berlin, 26 September 1938.

24 *Ibid.*, Stimmungsbericht Steyr u. Umgebung.

25 *Ibid.*

26 See Gerhard Botz, 'Der ambivalente Anschluß 1938–1939. Von der Begeisterung zur Ernüchterung', *Zeitgeschichte* 6 (1978), pp. 91–109.

27 See Florian Freund and Bertrand Perz, 'Fremdarbeiter und KZ-Häftlinge in der "Ostmark"', in Ulrich Herbert (ed.), *Europa und der Reichseinsatz. Ausländische Zivilarbeiter, Kriegsgefangene und KZ-Häftlinge in Deutschland 1938–*

1945 (Essen, 1991), pp. 317–50; Kirk, *Nazism*, pp. 71–85.

28 BA, R43 528, Sozialpolitik im Rundfunk. Sozialpolitischer Bericht für das 3. Vierteljahr 1938.

29 See Tim Mason, *Arbeiterklasse und Volksgemeinschaft. Dokumente und Materialien zur deutschen Arbeiterpolitik 1936–1939* (Opladen, 1975), pp. 1085–1232. The lengthy introductory commentary on these documents has now been translated as Tim Mason, *Social Policy in the Third Reich. The Working Class and National Socialism* (Providence and Oxford, 1993).

30 See Mason, *Arbeiterklasse*, pp. 734–844.

31 AdR, Rk 170, Wirtschaftlicher Wochenbericht Nr. 6, 1939.

32 *Ibid.*, Wirtschaftlicher Wochenbericht Nr. 8, 1939.

33 AdR, Rk 73, Antrag auf Erlassung einer Notstandsverordnung, 29 September 1939; Fernschreiben von Gauleiter Bürckel, Wien an Reichsleiter Bormann, München, 2 October 1939.

34 USNA, T-84, Roll 14, SD Wien, 18 December 1939.

35 German Federal Military Archives, RW 20-17/13 (12 July 1940).

36 DÖW 5732c.

37 DÖW 5732f.

38 See Ursula von Gersdorff, *Frauen im Kriegsdienst 1914–1945* (Stuttgart, 1969), pp. 375–89.

39 Ludwig-Boltzmann-Institut für Historische Sozialwissenschaft, Landesgericht Linz, HV 415/43.

40 *Ibid.*, HV 88/44.

41 DÖW Film 104, Meldungen aus dem Reichsgau Oberdonau, 30 January 1943.

42 See Francis Carsten, *Revolution in Central Europe* (London, 1972).

43 Mason, *Social Policy*, pp. 19–40.

44 John Boyer, *Political Radicalism in Late Imperial Vienna* (Chicago, 1981), pp. 411–21.

45 Cited in Botz, *Wien*, p. 130.

46 See Tim Kirk, 'Nazis and Workers in Hitler's Homeland', *History Today* (July 1996), pp. 36–42.

9 'HOMOSEXUAL' MEN IN VIENNA, 1938

1 Michel Foucault, 'Geschichte und Homosexualität', in *Freundschaft als Lebensweise. Michel Foucault im Gespräch* (Berlin, n.d.). See also Jörg Hutter, *Die Gesellschaftliche Kontrolle des homosexuellen Begehrens. Medizinische Definitionen und juristische Sanktionen im 19. Jahrhundert* (Frankfurt and New York, 1992).

2 Klaus Müller, *Aber in meinem Herzen sprach eine Stimme so laut. Homosexuelle Autobiographien und medizinische Pathographien im neunzehnten Jahrhundert* (Berlin, 1991), p. 45.

3 Hutter, *Gesellschaftliche Kontrolle*, p. 171.

4 Hanna Hacker, *Frauen und Freundinnen. Studien zur 'weiblichen Homosexualität' am Beispiel Österreich 1870–1938* (Weinheim and Basel, 1987), p. 18.

5 Müller, *Aber in meinem Herzen*, p. 57.

6 *Ibid.*, p. 83.

7 Kertbeny referred to himself as Ulrichs' *Kampfgenosse* ('comrade-in-arms').

Manfred Herzer, 'Ein Brief von Kertbeny in Hannover an Ulrichs in Würzburg', *Capri. Zeitschrift für schwule Geschichte* 1 (1987), p. 31. See also Manfred Herzer and Jean-Claude Féray, 'Karl Maria Kertbeny', in Rüdiger Lautmann, *Homosexualität. Handbuch der Theorie-und Forschungsgeschichte* (Frankfurt and New York, 1993), pp. 42–7.

8 Hutter, *Gesellschaftliche Kontrolle*, pp. 89ff.

9 *Illustrierte Kriminal-Zeitung* 21 (9 September 1907), p. 8.

10 The Vienna branch had been founded a year earlier, under the direction of the psychoanalyst, Wilhelm Stekel.

11 *Illustrierte Kriminal-Zeitung* 21 (9 September 1907), pp. 7ff.

12 *Ibid.*, p. 275.

13 Austrian State Archives, Allgemeines Verwaltungsarchiv, Bundeskanzleramt 22 N, Zl 12 9457/1 1923.

14 Hacker, *Frauen und Freundinnen*, p. 198.

15 Selections from *Der Eigene*, in English, are published in Harry Oosterhuis and Hubert Kennedy (eds.), *Homosexuality and Male Bonding in Pre-Nazi Germany. The Youth Movement, the Gay Movement, and Male Bonding before Hitler's Rise* (New York, 1991).

16 *Spartacus Gay Guide 1920, Der internationale Reiseführer* in *Capri. Zeitschrift für schwule Geschichte* 4 (June 1992), pp. 29ff.

17 Vienna State Archive (henceforth WStLA), Landesgericht für Strafsachen [I] Vr 3572/1936.

18 *Wiener Freie Worte. Freisoziales Organ zur Aufklärung und Befreiung des Volkes* 28 (26 August 1911).

19 WStLA, Landesgericht für Strafsachen [I] Vr 5477/38.

20 Dokumentationsarchiv des österreichischen Widerstands, Vienna (DÖW), Akte R 347.

21 WStLA, Landesgericht für Strafsachen [I] Vr 10421/36. Masturbation as a cause of homosexuality was a widespread idea. The striking feature of this case is that it is not made solely responsible, but is combined with the defendant's experiences in children's homes.

22 According to the Gestapo officer's report. WStLA, Landesgericht für Strafsachen [I] Vr 5639/1938.

23 See Müller, *Aber in meinem Herzen*, p. 51.

24 The records of 147 cases have survived from 1938 in the Vienna City Archive. According to the archive staff this is almost a complete collection. The records of thirty-six cases from 1936 can be assumed to constitute about half the cases in that year which were tried under Paragraph 129 I b. Since the other half, those of the second Vienna court, are catalogued only by name and not by charge, they have so far proved elusive.

25 'Zweiter Runderlaß des Preußischen Ministers des Innern', 23 February 1933, 'Dritter Runderlaß des Preußischen Ministers des Innern', 24 February 1933', in Günter Grau (ed.), *Homosexualität in der NS-Zeit. Dokumente einer Diskriminierung und Verfolgung* (Frankfurt am Main, 1993), pp. 56–60, Docs. 2 and 3. 'Reichsgesetzblatt 1933' No. 17, 23 February 1933, in Burkhard Jellonek, *Homosexuelle unter dem Hakenkreuz. Die Verfolgung von Homosexuellen im Dritten Reich* (Paderborn, 1990) p. 81.

26 Jellonek, *Homosexuelle*, pp. 102ff.; Claudia Schoppmann, *Nationalsozialis-*

tische Sexualpolitik und weibliche Homosexualität (Pfaffenweiler, 1991), pp. 180ff.

27 Jellonek, *Homosexuelle*, p. 331.

28 *Völkischer Beobachter* (Norddeutsche Ausgabe) 149 (28 May 1936), p. 2.

29 Gesetz zur Änderung des Gesetzes zur Verhütung erbkranken Nachwuchses, 26 June 1935, *Reichsgesetzblatt* I, p. 773, cited by Jellonek, *Homosexuelle*, p. 150.

30 Projektgruppe für die vergessenen Opfer des NS-Regimes in Hamburg e.V. (eds.), *Verachtet - verfolgt - vernichtet. Zu den 'Vergessenen' Opfern des NS-Regimes* (Hamburg, 1988), p. 54.

31 *Reichspost* 179, 2 July 1934.

32 *Neues Wiener Tageblatt* 178, 1 July 1934.

33 WStLA, Landesgericht für Strafsachen [I] Vr 2755/1938.

34 Wolfgang Neugebauer, 'Das NS-Terrorsystem', in Dokumentationsarchiv des österreichischen Widerstandes (DÖW) (ed.), *Wien 1938* (Vienna, 1988), pp. 222–45.

35 See, for example, the case of Josef Karas, one of the most frequently deployed Gestapo officers in Vienna, who was employed as a personal bodyguard for the Mayor of Vienna between 1934 and 1938. According to his court statement he was neither a member of the Nazi Party nor otherwise involved in the Nazi movement at that time. Witness statement Josef Karas, in the trial of Johann Weitschacher at the Volksgerichtshof Vg 12 I Vr 4490/1947; DÖW Akte E 19416.

36 Franz Weisz, "'Die geheime Staatspolizei Staatspolizeistelle Wien'" 1938–1945. Organisation, und personale Belange' (Phil. Diss., Vienna, 1991), Vol II /1b, p. 457.

37 WStLA, Landesgericht für Strafsachen [II] Vr 302/38.

38 What happened to him after the trial is not recorded. WStLA, Landesgericht für Strafsachen [I] Vr 5632/1938.

39 This deficit was mentioned, for example, in a case before the Municipal Court in Salzburg.

40 *Das Schwarze Korps* 15 February 1940, as cited in Grau, *Homosexualität in der NS-Zeit*, pp. 255ff (Doc. 65).

41 There was no provision for such a sentence even in German law at this time. Only in September 1941 did a 'Law for the Revision of the Reich Penal Code' introduce the death penalty for 'repeated approaches to children for the purposes of sexual gratification, whereby serious physical and psychological damage is caused to many children'. Cited in Jellonek, *Homosexuelle*, pp. 117ff.

42 Oberreichsanwalt Brettle to Dr Freisler, Reich Justice Ministry, 27 November 1941. Bundesarchiv Koblenz R22/970 Blatt 47; Grau, *Homosexualität in der NS-Zeit*, p. 261 (Doc. 67).

43 WStLA, Landesgericht für Strafsachen [I] Vr 5856/1938.

10 'THE YEARS OF CONSENT'? POPULAR ATTITUDES AND RESISTANCE TO FASCISM IN ITALY, 1925–1940

1 Renzo De Felice, *Mussolini il Duce*, vol. I: *Gli anni del consenso 1929–1936*

(Turin, 1974), p. 54.

2 Renzo De Felice, *Mussolini il Duce*, vol. II. *Lo Stato totalitario* (Turin, 1981), p. 209.

3 De Felice, *Gli anni del consenso*, p. 194.

4 *Ibid.*, p. 199.

5 The example is adapted from G. G. Ortu, 'Tensioni e conflitti nelle campagne sarde durante il fascismo', in M. Chiodo (ed.), *Geografia e forme del dissenso sociale in Italia durante il fascismo (1929–1934)* (Cosenza, 1990), p. 201.

6 See the articles by Paola Carucci, 'Arturo Bocchini', in Fernando Cordova (ed.), *Uomini e volti del fascismo* (Rome, 1980), pp. 65–103; 'L'organizzazione dei servizi di polizia dopo l'approvazione del testo unico delle leggi di pubblica sicurezza nel 1926', *Rassegna degli Archivi di Stato* (1976), pp. 83–113.

7 See Luciano Casali, 'E se fosse dissenso di massa? Elementi per un'analisi della "conflittualità politica" durante il fascismo', *Italia Contemporanea* 144 (1981), p. 101.

8 See, for example, Gianpasquale Santomassimo, 'Antifascismo popolare', *Italia Contemporanea* 140 (1980), pp. 44–5.

9 Palmiro Togliatti, *Lezioni sul fascismo* (Rome, 1970). Given in early 1935, the Italian Communist leader's 'lessons on fascism' marked an important point in the PCI's re-evaluation of fascism and the 'hold' of its mass organisations.

10 Simona Colarizi, *L'opinione degli Italiani sotto il regime, 1929–1943* (Bari, 1991). See also Simona Colarizi, *L'Italia antifascista dal 1922 al 1940. La lotta dei protagonisti* (2 vols., Rome, Bari, 1976), vol. II, pp. 423–38; Piero Melograni, *Rapporti segreti della polizia fascista, 1938–1940* (Rome, 1979); Alberto Aquarone, 'Violenza e consenso nel fascismo italiano', *Storia Contemporanea* 10 (1979), pp. 147–54; Alberto Aquarone, 'Lo spirito pubblico in Italia alla vigilia della seconda guerra mondiale', *Nord e Sud* 11 (1964), pp. 117–25.

11 See Franco Andreucci, '"Subversiveness"' and Anti-Fascism in Italy', in Raphael Samuel (ed.), *People's History and Socialist Theory* (London, 1981), pp. 200–4; Dianella Gagliani *et al.*, 'Culture popolari negli anni del fascismo', *Italia Contemporanea* 157 (1984), pp. 63–89.

12 Luisa Passerini, *Fascism in Popular Memory. The Cultural Experience of the Turin Working Class* (Cambridge, 1987). See also, by the same author, 'Work Ideology and Consensus under Italian Fascism', *History Workshop* 8 (1979), pp. 84–105; 'Soggettività operaia e fascismo: indicazioni di ricerca delle fonti orali', in Giulio Sapelli (ed.), *La classe operaia durante il fascismo*, Annali della Fondazione G. Feltrinelli, vol. XX (1979–80) (Milan, 1981).

13 See Dianella Gagliani, 'Forme di protesta e soggettività bracciantile in Emilia-Romagna', in Chiodo, *Geografia e forme del dissenso sociale*, pp. 245–77.

14 See the contributions in Pietro Laveglia (ed.), *Mezzogiorno e fascismo. Atti del convegno nazionale di studi promosso dalla regione Campania, 1975* (Naples, 1978); Piro Bevilacqua, *Le campagne del mezzogiorno tra fascismo e dopoguerra. Il caso della Calabria* (Turin, 1980), pp. 23–171.

15 Guido Quazza, *Resistenza e storia d'Italia. Problemi ed ipotesi di ricerca* (Milan, 1976), p. 73.

16 Mentioned in Gagliani, 'Forme di protesta', p. 269.

17 See Gagliani's contribution to 'Culture popolari', pp. 79–80.

18 See, for example, the various contributions to Sapelli, *La classe operaia durante*

il fascismo. Also other local and case studies, such as Giulio Sapelli, *Fascismo, grande industria e sindacato. Il caso di Torino 1929–35* (Milan, 1975); Paride Rugafiori, *Uomini, macchine, capitali: l'Ansaldo durante il fascismo 1922–1945* (Milan, 1981).

19 See, for example, Francesco Piva, *Contadini in fabbrica: il caso Maghera 1920–1945* (Rome, 1991).

20 Passerini, *Fascism in Popular Memory*, p. 140.

21 From a 1934 article reproduced in Colarizi, *L'Italia antifascista*, vol. II, p. 377.

11 SAINTS AND HEROINES: RE-WRITING THE HISTORY OF ITALIAN WOMEN IN THE RESISTANCE

1 Testimony of Gigliola Venturi in M. Alloisio, C. Capponi, B. Galassi Beria and M. Pastorino, *Mille Volte No! Testimonianze di donne della Resistenza* (Rome, 1965), p. 192.

2 This figure is based on the often-quoted statement by Resistance commander Arrigo Boldrini that in a guerrilla war fifteen support workers (mostly female) were needed for every fighting soldier.

3 This group's name is ambiguous, translating literally as Women's Groups for Defence and for the Assistance of the Freedom Fighters.

4 The debate surrounding these terms is too complex to go into here. Each encompasses a different vision of the meaning of the Resistance and of its legacy. Most recent controversies focus on the term 'civil war', which has been used both by the right to describe it as a war between two competing and equally valid political viewpoints, and also, in a very different manner, by historians such as Claudio Pavone to open up debate, although in a deeply anti-fascist vein, on the complexities and contradictions of the period.

5 On this question see Renate Siebert, 'Don't Forget: Fragments of a Negative Tradition', in Luisa Passerini (ed.), *Memory and Totalitarianism, International Yearbook of Oral History and Life Stories* (Oxford, 1992), vol. I, pp. 165–77, here p. 171.

6 These institutions, devoted to the history of the Resistance and anti-fascism, are located mainly in northern and central cities, with a few in the south, and a headquarters in Milan (founded by Feruccio Parri in 1949). As well as promoting the publication of studies and celebratory texts they collect documentation and oral testimonies.

7 The 'Resistance phenomenon', although an extreme example, reflects the highly politicised nature of historical writing in Italy. Whilst this can mean a refreshing absence of the sham of 'scientific objectivity', it can also lead to complacent, repetitive publications which stagnate in fixed positions.

8 One example was the huge controversy in the media after the television screening of *Combat Film* – footage shot by US troops during the Liberation. Shown in April 1994 shortly after the elections which brought a right-wing alliance including Fini's 'neo-fascists' to power, and just before the forty-ninth anniversary of the Liberation, this provoked massive debate as it was accused of depoliticising the Resistance by treating the death of Resistance martyrs and the execution of fascist spies as equally tragic events. See, for example, John Phillips, 'TV Film Enrages Anti-Fascists', *The Times*, 8 April 1994, p. 11.

9 Palmiro Togliatti, *Discorso alle donne* (Rome, 1945), pp. 15–16.
10 See, for example, Comitato provinciale dell'ANPI di Ferrara (ed.), *Le donne di Bondeno* (Ferrara, n.d., probably late 1945 or 1946).
11 UDI, *Eroine del secondo Risorgimento d'Italia* (Rome, 1944).
12 See, for a good example of this, Federazione provinciale comunista romana (ed.), *Le donne di Roma durante l'occupazione nazista* (Rome, n.d., probably late 1944 or early 1945).
13 On this backlash see Mirella Alloisio and Giuliana Beltrami, *Volontarie della Libertà* (Milan, 1981), pp. 279–88.
14 Admittedly Calvino's male characters are not meant to be heroes. His partisans are a pretty ragged band of misfits and their attitude to women may be intended as a device to underscore their immaturity. But this book cannot be seen as anything but deeply misogynous as there are no dignified female characters to offset the 'bad women', the female equivalents of the Resistance commander Kim.
15 Renata Viganò, *L'Agnese va a morire* (Turin, 1949).
16 Where Viganò does depict younger women activists, as in *Matrimonio in brigata* (Milan, 1976), she constantly emphasises, possibly with a dose of wishful thinking, how the men respected the women sexually.
17 In *Matrimonio in brigata*, a collection of short stories about the Resistance, almost as if to underline the thin line between fiction and non-fiction, she includes one explicitly autobiographical story and also a personal account of her own Resistance experiences, not as a preface or afterword, but simply as if it were another story. In this account she notes: 'I wrote Agnese as a novel, but I didn't invent anything. It is my war testimony – I didn't meet a women called Agnese who did what I wrote about her. But many 'Agnese' were with me . . . Agnese is a synthesis', p. 143.
18 Penelope Morris, 'Truth and the Resistance in Giovanna Zangrandi's "I giorni veri"', *The Italianist* 11 (1991), pp. 105–27.
19 Marina Zancan, 'Memorie e scrittura nella Resistenza', in A. Gigli Marchetti and N. Torcellan (eds.), *Donna lombarda* (Milan, 1992), pp. 265–74.
20 For a discussion of such conferences see David Ellwood and Anna Bravo, 'Oral History and Resistance History in Italy', in Paul Thompson (ed.), *Our Common History: The Transformation of Europe* (London, 1982), pp. 284–96.
21 There are numerous examples from both the 1950s and 1960s. For example, *Donne della Resistenza* (Reggio Emilia, 1953); A. Galante Garrone, *La donna modenese nella Resistenza* (Modena, n.d., probably 1965). Commissione femminile dell'ANPI provinciale di Torino (ed.), *Donne piemontesi nella lotta di liberazione. 99 partigiane cadute, 185 deportate, 38 cadute civili* (Turin, n.d., probably 1965). The celebratory style also permeated other books on this subject. See, for example, the book by former political prisoner Berardo Taddei, *Donne processate dal Tribunale Speciale 1927–1943* (Verona, 1968), a reference book recording names and a few details about each woman tried by the Special Tribunal (the Fascist political court). It presents the women as heroines, with model behaviour in prison.
22 Ada Gobetti, *Diario partigiano* (Turin, 1972; first published 1956). This is perhaps deservedly the best-known female Resistance autobiography.
23 For example, Adele Bei's *Perché i giovani sappiano* (no place, undated) is a

didactic, moral tale with easily identifiable forces of good and bad. The main themes of Bei's short autobiographical account of her anti-fascist experiences are the evil nature of fascism, the heroism of anti-fascists, female strength and the unity of men and women.

24 For example, see S. Morini, 'Masse femminili e propaganda antifascista', in *La donna reggiana nella Resistenza* (Reggio Emilia, 1965), pp. 43–51.

25 For example, S. Soglia, 'I problemi dell'emancipazione nei periodici clandestini', in L. Arbizzani, P. Mondani and L. Sarti, *Donne Emiliane nella Resistenza* (Bologna, 1964), pp. 43–6, here p. 43.

26 For example, see A. Galante Garrone, *La donna italiana nella Resistenza* (1964), p. 22. This was first given as a speech at a conference on 'L'emancipazione femminile in Italia', Turin, 27–29 October 1961.

27 See, for example, PCI (ed.), *Le donne italiane nella lotta per la libertà* (Rome, 1945).

28 *La donna reggiana*, pp. 13–17.

29 For example, Marisa Cinciari Rodano (a Catholic-Communist and leading figure in the Partito della Sinistra Cristiana during the Resistance period) asserted in 1965 that adding women to the political scene improved it, for women have new things to contribute: 'Continuità degli ideali della Resistenza', *La donna reggiana*, pp. 103–13.

30 See, for example, Movimento femminile della Democrazia Cristiana di Milano (ed.), *Donne cristiane nella Resistenza* (Milan, 1956).

31 The commander of Agnese's partisan unit refers constantly to her in this way. As if this was not enough, Viganò even includes a tale where a doctor mistook Agnese for her husband's mother.

32 See, for example, Una donna della Resistenza, 'I gruppi di difesa della donna a Pisa', in Amministrazione provinciale di Pisa (ed.), *Pisa dall'antifascismo alla Liberazione* (Pisa, 1965).

33 For example, the breathless and heroic account of T. Giacobini, *Sta Bona Tecla!* (Treviso, 1978). See also R. Chiarini and R. Scappini, *Ricordi della Resistenza* (Empoli, 1974); *La donna e la Resistenza* (Carrara, 1974), proceedings of a conference held 6–7 July 1974.

34 For example, Avvenire Paterlini, *Partigiane e patriote della provincia di Reggio nell'Emilia* (Rome, 1977), which is a kind of commemorative dictionary.

35 For example, Sezione centrale stampa e propaganda del PCI (ed.), *Partigiane della libertà* (Rome, 1973). See also the sections on women in Istituto storico della Resistenza 'Pietro Mario Beghi' (ed.), *La Resistenza nello Spezzino e nella Lunigiana* (La Spezia, 1973).

36 For example, Cesarina Bracco, *La staffetta garibaldina* (Borgosesia, 1976), a simply written account by a former Resistance activist, with little analysis or elaboration.

37 B. Giudetti Serra, *Compagne: testimonianze di partecipazione politica femminile* (2 vols., Turin, 1977). This collection of interviews with working-class left-wing women from Turin constituted a more rounded attempt to get at the realities of women's lives and to understand what led them to their political choices than the rhetorical celebratory use of oral testimony in previous years. For discussions of methodology see also Cristina Papa (ed.), *'La dimensione donna' nella Resistenza Umbra* (Perugia, 1975), p. 11.

234   *Notes for pages 190–193*

38 N. Spano and F. Camarlinghi, *La questione femminile nella politica del PCI 1921–1963* (Rome, 1972).
39 See, for example, Collettivo Rosa, 'Donne e Resistenza a Siena', in Comitato femminile antifascista per il XXX della Resistenza in Toscana (ed.), *Donne e Resistenza in Toscana* (Florence, 1978), pp. 305–23.
40 A. M. Bruzzone and R. Farina, *La Resistenza taciuta: dodici vite di partigiane piemontesi* (Milan, 1976).
41 G. Benelli, 'La Resistenza femminile in città', in G. Benelli *et al.* (eds.), *La donna nella Resistenza in Liguria* (Florence, 1979), pp. 79–117, here p. 82.
42 *Donne e Resistenza* (Pisa, 1979), p. 50, conference proceedings. Gisela Floreanini was the first female government minister in Italy, holding this post in the partisan Republic of Ossola.
43 *Ibid.*, p. 55.
44 *L'altra metà della Resistenza* (Milan, 1978).
45 For example, the speeches by Manzela Sanna and Laura Conti in *ibid.*, pp. 99–107 and pp. 64–7.
46 *Ibid.*, pp. 33–42. The divided attitude of female Resistance activists to the new feminists is also discussed in Alloisio and Beltrami, *Volontarie della Libertà.* The women interviewed for this book were asked if they considered themselves feminists. Replies varied but the overwhelming majority replied that although basically they did, they disliked the way the new generation was going about it, p. 290.
47 See M. Mammucari and A. Miserocchi, *Le donne condannate dal Tribunale speciale recluse nel carcere di Perugia* (Milan, 1979), p. 8.
48 D. Boccacci, 'Donne e Resistenza a Massa Carrara', in *Donne e Resistenza in Toscana.* The 'Resister-as-wife-and-mother' image was also strongly denounced by Franca Pieroni Bortolotti in her introduction to *Donne e Resistenza in Emilia Romagna* (Milan, 1978), p. 14.
49 See, for example, Alloisio and Beltrami, *Volontarie della Libertà*, p. 24. This was an important book as it was the first to present an 'analytic panorama' of female Resistance roles. Although not particularly conscious of methodological issues, it is undoubtedly the best overview that there is to date.
50 Some of the articles in *Donne e Resistenza in Toscana*, for example, look at how the pattern of female employment affected the way in which they were motivated to join the Resistance.
51 Bruzzone and Farina, *La Resistenza taciuta*, p. 12.
52 One fairly solitary example was Laura Mariani's well-researched study of female political prisoners, *Quelle dell'idea. Storie di detenute politiche, 1927–1948* (Bari, 1982).
53 For example, Giusto Peretta (ed.), *Donne della Resistenza. Elena Rasera: la partigiana 'Olga'* (Como, 1989) is the transcription of an oral testimony about the contribution [*sic*] of some women to the Resistance. It also includes documents and biographies (copied verbatim from another book without even deleting the cross references!) and no attempt at analysis is made.
54 On *Memoria*, see Perry R. Willson, 'In Memoriam Memoria', *Gender and History* 3 (1993), pp. 416–20.
55 Laura Mariani, 'Note di storia delle donne: l' "Enciclopedia della resistenza"', *Storia e problemi contemporanei* 4 (1989), pp. 7–16, here p. 9.

56 For a careful reflection on some aspects of this new debate by one of the Resistance's most important male historians see Claudio Pavone, 'La resistenza oggi: problema storiografico e problema civile', *Rivista di storia contemporanea* 2–3 (1992), pp. 456–80, esp. pp. 473–80.

57 For example, R. Anni *et al.*, *I gesti ed i sentimenti: le donne nella Resistenza bresciana* (Brescia, 1990). There is also an ongoing project in Bologna on 'Resistance and women's political passion'.

58 On this see Ersilia Alessandrone Perona, 'Sincronia e diacronia nelle scritture femminili sulla seconda guerra mondiale', *Passato e presente* 30 (1993), pp. 117–27, here p. 120–1. Access to such sources has recently been improved by the foundation of a special archive in Pieve San Stefano and by the flood of personal documentation sent to Italian state television after the transmission of a programme on 'My war'. See G. Sciola, 'Il Novecento degli Istituti. L'Italia nella seconda guerra mondiale', *Italia contemporanea* 190 (1993), pp. 199–203.

59 An important stimulus to much of this research has been the work of Luisa Passerini. See her *Fascism and Popular Memory: The Cultural Experiences of the Turin Working Class* (Cambridge, 1987). Some male historians too have begun to focus on 'subjectivity' in their study of the Resistance. The most influential example of this approach is an important and much discussed recent book by Claudio Pavone, *Una guerra civile. Saggio storico sulla moralità nella Resistenza* (Turin, 1991).

60 Luisa Passerini, 'Per una metodologia fedele alla memoria', in R. Anni *et al.* (eds.), *L'esperienza e la narrazione: un percorso di ricerca con le fonti orali* (Brescia, 1990), pp. 3–8, here p. 7.

61 This criticism could be made of Rolando Anni, 'L'attività delle donne nella lotta clandestina', in Anni *et al.*, *I gesti ed i sentimenti*, pp. 69–126.

62 See Anna Bravo, 'Simboli del materno', in Anna Bravo (ed.), *Donne e uomini nelle guerre mondiali* (Rome, 1991), pp. 96–134.

63 This view is put strongly in Anna Bravo, 'Guerre e mutamenti nelle strutture di genere', *Italia contemporanea* 195 (1994).

64 Some of the findings of this doctoral research was presented as 'Between the Saucepan and the Gun – "Private" and "Public" in the Resistance Narratives of 40 Left Women from the Veneto', conference on 'Donne, Guerra, Resistenza nell'Europa Occupata', Milan, January 1995.

65 For example, Delfina Lusiardi, 'Fuori del riparo: l'io e il noi nell'esperienza e nella narrazione', in Anni *et al.*, *I gesti ed i sentimenti*, pp. 165–210.

66 Passerini, 'La molteplicità dell'universo femminile nella Resistenza', introduction to Anni *et al.*, *I gesti ed i sentimenti*, pp. 7–18, here p. 13.

67 G. Sciola, 'Società rurale e Resistenza nelle vallate bresciane', *I gesti ed i sentimenti*, pp. 25–68, here p. 50–4.

68 Very little research has been done on this. But see Maria Fraddosio, 'La donna e la guerra. Aspetti della militanza femminile nel fascismo: dalla mobilitazione civile alle origini del Saf nella Repubblica Sociale Italiana', *Storia contemporanea* 6 (1989), pp. 1105–81.

69 F. Koch, 'Una tragedia muta. L'esperienza dello sfollamento nella memoria femminile', *L'Annale* (1992), pp. 13–24. Experiences of evacuation varied and some other research shows it as a happy period of peace away from bombings.

70 A. Scali, 'La memoria della strage nazifascista nelle donne di Civitella della Chiana', paper presented at the conference 'Donne, Guerra, Resistenza'.

71 See M. G. Camilletti, 'Quando le donne raccontano "il nemico" – il caso di Ancona', paper presented at the conference 'Donne, Guerra, Resistenza'.

72 On 'civilian resistance' see Jacques Semelin, *Unarmed Against Hitler: Civilian Resistance in Europe 1939–1943* (Westport, 1993).

73 This is not due to problems with the concept itself, but to some historians' use of it. Semelin's work makes it clear that 'civilian resistance' means actions stemming from conscious opposition to the plans of the occupying power.

74 L. Capobianco, 'La guerra e l'occupazione militare a Napoli: trame di quotidiana resistenza', paper presented at the conference 'Donne, Guerra, Resistenza'.

75 Scali, 'La memoria della strage' pp. 16–17.

76 M. G. Camilletti, 'Racconti delle donne di Ancona', *Italia contemporanea* 195 (1994), pp. 392–404, here p. 393.

Index

First German Homosexual Movement,
150, 158
Fist National Conference of Communist
Women, 183
First Republic (Austria), 135–8, 148
Fislar, 129
flags, 17, 18, 52
Floreanini, Gisella, 191
Floridsdorf, 137
food, 18, 23–8, 30, 115–16, 119–21, 181
41st Infantry Division, 15
Foucault, Michel, 150, 156
Franc-Tireurs et Partisans (FTP), 117
France, 8, 16, 97–119
Franco, General, 7
Frangos, Georgios, 129
Fraser, Margie, 195, 196
'Free Greece', 123, 127, 132
freemasons, 112
free speech, 51
Free Trade Hall, 50–1
Free Trade Unions, 133, 140, 142
Freikorps, 17, 20, 29, 30, 32
Freisler, 161
Fröhlich, Paul, 26, 30
Führerbeleidigung, 141
fund-raising, 141

Gaeta, Isotta, 191
Gaidartzis, Dimitri, 129
Gallacher, Willie, 57
Garda, 89
'Gaullists', 113, 117
Gayl, Wilhelm von, 38
gender, 10, 184, 194
Generalitat, 69
Generalstaatsanwälte, 35
German Armistice Commission, 107
German Labour Front, 134
Germany, 2, 5, 6, 35, 48, 67, 79, 91, 121,
137
and Austria, 153–4, 157–8
1918 revolution, 12–32
Gestapo (*Geheime Staatspolizei*), 43, 138,
139, 140, 141, 145, 156, 157, 159,
160
Gilmore, George, 88
Gladbeck, 29
Gleichschaltung (co-ordination), 35
Gobetti, Ada, 186
Goebbels, Joseph, 38
Goering, Heinrich, 39, 45
'going to the people' campaign, 168
Gollancz, Victor, 57
Gonne, Maud, 94
Gramsci, Antonio, 166

Great Britain, 85, 122
Greaves Lord, Walter, 51
Greece, 2, 8, 120–32
Greenwood, Arthor, 57
Griffith, Arthur, 83, 94
Groener, General, 20, 21, 22, 23, 29,
32
Großdeutsche Volkspartei (DGVP), 135,
136
Gruchmann, Lothar, 35
*gruppi di difesa della donna e per l'assistenza
ai combattenti della libertà*, 181
Grzesinski, Albert, 25
guerrillas (Greece) *see andartes*
Gumbel, Emil, 34, 41

Haase, 23, 30
Hacker, Hanna, 151
Halle, 29
Hamburg, 29, 31, 37, 45
'hamstering', 28
Hanotel, 110
Hanover, 25, 26
Hansen, Peter, 35
Hart, Janet, 131
Häusserer, 159
Heimwehr, 135, 142
Hénin-Lietard, 102
Hersin-Coupigny, 100, 102
Hesse, 27
Heuchin, 116
Heydrich, Reinhard, 159
High Command, 13, 15, 17, 19–26, 29,
31
high courts (*Oberlandsgerichte*), 35
Hildebrand, 43
Himmler, Heinrich, 157, 159
Hindenburg, General, 14, 16, 20, 25
Hippe, Oskar, 17
Hirschfeld, Magnus, 151, 152, 154
Hitler, Adolf, 1
Hobsbawm, Eric, 173
Holland *see* Netherlands
Home Office, 54
Home Secretary, 56
homophobia, 157
homosexuality, 9–10, 150–62
Hoover, Herbert, 18
Hotel Metropol, 159
Houdain, 100
Huber, Ernst Rudolf, 39
Hubertuskeller, 154, 161
Hulme, 51–2
Hungary, 2
Hüttenberger, Peter, 44